FRENCH: FROM DIALECT TO STANDARD

This book looks at the external history of French from its Latin origins to the present day through some of the analytical frames developed by contemporary sociolinguists. Although French is one of the most highly standardised of the world's languages, the author invites us to see the language as always having been a heterogenous rather than a monolithic entity. After an introductory section which examines the dialectalisation of Latin in Gaul, the four central chapters of the book are constructed around the basic processes involved in standardisation as identified by E. Haugen: the selection of norms, the elaboration of function, codification and acceptance. These provide a useful comparative grid for relating developments in French with those in other languages. The concluding chapter deals with language variability and the wide gulf that has now developed between French used for formal purposes and that used in everyday speech and suggests that standardisation is an ongoing rather than a finite process. Concentrating on the ordinary speakers of the language, rather than the statesmen or great authors as agents of change, the book combines a traditional 'history of the language' approach with a sociolinguistic framework to provide a broad overview of the problem of language standardisation.

R. Anthony Lodge is Professor of French at the University of Newcastle upon Tyne.

FRENCH: FROM DIALECT TO STANDARD

R. Anthony Lodge

London and New York

To Martin, Ben and Catriona

First published 1993
by Routledge
11 New Fetter Lane, London EC4P 4EE

Simultaneously published in the USA and Canada
by Routledge
29 West 35th Street, New York, NY 10001

© 1993 R. Anthony Lodge

Typeset in 10 on 12 point Palatino
by Florencetype Ltd, Kewstoke, Avon
Printed in Great Britain by
T. J. Press (Padstow) Ltd, Padstow, Cornwall

British Library Cataloguing in Publication Data
Lodge, R. Anthony
French: From Dialect to Standard
I. Title
440.9

Library of Congress Cataloging in Publication Data
Lodge, R. Anthony.
French, from dialect to standard/ R. Anthony Lodge.
p.   cm.
Includes bibliographical references and index.
1. French language – History. 2. French language – Standardization.
3. French language – Social aspects – France. 4. Latin language –
Influence on French.   I. Title.
PC2075.L75 1993

440′.9–dc 20   92-12237

ISBN 0-415-08070-3
0-415-08071-1 (pbk)

CONTENTS

List of figures   vii
List of maps   viii
Acknowledgements   ix
Phonetic symbols   x

1 VARIATION, CHANGE AND STANDARDS   1

2 THE LATINISATION OF GAUL   29

3 THE DIALECTALISATION OF GALLO-ROMANCE   54

4 SELECTION OF NORMS   85

5 ELABORATION OF FUNCTION   118

6 CODIFICATION   153

7 ACCEPTANCE   188

8 MAINTENANCE OF THE STANDARD   230

References   261
Index   279

FIGURES

1 A layperson's view of varieties of French 7
2 Language and dialect 16
3 The 'two-norm theory' 89
4 Diglossia in sixteenth-century France 151
5 A view of social stratification in seventeenth-century
   France 176
6a, 6b The decline of the *patois* 207
7 Population growth in France 221
8 The urban and rural population in France 222
9 A model of stylistic variation 231
10 A model of regional variation 231
11 Factors maintaining and inhibiting the standard 234
12 Regional and social variation 242

MAPS

1 The expansion of Roman power   32
2 Celtic place-names in Gaul   41
3 The romanisation of Gaul   43
4 The provinces of Roman Gaul   46
5 The Romance languages   55
6 Germanic settlement in Gaul   58
7 The new linguistic frontier   60
8 The Gallo-Romance dialects   72
9 Oc–Oïl isoglosses   76
10 Cultural boundaries within France   82
11 The principal towns of medieval France   110
12 Distribution of the -s/-z spelling variables   115
13 Expansion of the power of the French kings   121
14 Spread of the Parisian writing system   123
15 French-speaking departments in 1835   201
16 *Patois*-speaking departments in 1863   203
17 Rural bilingualism in 1968   208
18 Travelling time from Paris in 1765   226
19 Travelling time from Paris in 1780   227

ACKNOWLEDGEMENTS

Some books are written quickly and others at a much slower pace. Stendhal's *La Chartreuse de Parme* is said to have been composed in fifty-eight days. The present volume took a good deal longer, and its eventual emergence is by no means due to the unaided efforts of its author.

I would like to acknowledge, first of all, generous assistance from the British Academy and from the University of Newcastle upon Tyne's Research Committee which financed numerous visits to French libraries. These visits took me most frequently to Albert Dauzat's collection in the library of the Institut de Linguistique at the University of Clermont-Ferrand. Access to these facilities was always granted in a most helpful way by Mme D. Hadjadj and her colleagues, and similar help was frequently forthcoming from Jacques-Philippe Saint-Gérand of the Institut de Français in that same university. To these I wish to express grateful thanks.

On this side of the water, I would like to express my particular gratitude to James Milroy, John Charles Smith and Glanville Price, who made many wise suggestions for improving various parts of the text. Finally, I must thank several generations of students in Aberdeen and Newcastle who have been exposed to my ideas about the history of French over the years and who have every year given me cause to rethink them.

I would like to thank the following for permission to reproduce or redraw maps and figures: Editions Arthaud, Chatto & Windus, Armand Colin, Paul Elek (an imprint of HarperCollins Publishers), Flammarion, Editions Gallimard, Institut d'Etudes du Massif Central, Linguistic Society of America, Macmillan Publishers, Editions Ouvrières, Zeitschrift für Romanische Philologie.

PHONETIC SYMBOLS

a	p*a*tte, North of England p*a*t
ɑ	p*â*te, Standard English p*a*rt
ɛ	*fai*t
e	th*é*
i	s*i*
ɔ	c*o*l
o	p*ô*le
u	s*ou*s
y	t*u*
œ	doul*eu*r
ə	d*e*mande
ã	b*an*c
ɛ̃	p*ain*
œ̃	*un*
ω	*ou*i
ɥ	h*u*it
b	*b*al
d	*d*ans
g	*g*rand
ĩ	f*im* (Portuguese)
j	envo*y*er
k	*qu*and
l	*l*ent
m	*m*aman
n	*n*uit
p	*P*aul
r	*r*at (English)
ʀ	*r*ose
s	*c*ertain
t	*t*ant
v	*v*ous
ŋ	parki*ng*
ʃ	*ch*ose
ʒ	*g*ens
z	pe*s*er

1

VARIATION, CHANGE AND STANDARDS

This book treats a subject which, outside France, has lost much of its appeal: the history of the French language. The great discoveries made over the past century and a half by scholars exploring the historical links between French, Latin and the other Romance languages have now been largely assimilated, and the questions they raised pushed from the forefront of research by linguists with new preoccupations. The medieval language, which thirty years ago exerted a powerful fascination upon perhaps a majority of French-language specialists, nowadays sets off *frissons* of curiosity among only a diminishing band of researchers. Moreover, so many books bearing the title 'History of the French Language' have been published over the years that a bibliographer could be forgiven for classifying them as a separate *genre*. So, in view of all this, we are bound to ask why anyone should wish to start again on such a well-worn topic, in the last decade of the twentieth century. What more is there to say?

The very obvious answer to this question is that a subject as broad as this can never be exhausted. Even after all the work so far done in the history of French, a host of interesting problems remain unsolved, a great array of questions remain unanswered. On the one side, new linguistic data from the past are constantly coming to light (in the form very often of texts retrieved from archive shelves hitherto inaccessible to scholars) – and it is possible that there is a richer source of such data in France than in most European countries, given the size of France and its wealth and populousness in past centuries. On the other side, new hypotheses, new interpretations of the available data, are constantly being called for to enable us to square our ideas about language in the past with current theories about the nature of language in general.

The present volume will then venture into the somewhat unfashionable field of 'the history of the French language', for its author is confident that there are new things to be said and new patterns to be discovered. However, the scope of this book will be a good deal narrower than that covered by traditional histories: we will be concerned more with interpreting certain aspects of the history of French in a new way than with presenting data previously unknown to the world of scholarship. Furthermore, a distinction is usually drawn between the *internal*, linguistic history of French (the development of its sound-system, its morphology, etc.) and the *external*, sociolinguistic history of the language (the developing relationship between French and the population which uses it) – though the uncovering of a close relationship between language variation and language change has meant that the distinction between the linguistic and the sociolinguistic in the history of a language is now seen to be a good deal less clear-cut than it was previously. Whereas writers of 'histories of the language' have usually treated both of these aspects, in varying degrees of thoroughness, in this book we will be concerned more with the latter than with the former, more with the sociolinguistic than the linguistic, for the explosion of sociolinguistic research over the past thirty years has produced results which are proving very enlightening for the linguistic historian. Working on the basis of data drawn from languages currently in use, sociolinguists have developed insights and analytical frames which can be projected back in time to help us elucidate the changing patterns of language use in the remoter past. The area of sociolinguistic research, which is to provide the central theme of this book, is macrolinguistic rather than microlinguistic in scope, namely the topic of language standardisation.

The emergence of the great European standard languages has left a profound imprint on European culture, most obviously in the way Europeans subconsciously view language and its role in society: it has come to be widely accepted, for instance, that the ideal state of a language is one of homogeneity and uniformity (rather than diversity), that its ideal form is to be found in writing (rather than in speech), and that the ideal distribution of languages is for there to be a separate language for every separate 'nation' (see Deutsch 1968). This nexus of ideas was not present in pre-modern Europe, nor is it axiomatic in many non-European societies today. These ideas are bound up with the development of standard languages and the spread of literacy, and are the product of a particular series of sociocultural developments which occurred at a particular stage in European history. In no European society did they take deeper root than in France, and their mark is to be seen in many aspects of French culture, witnessed for instance in the profound respect felt for literary authors seen as creators of *la belle langue* and in the cultivation of the French language as a central part of the 'national patrimony'. They have also greatly influenced the way the history of the French language has hitherto been written. In this introductory chapter we will examine how subjective attitudes to language in France may have influenced the writing of French linguistic history, and then we will attempt to set out a different approach to the history of French.

SUBJECTIVE ATTITUDES AND HISTORIES OF FRENCH

When we examine subjective attitudes to language current in France at the present time, one of the most striking features we come across is the depth of reverence felt in many parts of society towards the standard language: linguistic prescriptivism (a readiness to condemn non-standard uses of the language) and linguistic purism (a desire to protect the traditional standard from 'contaminations' from any source, be they foreign loanwords or internally generated variation and change), have developed roots in French culture which go particularly deep. The belief that the ideal state of the language is one of uniformity and that linguistic heterogeneity is detrimental to effective communication is firmly entrenched, and as an expression of this belief the French language has acquired a rigidly codified standard form which exerts powerful pressures upon its users. While no one could claim that speakers of French in France hang upon every word which issues from the lips of a member of the Académie Française, it is nevertheless true that many of them have developed a strong sense of what is correct in French and what is not, and that, as a result, many French people are actually ashamed of the way they speak. Intolerance of variation

3

and hostility to language change run particularly deep in certain quarters and, paradoxically, it is probably because of this that the difference between the 'correct' and colloquial forms of French is now very considerable: oppressive norms are always an incitement to rebellion.

Moreover, it is widely believed that the French language exists in its purest form in writing and that speaking usually involves a falling away from the ideal. There seems to be general agreement, among non-linguists at any rate, that the standard (written) language as a linguistic system is inherently 'better' (clearer, more logical) than all other varieties current in the community – colloquial forms, regional forms, lower-class forms, *patois*, etc. The myth of the 'clarity' and 'logic' inherent in the standard French language is extremely pervasive. In many societies in the modern world, language usage is not at all so standardised and pressure to conform to social norms in speech is a good deal weaker. In view of the importance of attitudes to language in the rest of this book, let us look in more detail at the way the French layperson typically regards the different language varieties present in French.

The average layperson in France (like speakers of all languages) is acutely aware of the variation which exists within French. He or she is sensitive to the most subtle distinctions among the particular 'accents' and styles he or she encounters. However, when it comes to describing these different language varieties the terminology (or metalanguage) at his/her disposal is usually heavily laden with value-judgements derived from a long and powerful tradition of prescriptivism. This can be clearly seen when we look at the traditional terms used to discuss language variation in French. To a layperson in France the answer to the question 'What is the French language?' is straightforward: he/she identifies *la langue française* with the standard, normally the written, form of it. Although he/she will probably regard the informal speech of the educated middle classes (traditionally labelled *le français familier*) as coming within the general scope of 'the French language' – for standard languages are usually thought to have formal and informal variants – other varieties he/she will exclude. It is quite usual for French-speaking laypersons to regard slang or regional forms as not being French at all: 'Ce n'est pas du français ça, c'est de l'argot.'

The most pervasive of the 'non-standard' varieties identified by the layperson is possibly working-class speech, commonly labelled *le français populaire*. Its vocabulary is closely associated with *argot*, a large set of stigmatised lexical items thought to have originated in the Paris underworld. Beyond *le français familier* and *le français populaire* come the *dialectes* and *patois*, used by the rustic populace in the various provinces of France (Norman, Picard, Burgundian, etc.), and widely considered by the layperson to be 'debased, corrupt forms of French'. *Dialectes* usually have greater dignity than *patois*, for they (allegedly) possess a written form and a higher level of standardisation. For many a French layperson, in fact, the *patois* are the lowest form of language life, associated as they are with the despised culture of the peasantry, and subject as they are to infinite variability. Intermediary between the *patois* and the *langue française* come regional *accents*; these involve deviations in pronunciation from the Parisian norm and are commonly associated with the various *français régionaux* (regional varieties of French). The latter are obviously distinguished from the *langues régionales* (Basque, Breton, Flemish, Alsatian, Corsican, Catalan and Occitan) which are felt (rightly in some cases) to be genetically different from French and which enjoy various levels of prestige/stigmatisation.

As we can see, the layperson's metalanguage in this area contains a large judgemental element. The layperson tends not to view the different language varieties current in society in a detached way, instead attributing to each of them a *social* meaning based on culturally transmitted stereotypes. In most of our superficial day-to-day dealings with people, we judge them with reference to these stereotypes. Social attitudes to non-standard speech in France as in Britain are not always unfavourable. Non-standard varieties can be viewed with affection, inducing a sense of security and homeliness. For instance, positive feelings towards one's own local speech tend to be bound up with a sense of belonging to a small community within society at large. Informal style is normally taken to be more friendly than formal style. Rural varieties are often more favourably regarded than urban ones (see Ryan and Giles 1982: esp. 22–7). However, in France, as in Britain, such non-standard varieties are rarely given high status when judged by wider social norms of acceptability. In these countries institutional pressure to conform to standard linguistic usage has been strong for so long that people have come to believe that the standard language is the only authentic form of the language and that all non-standard varieties are merely failed attempts to express oneself properly. The layperson's model seems then to be something like that shown in Figure 1.

It is likely that the social norms presented by the French standard language derive much of their strength from the highly centralised nature of French society, strongly focused as it is on Paris. They are greatly reinforced, however, by the central role which language has played over the past two centuries in the definition of French national identity – the standardised variety of French is more than an efficient vehicle for communication across the vast length and breadth of France; it serves as a powerful symbol fostering among French people a sense of national solidarity (internal cohesion) and a feeling of their uniqueness in comparison with other nations (external distinction). In pursuance of the principle, first enunciated at the time of the French Revolution, that 'la langue doit être une comme la République' ('there should be a single language, just as there is a single Republic'), non-standard languages and dialects were until quite recently persecuted with great ruthlessness. The overwhelming dominance of the standard language which has resulted in France (see Grillo 1989) contrasts quite starkly with the situation holding in many other societies where the ideal of 'one nation – one language' is much further from being realised – that is to say that two or more languages are widely used within society, distributed either functionally (e.g. English and Hindi in India), geographically (e.g. English and French in Canada) or socially (e.g. Anglo-Norman and Middle English in medieval England). On the external scene, given that for many French people their language has come to stand for French national identity, French culture and France's position in the world, strenuous official efforts have been and are still being deployed to maintain the use of French as an international language, and to combat the effects of outside (usually lexical) influences on the language, as if they were a hostile invasion. In many other societies, including those of the Anglophone world, the symbolic potency of the national language is weaker: since it is less of a symbol of national identity, speakers have a somewhat more relaxed attitude to its role in the world and to foreign linguistic influence upon it.

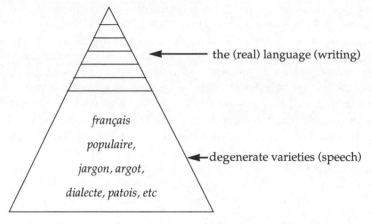

Figure 1   A layperson's view of varieties of French

Reverential attitudes towards the standard language, such as those we have just outlined, are to be found to some degree in most European societies, sharing as they do similar attitudes to literacy and to nationhood. However, it is clear that these beliefs are particularly pervasive in France, and that they are not only apparent in the language attitudes of laypersons but are also to be found lurking in an insidious way in work published about the French language by respected scholars, notably in histories of the language.

It is not unfair to maintain that the way in which the history of the French language has traditionally been written (principally in France, but elsewhere too) has in fact been heavily conditioned by reverential attitudes to the standard language and by linguistic prescriptivism. Let us attempt to substantiate this by looking at certain basic features shared by many traditional histories of French: (1) the unidimensional nature of many of these histories; and (2) their tendency to a belief in the fundamental uniqueness of France and the French language.

When we probe traditional histories of French on the very basic question of what they mean by 'the French language', explicit definitions are hard to find, but the implicit scope of the term is commonly restricted to 'the standard language' (normally extended backwards in time to include what the historian regards as its legitimate antecedents, e.g. 'Francian', the medieval dialect of the Paris region). Many of these studies are in

7

essence histories of the standard variety only (principally in its literary manifestations), implying that other varieties of French (e.g. colloquial, popular and regional forms) are of little interest. Of course, the freedom of linguistic historians to explore spoken forms of the language in past centuries is severely limited by the nature of the surviving data, but this does not justify the assumption all too commonly made that the variety of French found in written (and especially literary) texts constitutes 'the quintessential form of the language', and that the linguistic usage of the upper social groups is the only one possessing real historical significance. There is as yet no comprehensive 'history of colloquial French' to compare, for instance with Wyld's *A History of Modern Colloquial English* (Wyld 1920, but see Stimm 1980).

This concentration on the evolution of a single variety of French often cloaks a teleological yearning on the part of the historian for linguistic homogeneity. This is to say that many traditional histories seem to have had as their underlying purpose to trace the gradual reduction of obstacles to linguistic uniformity and to point the way to the seemingly inevitable triumph of the standard language. In some cases one even feels that this purpose was actually to legitimise the triumph of the standard (see Bergounioux 1989). Such an approach has a long pedigree: an (unstated) function of early histories of French (they began to be written in the sixteenth century) was quite evidently to confer historical legitimacy upon the newly forming standard language, in its rather unequal relationship with the non-standard varieties current in the community, and in its competition for status with other more dignified languages like Latin, Greek and Italian. A remarkable early example is to be found in Claude Fauchet's *Recueil de l'origine de la langue et poésie françoise, ryme et romans* (1581). It should be said, in fairness, that this approach to language history is by no means monopolised by historians of French: standard languages commonly acquire what can be termed 'retrospective historicity', that is they are given, after the event, a glorious past which helps set them apart from less prestigious varieties current in the community (see Haugen 1972).

A multidimensional history would not be so narrowly focused. It would assume that no speech community is ever linguistically homogeneous, and so would attempt to trace, within the severe limits imposed by the evidence available, the development of the whole amalgam of varieties which make up 'the language'. This raises of course the general problem of 'idealisation' in linguistic description – the degree to which linguists ignore aspects of the variability of their data. If general statements are to be made about linguistic evolution, then some degree of idealisation is inevitable. However, traditional histories have tended to evacuate too many variable elements from the data they have wanted to consider, insufficiently aware perhaps that language change has its very roots in language variation (see below, p. 19).

Great impetus to the writing of histories of French was provided in the first half of the nineteenth century by the development of comparative philology and the general diffusion of the ideas of Romantic nationalism. Influenced no doubt by W. von Humboldt's (1836) view of language as an expression of the spirit of a people, a great deal of effort began to be devoted at that time to exploring and defining France's cultural specificity, i.e. what made the French people unique, what constituted 'le génie du peuple français' ('the genius of the French people'). Since the French language had come (quite recently in most people's eyes) to symbolise French national identity, many came to the view that the rise of the French language signified the rise of the French people. It was entirely consistent with this approach, therefore, that linguistic historians should have sought to correlate events in the external history of the French language with the particular sequence of events which they considered to be milestones in the political, social and literary history of the people of France. Each was felt to be inextricably bound up with the other, and both were conceived of as fundamentally unique.

This essentially Romantic vision of history seems to have set the agenda and laid down the ground rules in histories of the language for 150 years. Even histories of French written very recently seem to share this approach at a very fundamental level. This is evident when we consider the now traditional period divisions in the history of the language which continue to condition historians' vision of France's linguistic past:

AD 500–842	Proto-French
842–1100	Early Old French
1100–1350	'Classical' Old French
1350–1500	Middle French
1500–1600	Renaissance French
1600–1789	Classical French
1789–present day	Modern French

(See, for example, Picoche and Marchello-Nizia 1989: 341–65; Rickard 1989; Caput 1972: I, 317–19; Chaurand 1972.)

When we examine the bases for these periods we discover that they have been fixed with reference to a diverse set of criteria geared sometimes to political, sometimes to literary and occasionally to linguistic events. The year 842 is the date of the swearing of the 'Strasbourg Oaths'. If the transcription of them in a manuscript dated 1000 is reliable (and we have no very strong reasons to doubt it), this text is the first one to attest the existence of French as a 'separate language' from Latin; the 'Classical' Old French period and the Classical French period correspond to centuries which produced literary texts which have come to be highly valued in French culture; the Middle French period is seen as a 'transitional phase' when the linguistic structures of French lurched from an alleged stability in the thirteenth century to the imposed stability of the seventeenth; the sixteenth-century Renaissance was one of great aesthetic activity; the date of 1789 is purely political. It is highly likely that this periodisation owes more to political and literary history and to French nationalist 'mythology' than to the reality of linguistic or sociolinguistic development (see Citron 1987).

Very often approaches to the periodisation of the history of French are dominated by particular metaphors. Sometimes these are architectural: the language is viewed as a castle which has its rough foundations laid in the ninth century, becomes a feudal fortress in the thirteenth, a Renaissance *château* in the sixteenth, and a symmetrical Classical edifice a century later. Sometimes they are anthropomorphic: the language becomes a child growing to manhood, who makes his 'premiers balbutiements' ('first halting efforts to speak') in the ninth century, becomes a lusty young lad in the thirteenth, a wayward adolescent in the fifteenth and sixteenth centuries, reaching a sober maturity in the seventeenth (see Guiraud 1966: 13). Such approaches are of course steeped in prescriptivism and, even more importantly, they are not ideologically innocent (that is, they make assumptions about the relative importance of particular historical events which may be disputed by someone with a different political or philosophical outlook). They appear, for instance, to give special prominence to epochs presided over by the great centralising rulers of France: Charlemagne (768–814), Philippe-Auguste and Louis IX (1180–1271), Louis XIV (1643–1715) and the Revolution and Napoleon (1789–1815).

One of the consequences of this approach to the history of the language is that we are often given not so much 'French linguistic history' as 'a history of France from the point of view of the language' (with strong emphasis on tracing and no doubt legitimising the diffusion of the Parisian standard). Another consequence is that since the (usually unstated) object of the exercise was ultimately to highlight the uniqueness of France and its national language, few attempts were made to see in the sociolinguistic development of French parallels with the historical development of other languages. A case in point is provided by the central problem of language standardisation. Traditional histories carefully chart the stages whereby French passed from 'dialect' to 'standard' (under chapter headings like 'L'extension du français en France'), but the way they do it makes it appear as though French is alone among the world's languages in having undergone such a process. Recent work on standardisation across a range of languages shows that while the historical development of French was in many respects specific to itself, nevertheless it follows underlying patterns of evolution which are widely attested elsewhere. One of the central aims of this book will be to see the 'external' history of French not in terms which are ethnocentric (i.e. specifically French), but in a more generally applicable sociolinguistic framework, particularly that provided by recent work on the theory of language standardisation.

We will devote the second part of this chapter, therefore, to explaining the general theoretical framework within which the later chapters have been conceived, and to discussing the principal technical terms we will be using. We will find ourselves looking at ideas which have long been central to the preoccupations of sociolinguists, and it may appear to some that they are so well known and basic that they hardly warrant the space devoted to them. However, we will defend our approach on the grounds that sociolinguistic thinking on these matters, while it may be commonplace in work on the history of English (see Leith 1983), has so far not been applied widely and systematically to French linguistic history. The general ideas in question concern the susceptibility of language to variability and change, and the problem of language standardisation.

LANGUAGE VARIATION AND LANGUAGE CHANGE

Sociolinguists have come to view language variation in a totally different way from the layperson. They regard the idea of the homogeneity of a natural language as a pure fiction. For them, it is the standardised varieties which are 'unnatural' – they are 'pathological in their lack of diversity' (Hudson 1980: 34). Sociolinguists' attitude to the different language varieties they encounter are descriptive rather than evaluative or prescriptive. They consider that, from a linguistic point of view, all language varieties are equally valid as communication, provided they are used for the appropriate purpose and in the appropriate context: speakers of non-standard varieties by definition break the rules of the standard, but their speech remains rule-governed – it is governed by the rules of the dialect or style in question. As we have seen, this egalitarian view of dialects and styles is not one shared by laypersons, who unfailingly arrange language varieties in a hierarchy of prestige, mirroring the structure of power in society: they attribute social meaning to the different dialects they encounter. For a long time, linguists played down the importance of laypeople's attitudes to language on the grounds that they are unscientific and the reverse of value-free. It is now becoming clear, however, that these subjective attitudes have a major role to play in people's linguistic performance (see Giles 1970). The social consequences of prescriptive attitudes to language are in fact far-reaching: since speakers of the standard tend to be credited with greater intelligence, trustworthiness, etc., than those who cannot 'rise above' the other varieties, upward social mobility can be denied to non-standard speakers. A good deal of space in this book will therefore be devoted to tracing the evolution of social attitudes towards particular varieties of Gallo-Romance.

In order to study variability in language, sociolinguists have had to evolve a highly sophisticated terminology to help them.

Natural languages like English and French are not neat, monolithic entities, but fluid amalgams of varieties. 'Variety' is a very general sociolinguistic term denoting the multifarious manifestations of language, be they different 'styles' or different 'dialects', etc. The variable elements which give rise to particular language varieties are sometimes classified under the headings 'Variation according to use' and 'Variation according to user' (see Halliday 1964).

Language variation derives importantly from the different *uses* to which a language is put (writing as opposed to speech, formal as opposed to informal contexts, planned, message-oriented discourse as opposed to unplanned, listener-oriented discourse, etc.), and receives such labels as 'mode', 'style' and 'field'. Implicit in this approach is the notion of the individual speaker's 'verbal repertory': 'Parler sa langue consiste à en acquérir, ne serait-ce que passivement, un répertoire de variétés' ('Speaking one's own language involves acquiring, if only passively, a whole repertory of varieties') (Valdman in Vermes 1988: I, 15). A central feature of a speaker's communicative competence is the capacity to modify speech in the presence of others (on 'accommodation theory', see Trudgill 1986: 1–38), to *shift styles* according to the situation of use, or to *switch codes* in the case of people living in bilingual or 'diglossic' communities.

The term *diglossia* was given widespread currency by Charles Ferguson (1959) in his endeavour to describe the sociolinguistic situation found in, for example, German-speaking Switzerland and in the Arab-speaking countries. Here, two distinct language varieties are widespread throughout the community – one, which Ferguson labelled High (H), is used in formal contexts, and the other, labelled Low (L), is used in informal contexts. Ferguson distinguished H and L in the following ways:

(1) Functions	H	L
Religion	+	
Conversation		+
Education/Learning	+	
Administration/Law	+	
Instructions to servants		+
'Real' literature	+	
Folk literature		+

(2) *Prestige*

H is felt to be more beautiful, more logical, better able to express important thoughts than L. It has a strong association with religion.

(3) *Literary heritage*

H possesses one, L does not.

(4) *Acquisition*

H has to be explicitly taught.
L is learnt at mother's knee.

(5) *Standardisation*

H is codified, uniform (grammars, etc.).
L is marked by dialectal fragmentation/variation.

(6) *Stability*

Diglossia is a stable language situation typically persisting for at least several centuries.

Since Ferguson's classic work on diglossia, other sociolinguists have attempted to apply the term to analogous but slightly different sociolinguistic situations. Ferguson's 'classic diglossia' involved switching from divergent 'dialects' of the 'same language', according to the domain of use. We have already hinted at problems involved in distinguishing between 'language' and 'dialect'. Fishman (1967) sought to extend the term to situations of 'superimposed bilingualism' where switching occurs between 'separate languages' (e.g. Spanish and Guarani in Paraguay). Finally, Fasold (1984) saw little difficulty in extending the use of the term 'diglossia' to cover shifting between different styles of the 'same language'. Whether one agrees to use the term 'diglossia' for all of these sociolinguistic situations or not, it seems to be a widely attested fact that highly valued parts of a society's linguistic repertoire are reserved for situations which are formal and guarded, whereas less highly valued items are used in more informal situations.

Situations of diglossia or of other forms of societal bilingualism may be of varying degrees of permanence. Diglossia, according to Ferguson, is a relatively stable situation, but no sociolinguistic state is immune to change. In the course of time leakage of function can take place between H and L languages;

the balance between two languages widely used through a society may shift to the benefit of one and to the detriment of the other. This can lead to the population's abandoning the use of one language altogether, as we shall see shortly when we consider how the Gauls gradually abandoned their Celtic language in the first 500 years AD in favour of the Latin introduced into Gaul by the Romans. When this occurs we are dealing with what has been termed *language shift* (see Gal 1979), or, seen from the point of view of the abandoned language, *language death* (see Dorian 1973). It has been noted that almost all cases of language shift come about through intergenerational shifting (see Weinreich 1968: 106–10). In other words, bilingual speakers tend not to give up completely the use of one language and substitute another during the course of their own lifetime. Typically, one generation is bilingual and passes on only one of its two languages to the next. However, bilingualism may survive for decades or centuries before one language is lost. Indeed, the presence of societal bilingualism does not necessarily mean that language shift will take place.

Language variation derives not only from the different uses to which a language is put, but also from its *users*, i.e. from 'speaker variables' such as their geographical origin, their social class, their ethnic group, their age, sex and so on. A term frequently used here is 'dialect'. We have already seen how the term 'dialect' is widely used by laypeople with particular (usually negative) connotations and associations. We shall now see that sociolinguists use this same term, but in a markedly different way, and in doing so they alter fundamentally the relationship between the two terms 'dialect' and 'language' (see Chambers and Trudgill 1980: 3–14).

'Dialects' have acquired a very broad definition as 'varieties of a language used by groups smaller than the total community of speakers' (Francis, 1983: 1). In contradistinction to a traditional view of dialect, the relationship between 'dialect' and 'language' is inclusive rather than exclusive. 'Language' is a generic or superordinate term embracing any number of dialects and styles (see Figure 2).

We shall look at the tricky problem of which dialects are to be included in 'the language' shortly, but let us first look at the relationships of different dialects of a language with each other. According to this view of language and dialect, the standard

15

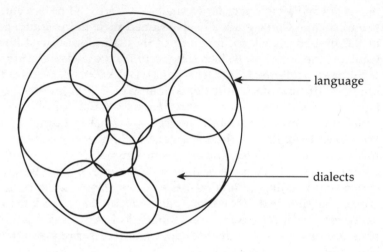

Figure 2 Language and dialect

language is simply a dialect along with all the others: everyone speaks a dialect, even if that dialect is the standard language. It has been estimated that in Britain in fact only about 3–5 per cent of the population speak something closely approximating to standard English. Dialectal diversity tends to increase proportionately to the degree of communicative isolation between groups. Barriers separating groups of people from one another may be geographical, but they may also be divisions of social class: thus dialects may be geographically based (e.g. Norman, Picard, etc.) or socially based (e.g. the peculiar speech of the *haute bourgeoisie*, of public schools, etc.). Some linguists use the term 'sociolect' to refer to the latter. Ultimately, every individual speaker possesses a personal repertory of varieties referred to as his or her 'idiolect'.

Contrary to the impression which may be given by Figure 2, the different varieties which make up a language are not in reality discrete circumscribed entities; they merge the one into the other to form *continua*. We can talk of *spatial continua* when

16

we consider, for instance, the old rural dialects of France: they differ massively from north to south and from east to west, but clear-cut boundaries are rare.

> Du bout à l'autre du sol national nos parlers populaires étendent une vaste tapisserie dont les couleurs variées se fondent sur tous les points en nuances insensiblement dégradées.

> (From one end of our national territory to the other our popular spoken language lays out a vast tapestry whose various colours merge into one another at all points in imperceptible gradations.)

> (Paris 1888: 3)

Likewise, we have to speak of *social continua* – the speech of lower working-class people merges with that of upper working-class people, and so on through lower middle-class people to upper middle-class people – and *stylistic continua* – moving through a spectrum of styles from highly informal to stiffly formal (see Joos 1962). In this way use of the traditional labels *le français familier, le français populaire*, can be very misleading, for they carry implications of neatly circumscribed language varieties. Not only do spatial, social and stylistic variables generally throw up continua with few natural breaks, they also generally operate conjointly, further widening the parameters of variability.

Just as varieties *within* a language commonly merge into one another without natural breaks, so delimitations *between* languages are not always easy to establish on linguistic grounds. How are we to decide whether such and such a dialect is to be 'included' in language A or to be seen as belonging to or forming a 'different language' B? The commonsense approach would be to invoke the criterion of mutual intelligibility. Everyone will agree that Welsh, English, French and Basque represent 'separate languages', for they are not genetically related (not closely at any rate) and, more importantly for the layperson, mutual intelligibility is not possible between them. However, with genetically related languages the distinctive criterion of mutual unintelligibility is not always so easy to apply. Coquebert-Montbret observed in the early nineteenth century that

lorsqu'on passe d'un pays de langue française à un pays de langue italienne, ou espagnole: ce n'est plus alors une ligne tranchée qu'on franchit mais une bande plus ou moins large, où le type de la langue française, déjà altéré à mesure qu'on approche des frontières, par l'effet des divers patois, continue à changer plus ou moins rapidement, toujours par une succession de nuances à peine sensibles. C'est ainsi que l'italien succède peu à peu au provençal, et le castillan au gascon.

(When we pass from a French-speaking country to an Italian- or Spanish-speaking one, we do not cross a clearly defined line, but rather a band of greater or smaller breadth, where French-type speech, already modified as we approach the frontier by the effect of the various *patois*, continues changing more or less quickly, and always through a succession of barely perceptible nuances. In the same way Italian gives way gradually to Provençal, and Castilian to Gascon.)

(Coquebert-Montbret 1831: 9)

The old Romance continuum which obtained from Belgium to Sicily has now been largely broken by the imposition of mutually *un*intelligible standard languages from the centre right up to the political frontiers. However, cases can still be found of spatial dialect continua straddling 'language' boundaries – Occitan and Catalan; Galician and Portuguese; Low German and Dutch; Danish, Norwegian and Swedish. These varieties merge imperceptibly the one into the other, but despite a high degree of mutual intelligibility, the communities which speak them frequently insist that they speak 'separate languages'. For the linguist analysing the internal structure of the varieties in question it may be of little consequence whether Galician and Portuguese represent 'separate languages' or dialects of the 'same language', but for speakers of these varieties this question often matters a great deal. Why should this be so?

Languages serve as more than vehicles for the communication of information – they commonly act as symbols of identity. A group such as a 'nation' will often use language as a way of drawing lines around itself to distinguish itself from other 'nations'. A state may adopt a dialect as its 'national' or 'official' language, and citizens loyal to that state will generally prefer to call that dialect not a 'dialect' of some other language (shared with a perhaps alien group) but a 'language' in its own right, the latter possessing greater dignity. Thus the decision about whether to refer to a variety as a 'dialect' or as a 'language' is usually tied in with questions of group identity and dialect status. We shall return to the question of language and group identity shortly. As for the social status of a dialect, this is generally linked to such things as the political and economic power of the people who speak it ('a language is a dialect with an army and a navy'; 'a language is a dialect which has risen in society and the other dialects are its poor relations'), to the prestige of the writers who have used it for literary purposes, and perhaps most importantly to the degree of standardisation and uniformity which it has achieved. At all events, the distinction between 'dialect' and 'language' is often a sociopolitical rather than a linguistic one.

The existence of *language variation* in a society has as its necessary and inevitable consequence *language change*. Purists are as hostile to language change as they are to language variation. For them, language change represents corruption, a decline from the high standards in grammar, vocabulary and pronunciation allegedly achieved in 'former times'. However, it is more realistic to regard language change as a fact of *life*, and the absence of change as the defining characteristic of a *dead* language. The variability and instability inherent in a language which is in constant use automatically entail linguistic change. Saussure (1915: 138) expressed this idea in reverse perspective when he stated: 'Tout ce qui est diachronique dans la langue ne l'est que par la parole' ('all language change has its origins in individual variations').

Much historical linguistic research has been devoted to investigating the origins and internal mechanisms of innovations. Broadly speaking, these have been seen as either internally or externally generated. Internally generated changes are those triggered by a speaker's tendency to maximise communication with a minimum of effort (e.g. the dropping of unstressed vowels in late Latin, *computàre* → *compter*), or by structural adjustments made necessary by changes elsewhere in the system (e.g. analogical changes: for instance, there existed in Old French a class of adjectives which to all intents and purposes did not distinguish masculine from feminine, thus masculine *grant*,

19

feminine *grant*. This class was eventually brought into line with the majority of adjectives which had come to mark the feminine with the addition of *e*, masculine *rond*, feminine *ronde*, etc., giving *grand* ~ *grande*). Externally generated changes are those triggered by interference from other dialects or languages existing in a variety of contact situations (see Weinreich 1968). The traditional terms used to denote different types of linguistic interference were drawn from the field of geology: *adstratum* influences – occurring when two languages exist side by side in more or less permanent contact (e.g. French and Flemish in Belgium); *substratum* influences – occurring when speakers of a native language shift to an 'invading' language (e.g. Occitan speakers shift to French); *superstratum* influences – occurring when speakers of an 'invading' language shift to the language of the native population (e.g. the Normans who conquered England shifted to English during the twelfth century).

Extreme cases of language interference are to be found in what are termed 'pidgin languages'.

A pidgin language is a *lingua franca* which has no native speakers. Chronologically speaking, it is derived from a 'normal' language through simplification: most often reductions in vocabulary and grammar, and elimination of complexities and irregularities. There is usually a certain amount of admixture, often considerable, from the native language or languages of those who use it, especially as far as pronunciation is concerned. Normally in the first stages of development at least, it is used only in trading or other limited-contact situations.

(Trudgill 1983: 179)

Sociolinguists are themselves very interested in language change. However, instead of concerning themselves primarily with the *origins* and internal mechanism of linguistic innovations, they pay particular attention to the manner of their *diffusion* through the community. The presence of language variation can to an extent be explained on the basis of differential rates of change in certain social groups or in certain styles: not all varieties of a language evolve at the same rate (for instance, many features of standard dialects are by definition slow-moving and conservative). It takes time for an innovation initiated in one part of the language to be diffused through the rest, just as it takes time for an innovation initiated in one part of the speech community to be adopted by the others (see Aitchison 1981: 63–107). The speed of language change in a given society is determined to a large extent by the length of time it takes a particular language change to be diffused throughout the community. The sociolinguist then asks what determines the rate of diffusion of particular innovations.

If we follow the argument of J. and L. Milroy, the time taken for an innovation to be diffused (if indeed it gains wider diffusion at all) will depend on the social structure of the group concerned and the nature of social networks within it. What is meant by 'social networks'? Any human group possesses a set of structural properties which may be characterised in terms of the 'density' and 'multiplexity' of the relationships holding between its members. 'A network is said to be relatively dense if a large number of the persons to whom ego is linked are also linked to each other' (Milroy 1987: 50). The nature of the link needs of course to be specified. If the link in question bears only on one single strand of the individual's existence (e.g. the economic tie linking him or her with the newsagent) then this relationship is said to be *uniplex*. If on the other hand the link in question bears upon several strands of the individual's existence, then this relationship is said to be *multiplex*. 'Relationships in tribal societies, villages and traditional working-class communities are typically multiplex and dense, whereas those in geographically and socially mobile industrial societies tend to uniplexity and spareness' (Milroy 1987: 52). What has this to do with language change? Relatively dense networks are generally considered to function effectively as norm-enforcement mechanisms, an idea which anticipates what we shall say shortly (p. 24) about the strength of linguistic norms in 'highly focused societies'. In other words, relatively dense networks are a conservative force slowing up the diffusion of linguistic changes, while relatively loose networks have the opposite effect. 'Linguistic change is slow to the extent that the relevant populations are well-established and bound by strong ties, whereas it is rapid to the extent that weak ties exist in populations' (Milroy and Milroy 1985b: 375).

Occasionally in the history of a language a cataclysmic event like a massive foreign invasion (e.g. the Germanic invasion of Roman Gaul in the fifth century AD) may have a devastating impact upon the social networks in the invaded country. As a result the rate of linguistic change becomes extremely rapid. Normally, however, language change is gradual, and its gradual and piecemeal nature makes it difficult to use internal, linguistic criteria in order to divide up the periods of a language's history. Hence the rather arbitrary nature of the period divisions we find in traditional histories of French (see above, pp. 9–10). The linguistic historian in fact comes up against analogous problems to the ones encountered by the linguistic geographer attempting to detect clear-cut boundaries within the spatial continua of geographical dialects. Despite the fact that the language is constantly changing, mutual intelligibility between successive generations of speakers is, as a rule, permanently maintained. In this book, therefore, the chapter headings will not be linked in any way to internal changes within the structure of the French language. Instead they will be derived from the external, sociolinguistic processes involved in language standardisation.

LANGUAGE STANDARDISATION

Linguists seem generally anxious to assume that the internal structures of different languages (if we exclude special languages like pidgins) are by and large all equally complex. For example, English may well have a simpler morphology than Latin, but this is amply compensated for by the relative complexity of its syntax. From a purely *linguistic* point of view, linguists are keen to agree that there are no 'primitive languages'. However, when we consider the *sociolinguistic* structure or profile of different languages, no such egalitarianism is possible: languages mirror the complexities of the populations which use them and can quite properly be compared with one another with respect to the number of their speakers and the range of functions they are equipped to carry out. A. Valdman (in Vermes 1988: I, 17) discusses four broad language functions: vernacular (informal colloquial, for use within the group), vehicular (for inter-group communication), referential (for official use and for the transmission of knowledge and cultural values) and religious (for liturgical use). Oral vernaculars serving the colloquial needs of local populations can be seen without prejudice to be 'less developed' than standardised languages used by large populations, and performing a wide range of sociolinguistic functions. Ferguson (1968) explains the difference between 'less-developed' and 'developed' languages by pointing out that the latter have been the object of three processes: (1) graphisation (the development of a writing system); (2) standardisation (suppression of variation) and (3) modernisation (the development of a range of linguistic tools, syntactical and lexical, to cope with the needs of an advanced urban society).

Standardisation in any sphere of activity involves the imposition of uniformity upon a class of objects, the suppression of variation. Standard languages grow up as a group of speakers perceives the need for a set of shared linguistic norms. In the case of the early history of English and French, the process of standardisation was in a sense spontaneous, but in that of countries standardising their language in the modern world it often occurs as the result of deliberate government policy. The existence of linguistic diversity, in whatever form, causes problems for the modern state, obliging it to intervene with policies of *language planning* ('corpus planning' and/or 'status planning'). There are various attitudes which the state can adopt towards the languages used within its borders. At the one extreme it can adopt a policy of *linguistic assimilation* whereby all languages other than that of the state are marked out for suppression. This was, until recently, the policy practised by the French state with regard to the minority languages used within its borders. Alternatively, the state can adopt various policies involving *linguistic pluralism*. Two or more languages can be given 'official status', as in Belgium (French, Dutch) and Canada (English, French) where, theoretically at least, each language is permitted in all domains of use throughout the community. Alternatively, a language may have official status only on a regional basis (e.g. Romansh in the canton of the Grisons in Switzerland). In other societies a minority language may be awarded 'promoted status', that is it may be used by various authorities for specific purposes only (e.g. Spanish in New Mexico). It may be given 'tolerated status', i.e. be neither promoted nor proscribed (e.g. Basque in France) (see Wardhaugh 1986: 337–8). From this it may perhaps be clear that 'national languages', 'official languages' and 'standard languages' are not all the same thing.

The need for shared linguistic norms springs in part from pressures for functional efficiency (as with the adoption of a standardised system of weights and measures, e.g. the metric

system in France at the time of the French Revolution): suppression of variation in language will ensure communication
over longer distances of space and time with a minimum of
misunderstanding. In addition, however, the needs of the
group may call for a uniform language to act as a badge or
symbol of group identity. Social groups, be they 'nations',
oppressed minorities, marginalised groups like a criminal fraternity, or dominant elites, use language as a way of defending
their identity (and in some cases their power) against the
encroachments of other groups. In some circumstances they use
language aggressively in order to impose their identity upon
other groups. Le Page and Tabouret-Keller (1985) have observed
that groups with a strong sense of shared linguistic norms have
a number of features in common which enable them to be
labelled 'highly focused communities'. Factors promoting
'focusing' are: (a) tight social networks within the group; (b) an
external threat leading to a sense of common cause; (c) a powerful model (for example, a strong leader or prestige group).
Feelings of language loyalty can be very strong, as the examples
of French in Belgium and Canada show most clearly. However,
the general point being made here is that standardisation of
languages arises as much from subjective pressures (group
identity) as from objective ones (functional efficiency).
Language serves a demarcatory as well as a communicative
function. Individuals or institutions concerned with promoting
the standard language in Britain and France are always insistent
upon the importance of the latter function; they are often more
coy about the role played by the former.

For obvious reasons, standardisation is more easily achieved
in writing than in the speech. Although the invention of the
printing press in the fifteenth century brought about the easy
production of homogenised pieces of written language, variation in speech was not so easily suppressed. What norms were
to be followed? Models for 'correct' speech tend to be provided
by prestige groups in society, but these models cannot be relied
upon to be stable or homogeneous. This has given rise to the
tendency to regard the more stable written language as the
ultimate model for speech, and hence to the widespread belief
that writing is a superior form of language to speaking.
Sociolinguists are not agreed, however, on the precise definition
of what standard languages are. Leith (1983: 33) argues that 'like

any variety, the standard has its dimensions of variation, including that of informality–formality, since for many people it must function as the medium of everyday conversation. . . . The standard is less fixed and monolithic than many suppose.' On the other hand, the fact that absolute standardisation of a spoken language is never achieved has led Milroy and Milroy (1985a: 22–3) to declare that 'it seems more appropriate to speak more abstractly of standardisation as an *ideology*, and a standard language as an idea in the mind rather than a reality – a set of abstract norms to which actual usage may conform to a greater or lesser extent.'

The approach to standardisation adopted in this book is a rather broad one proposed by a Scandinavian linguist, E. Haugen, in an influential study published in 1966 entitled 'Dialect, language, nation'. Haugen distinguishes two broad types of process at work in standardisation: social processes and linguistic processes.

Social processes concern modifications to the status of a particular variety adopted as the standard in a given speech community. In an initial phase we have the *selection*, from among the dialects spoken over a particular area, of one dialect for privileged use in the political and economic sphere. The dialect chosen will normally be that of the dominant group in the society in question. The dialect selected does not possess any intrinsic superiority which makes it preferable to the others, though it may have achieved *lingua franca* status through a central geographical location. Once selected, this variety has to be diffused and gain *acceptance* throughout the relevant population. The definition of what is 'the relevant population' raises problems here, because as the dominant group extends its power over neighbouring groups it transforms the nature of itself as a group. The community is extended beyond primary groups to embrace a larger geopolitical unit: this is commonly associated with the growth of wider markets in a developed economy and with the development of what has come to be known as the 'nation-state'. The standard language thereafter becomes a symbol of this new 'national' identity, serving the twin purposes of internal cohesion and external distinction – binding together in common allegiance the new 'national' grouping and serving to distinguish the 'nation' from surrounding 'nations'.

Linguistic processes involved in standardisation concern developments within the corpus of the language itself. Haugen distinguishes two processes here – *elaboration of function* and *codification*. If an oral vernacular is to become the omnifunctional language of a developed society, it has to develop the linguistic tools needed to perform its extended range of functions: it has to develop a written form (graphisation), it has to develop the syntax required in written documents (the grammar of writing functions in a quite different way from the grammar of speech), and it has to develop its lexicon in order to function in a wider range of fields. This is not to say that oral vernaculars do not possess extremely complex and sophisticated vocabularies in the fields which are culturally important for the communities concerned (e.g. the vocabulary of animal husbandry, haymaking and basket-work is extremely elaborate in some traditional rural societies). It is simply to claim that oral vernaculars each have only a narrow range of such lexical sets and that there are whole areas of human activity in advanced technological society which they do not cover. Even after the variety destined to be the future standard has been given special status with regard to others, it will still contain within itself considerable fluidity. This variability has to be suppressed for it to act as a standard – an important means to this end lies in grammatical legislation (*codification*) whereby grammarians prescribe what forms (grammatical and lexical) are to be considered 'correct' and stigmatise deviant forms. Haugen (1966: 107) defines the goals of the linguistic processes of standardisation as 'maximal variation in function but minimal variation in form'. He summarises his whole model of standardisation in the following way:

	Form	*Function*
Society	Selection	Acceptance
Language	Codification	Elaboration

In this book we will attempt to trace the development of French from 'dialect' to 'standard' with reference to the model proposed by Haugen. In one respect, however, we will go beyond Haugen, for language standardisation is not a historical process which is ever completed. Once the standard variety has been 'accepted' by the whole community, there is a permanent struggle to *maintain* the standard in its pre-eminent position. While there may be strong forces promoting the maintenance of the standard, there are likely to be equally strong countervailing forces *inhibiting* its dominance of linguistic performance in society. In centralised, urbanised and socially stratified societies like Britain and France, there is strong institutional pressure to comply with wider social norms of language behaviour. However, this status-based ideology, linked to 'overt prestige', is counterbalanced by the needs of individuals to find identity in smaller groups within society at large. These groups (class, regional, ethnic, age, etc.) tend to use non-standard language as a badge of group solidarity. Prestige within the group (referred to as 'covert prestige') will be linked with the speaker's ability to comply not with wider social norms, but with community norms. It may be that the greater the power of the ideology of the standard, the greater the pressure on groups within society to protect and tighten their community norms of linguistic behaviour.

THE PLAN OF THIS BOOK

In preparing this book, which deals above all with the socio-linguistic development of French, we found that the traditional period divisions we listed above (see pp. 9–10) are not at all helpful. We have attempted to organise our various chapters, therefore, not around them, but around the fundamental socio-linguistic processes involved in standardisation, especially those isolated by Haugen (see pp. 25–6). The first two chapters will be concerned with the dialectalisation of Latin; the central section will examine the development of the French standard, that is the processes of 'Selection', 'Elaboration of function', 'Codification' and 'Acceptance'; the final chapter will consist of a discussion of the problems of the 'Maintenance of the standard' in contemporary France.

Our approach, however, cannot be quite as neat as this simple summary implies. In practice it is not possible to make sense of the *linguistic* processes involved in standardisation ('elaboration of function' and 'codification') without reference to the *social* processes ('selection' and 'acceptance') which were taking place

27

at the same time – linguistic developments and changing social needs have never been independent of one another. The order we shall follow then will be broadly chronological: we will present particular sociolinguistic processes (e.g. 'selection of norms', 'elaboration of function') as being dominant at particular historical periods. However, it is important to bear in mind that a process dominant at any one time is not exclusive. It needs to be emphasised, in addition, that the processes involved in standardisation are continuous and not separated from one another by clear period divisions. For example, the process of 'selection of norms' merges imperceptibly into that of 'acceptance'. Finally, we need to be aware that the 'acceptance' of particular norms across the community is never fully achieved, since existing norms are permanently being challenged by the development of new norms. Likewise, new linguistic functions are constantly being 'elaborated', entailing a constant need for the revision of previous 'codifications'.

It will be objected, with complete justification, that this book is excessively Gallocentric, little space being devoted to the use of French outside the present-day political borders of France – in Anglo-Norman England, present-day Belgium, Switzerland, Canada, Francophone Africa, etc. The reason for this specialisation is essentially one of space: the sociolinguistic histories of French in these countries are too interesting to warrant anything less than a second volume (see Valdman 1979), and it is worth noting that a valuable contribution to this 'greater Francophonia' approach has recently been made by Picoche and Marchello-Nizia (1989). The fact remains, however, that the standardisation of French, which is our principal concern here, took place, until recently at any rate, essentially in France.

2

THE LATINISATION OF GAUL

French is a member of the group of languages, derived from Latin, which gradually came into existence after the final disintegration of the Roman Empire in the fifth century AD. Languages derived from the speech of the Romans are referred to as the 'Romance languages', the main ones being French, Italian, Spanish, Portuguese, Rumanian, Catalan, Occitan, Sardinian and Rheto-Romance (see Harris and Vincent 1988). It makes sense to begin a discussion of the development of French from dialect to standard with a section devoted to the formation of the Gallo-Romance dialects, so this is what we will undertake in the next two chapters. However, since the question of the linguistic fragmentation of Latin occupies a central place in Romance linguistics and has thrown up a correspondingly large bibliography, it is unlikely that the two chapters which follow will avoid the twin pitfalls of unoriginality and superficiality.

For a long time discussion of the process of dialectalisation in the Latin of Gaul turned around the *substratum–superstratum* controversy (see Jochnowitz 1973: 152–9): one side, with its flag-bearer Auguste Brun, maintained that the dialectal divisions in Gallo-Romance are extremely ancient and result primarily from the *substratum* influence of earlier languages (notably Gaulish) upon the Latin brought into Gaul by Roman colonists and tradespeople (see Brun 1936); the other side, represented by Walter von Wartburg, argued that dialectal fragmentation of Latin took place later and was primarily the result of *superstratum* influence from the languages of the Germanic invaders who overwhelmed Roman Gaul in the fifth century AD (see Wartburg 1939, 1967). In what follows we will see that while the most spectacular stages of dialectalisation occurred during the prolonged period of social and economic disruption following the collapse of the Roman Empire, nevertheless the origins of the process have to be sought earlier – Latin, like any natural language, was a variable entity and the sociolinguistic conditions under which it was diffused into Gaul varied so much with space and time that it is not possible to envisage a Latin-speaking Gaul which did not prefigure, however vaguely, the dialectal fragmentation of the post-Imperial period. We will argue, however, that in order to understand this process of dialectalisation it will not be sufficient simply to consider direct interference phenomena (*substratum* and *superstratum* influences), but to take account also of sociolinguistic factors like the strength of Latin norms in a given area, the stability or otherwise of social structures in the region, together with the social networks and patterns of communication within and between them. It needs to be understood from the outset, however, that the absence of direct written evidence means that all the statements we make about the way people spoke at this very early stage in the French language's development will be largely conjectural.

LATIN AND THE ROMAN EMPIRE

The term 'Latin' is derived from the toponym 'Latium' which designated the area around the mouth of the river Tiber in central Italy where Rome is located. The city of Rome was founded, so legend has it, in 753 BC. Gradually its power grew, and by 270 BC its citizens had subjugated all the other peoples of southern and central Italy. The islands of Sicily, Corsica and Sardinia were conquered soon after. During the next two centuries the Romans constructed an empire which was not only the most powerful and durable of the Ancient World, but which continued to exert a profound cultural and linguistic influence on Europe for more than a thousand years after its demise as a political entity. The second century BC saw the defeat first of the Carthaginians and then of the Greeks: Spain, Illyria (modern Yugoslavia), north Africa, Greece, Asia Minor successively fell under Roman control. In 120 BC the coastal area between the Alps and the Pyrenees was annexed to act as a bridge with the province of Spain. In the first century BC came the conquest of the Celtic peoples of north Italy (Cisalpine Gaul) and of what we shall call Gaul proper (Transalpine Gaul). With the conquest of Egypt and Syria shortly after, Rome became the master of the entire Mediterranean world. In the first century AD it extended its power into southern Germany, Britain and Dacia (modern Rumania). See Map 1.

The Roman armies, tradesmen and colonists carried their language with them to all the corners of the Empire, so that wherever the Romans exercised power they did so through the medium of Latin. Latin had acquired a written form in the course of the early history of Rome – the first inscription in what can be called Latin has been dated c. 600 BC (see Meillet 1928: 95–7). Written Latin was gradually standardised and eventually became virtually the sole language of writing in the western part of the Empire. It was to remain the principal written language of western Europe until the sixteenth century AD. From about the third century BC a literary variety of Latin developed, conservative in syntax, but showing signs of strong influence from Greek, particularly in lexis (Meillet 1928: 191 ff.). This highly refined literary variety, codified by generations of grammarians and hallowed by the compositions of prestigious authors like Cicero, Caesar, Ovid, Virgil, has come to be known as 'Classical Latin', for it has been held up as a model for imitation in 'class' throughout the Middle Ages right down to modern times. Around it was generated the myth of Latin – a language superior to all others, supremely adapted to the expression of higher thought, immune from continual change and variation.

This picture of Latin as the ideal language, uniform and unchanging, has had a profound influence on the way language and culture are perceived in Europe and the western world, but it greatly distorts our view of the linguistic realities of Ancient Rome. Before examining the process of the latinisation of Gaul, let us rapidly 'demythologise' our picture of the Latin which was exported from Rome to the Empire – on the one hand the sociolinguistic functions it came to acquire varied greatly across the diverse ethnic, cultural and linguistic groups which made up the Roman Empire; on the other hand, Latin, like any other natural language, was subject to the normal pressures for variation and change.

Throughout the Empire, Latin was used as a language of administration and officialdom. However, the degree to which it assumed other functions in society varied considerably from

conquered before 200 BC

conquered between 200 and 100 BC

conquered between 100 BC and AD 1

conquered between AD 1 and 200

Map 1   The expansion of Roman power

province to province. The situation in the eastern part of the Empire was particularly complex, for Latin, despite its status as an official language, never eliminated Greek as the principal language of government, learning and commerce. In the western provinces the sociolinguistic position of Latin varied according to the period of annexation and intensity of romanisation. It used to be thought that the provinces annexed early and subjected to intense romanisation became monolingual in Latin by the middle of the first century BC – Italy, Corsica, Sardinia, Sicily and the Mediterranean seaboard of Gaul and Spain. This would be too simple, however, for, to quote but one example, we have indications that a language located as close to Rome as was Etruscan (see Bonfante and Bonfante 1983) was still in use in the first century AD, some even claiming its survival as late as the fifth century (see Doblhofer 1959: 311). Evidence suggests that, further afield, communities like Gaul remained diglossic for a long time, with Latin acting as the official language and with numerous local vernaculars continuing to serve the needs of local populations. In Britain the use of Latin as a spoken language replacing Celtic was probably very limited. It is more accurate, therefore, to see the Roman Empire as a sprawling multilingual and multicultural community than as a sociolinguistic monolith built around a Latin free of variation.

Although the growth of an educated, urbanised elite in the Rome of the first century BC led to the development of a highly standardised written language, suppression of variation in speech could never reach the same degree of completion. The nature of colloquial Latin is of great interest to Romance linguists because it is here essentially that they must look for the genesis of the languages which concern them. It is highly likely in fact that the Latin language was diffused in the western Empire more in its informal, colloquial form than in that of the high-prestige standard: greater use is made of language in informal speech than in writing or in formal social situations. This process has been observed in modern Switzerland where

> several generations of Rhaetoromans have known standard German, but . . . it is the knowledge of unstandardised Schwyzertutsch which poses the threat of a substantial shift (from Rhaeto-Romance) in some areas. It would appear, then, that an unstandardised vernacular is

sometimes more apt to be adopted than a standardised language whose functions do not include everyday speech.

(Weinreich 1968: 107)

The term traditionally used to denote the non-classical varieties of Latin current in the Ancient World is 'Vulgar Latin' (see Herman 1967). This term is rather problematic, so requires a little discussion. The word 'vulgar' corresponded with the Latin *vulgus* ('mass, crowd, people') and in Latin meant simply 'of the populace' without any necessary prescriptive connotation. It made its first appearance in philological writing in the nineteenth century (Lloyd 1979 offers the date 1842), for it was only around that time that scholars began fully to appreciate the heterogeneity of Latin – they were led to this essentially by the development of Romance philology and were no doubt further encouraged by archaeological excavations in places like Pompeii and Herculaneum where significant numbers of graffiti written in a Latin which departs a long way from the norms of Classical Latin were discovered. However, sources of information about non-standard varieties of Latin were to be found elsewhere too – for example, in the language of illiterate speakers depicted by the author Petronius, in the replication of colloquial speech found in playwrights like Plautus and Terence, in the prescriptive comments made by grammarians, etc. Early uses of the term 'Vulgar Latin' imply a simple dichotomy on social lines between high-class literary Latin on the one hand and low-class uneducated Latin on the other. Subsequently, definitions of Vulgar Latin have proliferated: it has been seen in turn as lower-class Latin, middle-class Latin, colloquial Latin, spoken Latin, Latin of the non-Roman inhabitants of the Empire, reconstructed Latin. Some of these clearly contradict one another, and others are unacceptably vague. The root causes of problems with the term, however, are the vast and fluid nature of the linguistic reality it is called upon to denote and the paucity of direct evidence.

The parameters of variation in spoken Latin appear to have been the same as those found in other languages. The rhetoricians of the Classical period (*c.* 100 BC–*c.* AD 100) such as Quintilian, and scholars like Varro, were highly sensitive (with a strong prescriptive bias) to the variability of the Latin language –

the 'Latinitas est incorrupta observatio loquendi secundum Romanam linguam' ('True Latinity is to be found in the pure observation of speech after the language of Rome') (quoted by Richter 1983: 439). They saw variability primarily in social/ geographic terms (town versus country, educated versus uneducated), as witnessed by their labels: *sermo urbanus, sermo rusticus, sermo plebeius* and *sermo vulgaris* (Latin *sermo* = speech). They were aware also of variation according to context ('style'): their label *sermo cotidianus* implies a scale of formality whereon the language of private, everyday conversation is distinguished from that used on formal, public occasions. They were aware also of spatial variation (in the form of regional accents). As early as the first century BC, Cicero refers to a distinctive Spanish 'accent' perceptible even among highly literate speakers:

> [Metellus Pius] . . . qui praesertim usque eo de suis rebus scribi cuperet ut etiam Cornubiae natis poetis pingue quid- dam sonantibus atque peregrinum tamen aures suas dederet.

> ([Metellus Pius] . . . particularly considering that he so desired to have his exploits written about that he gave full attention even to poets born in Cordova with their heavy, foreign-sounding accents.)

> (*Pro Archia*, 10.26)

We shall return to the question of regional diversity later; all we wish to establish here is that Latin, like any natural language, was an amalgam of varieties, not the homogeneous monolith depicted in the 'Latin myth'.

The natural concomitant of language variation is language change. It was for a long time felt that Latin, like the 'Eternal City', escaped large-scale evolution until the end of the Empire (fifth century AD). While it is true that the pressure of a norma- tive tradition inhibited change in the literary form of the lan- guage and maintained a high degree of stability in the writing system, nevertheless the evolution of speech inevitably went on apace (see Janson 1979). Analysis of graffiti (see Väänänen 1959) and of informal writing such as the letters of Claudius Terentianus (early second century AD) (quoted by Wright 1982: 48) makes it clear that major linguistic changes, as far-reaching as those one would expect in any spoken language, were well in train during the Imperial period. The distance between the ends of the spectrum of styles in Latin thus became progressively wider so that organisations such as the Church, concerned to proselytise the unlettered populace, eventually had recourse to a variety of Latin which deviated substantially from the slow-moving norms of Classical usage. The written form of Latin used by the Early Church is sometimes termed 'Low Latin', an example of which is to be found in the 'Vulgate' version of the Bible translated by St Jerome in the fourth century. The language of this text is highly interesting, for apart from showing the influence of its Hebrew and Greek originals, it also reflects many features of spoken Latin, particularly in its syntax. In the words of another of the Church Fathers, St Augustine, writing in the fifth century: 'Melius est reprehendant nos grammatici quam non intelligant populi' ('It is preferable that grammarians criticise us rather than that the masses should not understand'). A written text which mirrors the changes in spoken Latin even more than the Vulgate is *A Pilgrimage to the Holy Places*, thought to have been composed in the early fifth century by a Spanish nun named Egeria (see Löfstedt 1959). Thus, not even during the many centuries when the Empire stood more or less intact could the Latin language remain immune from change. The Latin exported from Italy in the second century BC was certainly not the same Latin as that exported two centuries later, and this was to have important consequences for the latinisation of the different provinces of the Empire. Before taking the matter further, it might be helpful to illustrate some of the linguistic changes which came about in colloquial Latin over this period.

On the level of *phonology* the most profound changes affected the vowel system: in earlier forms of Latin, vowels were distinguished not simply on the basis of how they were articulated (i.e. tongue position, lip position, etc.) but also on the basis of their length. In the Latin found in the writings of the great authors of the first century BC, it is clear that the length of a vowel affected meaning, e.g. *pŏpŭlum*, 'the people'; *pōpŭlum*, 'a poplar tree'. All vowels in fact occurred in two forms: a long form (indicated in modern editions by ‾), and a short form (indicated by ˘). These distinctions of vowel length (sometimes referred to as vowel quantity) were gradually effaced in colloquial Latin which came to base its distinction between vowels solely on differences of vowel quality (that is whether the point

36

of articulation of the vowel in the mouth was high or low, back or front, etc.). Thus:

Classical Latin			Late Latin
ă ā	}	→	/a/
ĕ		→	/ɛ/
ē ĭ	}	→	/e/
ī		→	/i/
ŏ		→	/ɔ/
ō ŭ	}	→	/o/
ū		→	/u/

On the level of *morphology*, earlier forms of Latin were characterised by a highly inflected system of verbs, nouns and adjectives. Verbs had separate endings for each person:

Present indicative		Imperfect indicative	
amo	('I love')	amabam	('I loved')
amas	('you love')	amabas	('you loved')
amat	etc.	amabat	etc.
amamus		amabamus	
amatis		amabatis	
amant		amabant	

Each verb had a distinct set of endings for each mood (indicative/subjunctive), for each voice (active/passive) and for each tense (present/future/perfect/imperfect, etc.). All nouns and adjectives modified their endings in up to five different ways according to the grammatical function (case) which they were performing. The six cases found in Classical Latin are: the nominative (subject case), the vocative (addressing case), the accusative (object case), the genitive (possessive case), the dative (the 'giving to' case) and the ablative (the 'taking away from' case). Thus:

Case	1st declension	2nd declension	3rd declension
Nominative	*femina*	*amicus*	*miles*
Vocative	*femina*	*amice*	*miles*
Accusative	*feminam*	*amicum*	*militem*
Genitive	*feminae*	*amici*	*militis*
Dative	*feminae*	*amico*	*militi*
Ablative	*femina*	*amico*	*milite*
	'woman'	'friend'	'soldier'

As time went on, this highly inflected system was simplified in colloquial Latin. The number of verb tenses was reduced, the separate passive conjugation disappeared and the six cases were reduced, broadly speaking, to two – the nominative and the accusative.

These morphological changes had simultaneous repercussions on the *syntax* of colloquial Latin: the genitive and dative functions came now to be expressed by prepositions instead of by flectional endings, e.g. *amici* → *de amicum* ('of a friend'), *amico* → *ad amicum* ('to a friend'), and subject and object came to occupy fairly fixed positions in the sentence: e.g. *Brutus militem necavit* → *Brutus necavit militem* ('Brutus killed the soldier').

The sound changes we mentioned earlier undoubtedly had a role to play in triggering morphological and syntactic changes of the type we have just described. However, it is also known that morphological structures can *inhibit* the spread of sound changes, presenting the historical linguist concerned with causality with a 'chicken or egg situation'. The 'causes' of all these developments are therefore likely to be found at a more abstract level, and this is seen in a shift in the underlying structure of Latin from a synthetic one to an analytical one. In an ideal 'synthetic' language individual words carry their load of information (lexical and grammatical) largely in the form of flexional additions to their stems, e.g. Classical Latin *militi* carries the lexical information 'soldier' in its stem (*milit-*) and grammatical information about singular number and dative case in its ending (*-i*). In an ideal 'analytical' language each separate word carries less information as the lexical and grammatical ideas to be communicated are analysed out and allotted to individual words. Thus in colloquial Latin the dative *militi* was 'analysed' out to give *ad militem* ('to a/the soldier').

In addition to changes in the phonological, morphological and syntactic systems of the language, the *lexical* system of Latin underwent constant modification and renewal. Thus old words like *equum* ('horse'), *virum* ('man'), *uxorem* ('wife') were replaced by the forms *caballum, hominem* and *sponsam* which we can relate quite easily with their modern French developments, *cheval, homme* and *épouse*.

THE LATINISATION OF GAUL

The geographical area which the Romans referred to as 'Gaul' (*Gallia*) coincides neither with the political frontiers of modern France, nor with the modern linguistic boundaries of French-speaking Europe. Transalpine Gaul (*Gallia Transalpina*) embraced all of modern France but also included modern Belgium, Germany as far as the Rhine, and Switzerland from Geneva to Lake Constance. Cisalpine Gaul (*Gallia Cisalpina*) was a sizeable area of northern Italy inhabited by Celts. To avoid confusion in what follows we will limit our use of the term 'Gaul' to Transalpine Gaul, bearing in mind the wide geographical reference of this term.

The huge geographical area covered by Gaul and the diverse nature of its physical terrain virtually guaranteed the ethnic and linguistic diversity of the region. When the Romans began extending their power into Gaul in the second and first centuries BC they found a region inhabited by at least four different peoples. In the coastal area south of the Alps and the Cévennes, they encountered alongside the Gauls an ancient Mediterranean people, the Ligurians, but little is known either about them or about their language. More significantly, the littoral hosted a number of important trading-centres (Agde, Marseille, Antibes, Nice) established and inhabited by Greeks as early as the seventh century BC (see Duval 1972: 31). The Greek alphabet was used in Gaulish inscriptions (see Whatmough 1970: 60–1). To the west from the Garonne to the Pyrenees and the Atlantic coast was Aquitania, inhabited by a population related to the Iberians of Spain and speaking a pre-Indo-European language, assumed to be the ancestor of Basque (see Rohlfs 1970: 17–22). The land north of those areas was inhabited principally by Celts who had migrated into various areas of Europe (Ireland, Britain, Gaul proper, north-west Spain, north Italy) from a focal area in southern Germany, from about the eighth century BC (see Duval

1972: 31). The Celts in Gaul were not a homogeneous group. While much of Celtic Gaul was inhabited by Gauls proper (*Galli*), north and east of the Seine and Marne rivers lived other Celtic peoples known to the Romans as *Belgae*. These had more recently (fourth century BC) migrated into Gaul from across the Rhine, and it is quite likely that their population contained a sizeable number of Germanic-speakers (see Whatmough 1970: 37).

Although the *Galli* and the *Belgae* appear to have had a common Druidic religion and to have spoken related Celtic dialects (see Dottin 1920), the bonds of cohesion within their society were loose.

> The large three-fold subdivision of the three Gauls . . . the *Belgae*, *Celti* and *Aquitani*, rested on a corresponding grouping of tribes (*civitates*) and each tribe was made up of an aggregate of communities, called *pagi* in Latin, whose relationship to one another might be based on nothing more than that of neighbourhood, though usually it implied blood-kinship, real or assumed. The population was scattered in small village groups with few urban communities of any size. The economy was largely agricultural based on a work-force of slaves.
>
> (Whatmough 1970: 46)

The Gaulish language was what could be termed an 'undeveloped vernacular'. It was rarely written down, for the Gauls, perhaps for religious reasons, never developed their own writing system (see Whatmough 1970: 47), and was no doubt subject to extensive dialectal variation. Evidence for this is only indirect, but there is no reason to doubt Caesar when he writes: 'Hi omnes lingua, institutis, legibus inter se differunt' ('These (peoples) are all different from each other in language, institutions and laws') (*De Bello Gallico*, 1.1). Traces of the old Gaulish language are still to be found in modern French: seventy or so 'common names' designating plants, trees, agricultural implements (e.g. *bouleau* ('birch'), *chêne* ('oak'), *arpent* (land measurement, roughly an acre), *bief* ('canal reach'), *charrue* ('plough'), *benne* ('bucket'), *charpente* ('timber framework')) and more importantly vast numbers of place-names designating rivers (e.g. *Marne*, *Seine*, *Oise*), mountains (e.g. *Cévennes*, *Vosges*), towns (e.g. *Bordeaux*, *Carpentras*, *Melun*, *Charenton*). The distribution of Gaulish place-names is very often the only clue

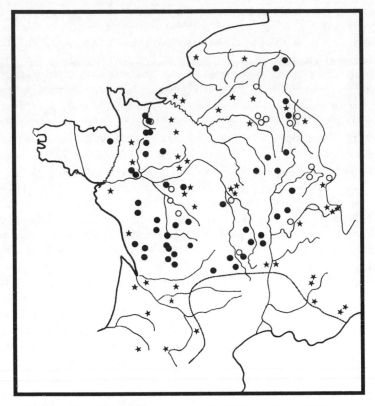

Map 2   Celtic place-names in Gaul (from Brun 1936)

- -icoranda
- o -duros
- ⋆ -dunum

we have concerning the areas inhabited by the Gauls. See
Map 2.

The military conquest of Gaul by the Romans took place in
stages. Towards the end of the second century BC (118 BC) the
Romans took control of the Mediterranean area from the Alps to
the Pyrenees. This created a land-bridge from Italy to the newly
conquered province of Spain, along the strategic roads known
as the *Via Domitia* and the *Via Aurelia*. The new Roman province
of southern Gaul was governed from Narbonne and was hence
referred to as *Provincia Narbonensis*. In so far as it was the
principal Roman province outside Italy – the 'Province' *par
excellence* – it was known simply as *Provincia* (→ *Provence*).

41

During the next seventy years the rest of Gaul experienced a period of 'peaceful' romanisation until in 55 BC Julius Caesar carried out his celebrated military conquest of the *Aquitani*, the *Celti* and the *Belgae*. In the wake of the military annexation of Gaul, the related processes of romanisation and latinisation gathered momentum. Detailed research has been carried out by historians on the progressive romanisation of Gaul (see Hatt 1959, 1972). Here is not the place to review the question in detail. We simply refer the reader to Map 3 on p. 43 where the historical geographer P. Bonnaud (1981: I, 109–10) offers a visual summary of the general directions of romanisation in Gaul.

The rich archaeological record surviving from the Gallo-Roman period enables historians to trace the spread of Roman civilisation in Gaul in some detail (see Thévenot 1948). The process of latinisation undoubtedly followed the same paths as that of romanisation, but direct evidence related to the linguistic history of the period is scanty. The fact that from the beginning almost all written documents were in Latin should not lead us to suppose that the process of language shift from the indigenous languages to Latin was either rapid or uniform. Recent work on language shift in modern well-documented situations makes it clear this cannot have been the case (see Weinreich 1968: 106–9). In all probability the latinisation of Gaul was very *gradual*, as the indigenous populations passed through various stages of bilingualism; it is also likely to have been very *patchy*, as Latin diffused (a) across different sociolinguistic functions (that is, different domains of language use like trade, administration, writing, informal speech, etc.), (b) through the different social strata, and (c) across geographical space. We will consider each of these in turn, spending more time on (c) than on the other two for the simple reason that evidence related to this aspect is somewhat more plentiful.

What can be said about the *functional* diffusion of Latin into Gaul? By virtue of the Roman annexation, Latin promptly became the language of writing, administration, politics and the law (although Gaulish was still permitted in private contracts at the beginning of the third century AD (see Berschin *et al.* 1978: 16)). As urban communities grew, schools were set up to equip a proportion of the upper-class natives with the linguistic and social skills necessary for advancement in the Roman world (see Haarhoff 1958: 33–8; Duval 1952: 201–2). For purposes of

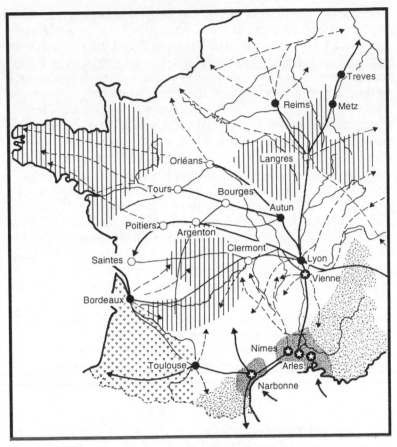

Map 3 The romanisation of Gaul (from Bonnaud 1981)

⊙ Principal urban centres involved in the initial phase of romanisation

▨ Initial zones of romanisation (Provence, Narbonnais).

● Great urban centres involved in the general romanisation of Gaul (Lyon, Autun, Toulouse, Bordeaux, Reims, Metz, Trèves)

○ Important regional centres of romanisation (Saintes, Poitiers, Argenton, Clermont, Bourges, Orléans, Tours, Langres)

↗ Principal avenues of romanisation

▥ Zones where complete romanisation came very late (eighth to tenth centuries), to which should be added Aquitaine

▒ 'Aquitanian' *substratum* (Paleo-Basque)

▦ Various *substrata* in southern Gaul which are difficult to locate with any precision (Ligurians, Iberians)

43

interregional trade, it is likely that Latin had been used in the north of Gaul even before the annexation: its use was clearly facilitated by the creation of military roads and the imposition of *pax romana*. However, the use of Latin in purely local transactions was probably slower in coming. Illustration of this is to be found in the Gaulish words retained in French: in general they denote items of purely local or domestic concern (agricultural implements, e.g. *char* ('cart'), *soc* ('ploughshare'), *charrue* ('plough'); features of the rural environment, e.g. *if* ('yew-tree'), *bouleau* ('birch'), *chêne* ('oak'); products produced or consumed in the home and not offered for sale to a wider market, e.g. *suie* ('soot'), *lie* ('dregs'), and *mègue* ('whey'), a word which survives in various modern dialects and which is more widely known through its colloquial French derivative *mégot* ('cigarette end') (see Monfrin 1972: 746–7)). Likewise, whereas Latin quickly became essential in public life, the local vernacular probably sufficed for a long time for informal discourse (see Hubschmied 1938). In other words, Gaul after the Roman conquest moved into a diglossic situation of variable duration, with Latin performing the H functions in society and oral vernaculars (principally Gaulish) the L. For an explanation of these terms see above, pp. 13–14.

Let us now look at *social* diffusion. After the military conquest of Gaul, Latin speakers migrated into the country as administrators, traders, soldiers, followed eventually by Italian-born peasant farmers and ex-soldiers (from all over the Empire) attracted by offers of land in the *coloniae*. However, the proportion of native-speaker immigrants should not be exaggerated. Duval (1952) puts them at less than 500,000 out of a population in the second century AD which has been estimated at some 12 million. They made no attempt to forcibly assimilate the Gauls – in most areas they were far too few in number to contemplate this, anyway. They were more interested in tapping the natural resources of their Empire than in imposing cultural uniformity. Accordingly they allowed the natives a considerable measure of self-government, supporting the maintenance of local culture and religious practices, and governing through the existing power structures (with the exception of the Druids who no doubt posed too great a political threat and who were outlawed). In this way the traditional Gaulish aristocracy survived the invasion, and found in Rome a means of perpetuating its dominant role. The association of Latin with Roman citizenship and political power meant that members of the social elite of Gaul were strongly motivated to learn it. They quickly romanised themselves and were attracted to the towns by the prospect of political office and Imperial recognition. Latinisation of the rest of the population was more piecemeal, however. It seems that much of the rural population remained ignorant of Latin until as late as the fourth century when Christian preachers began to proselytise the countryside through the medium of Latin (see Polomé 1983: 530–1). The process of language shift undoubtedly involved a period of bilingualism and intergenerational shifting, but evidence about this and about, for instance, the latinisation of women is simply not available.

The *spatial* diffusion of Latin in Gaul was, not surprisingly, a slow and uneven process. Let us begin with a glance at the administrative divisions imposed on Gaul by the Romans. Roman Gaul was divided in the early Empire into four provinces: *Narbonensis* (capital Narbonne), *Lugdunensis* (capital Lyon), *Aquitania* (capital Bordeaux), and *Belgica* (capital Autun) (see Map 4, p. 46). The regional metropolis was Lyon. The Roman administration tolerated considerable cultural diversity within an overall Roman framework. Thus, existing tribal boundaries were on the whole respected: each province was divided into 'cities' (*civitates*). Each 'city' had its own 'capital' and was further subdivided into *pagi* and *vici* (generally mirroring pre-Roman social units).

The eventual distribution of Latin-speaking settlers in Roman Gaul was apparently far from uniform (see Duval 1972: 28). Romans established themselves most densely in the south of the country between the Alps and Spain and in the east between the Rhône valley and the Moselle. Attention has been drawn to the varying importance of particular trade-routes in the latinisation of the country (see Lüdtke 1962), but the focal points of latinisation were the towns. The distribution of Roman towns across Gaul showed considerable regional disparities. Reichenkron (1965: 171) compares the proportion of towns to tribes in the four Roman provinces of Gaul and finds a ratio of 1:1 in the Narbonensis, 1:2 in Aquitania, 1:4 in the Lugdunensis and 1:3.5 in Belgica. As centres of commerce they attracted traders from widely different linguistic backgrounds, and Latin (mainly, we must assume, in its informal, colloquial variety) had a major role to play as a *lingua franca*. In frontier areas like the Rhine there is

Map 4   The provinces of Roman Gaul (from Drinkwater 1983)

evidence that a process of pidginisation occurred. However, the mass of the indigenous population of Gaul (90 per cent in the opinion of Braudel 1986: II, 75) were rustics who only occasionally had dealings with the towns and officialdom, and who, as we have seen, appear in places to have continued to use their local vernacular for centuries after the Roman conquest. Let us now consider the question region by region.

The population of the *Narbonensis* was latinised early, symbolised by the rapid adoption by urban leaders here of the Roman toga. This distinguished them from the aristocracy of the rest of Gaul who continued to wear the traditional trousers (*braccae* or 'breeks'). The Narbonensis was in fact referred to as *Gallia togata* ('toga-wearing Gaul') as distinct from *Gallia comata* ('long-haired Gaul') or *Gallia braccata* ('breeks-wearing Gaul'). Romanisation began in the trading settlements of Narbonne and the mouth of the Rhône, established in proximity to the long-standing Greek settlements of Agde, Marseille, Antibes and Nice. In time, the Romans took control of the whole coastal area from the Alps to the Pyrenees. The density of Roman settlement here was far superior to what it was to be in the northern provinces. The names given to urban settlements in Gaul are interesting in this respect. In the deeply romanised Narbonensis, latinised or Latin place-names have survived down to our own day (e.g. *Nemausus* (Nîmes), *Aquae Sextiae* (Aix), *Apta Julia* (Apt)). In the less romanised north, towns commonly had 'double-barrelled names' with the second element containing a reference to the local Gaulish tribe, e.g. *Lutetia Parisiorum* (Paris), *Agedincum Senonum* (Sens), *Avaricum Biturigum* (Bourges), *Limonum Pictavorum* (Poitiers), *Caesarodunum Turonum* (Tours). It is significant that after the so-called 'third-century crisis' when Franks and Alamans breached the Rhine frontier and penetrated deep into Gaul, many of these northern towns dropped their official Roman names and reverted to their old tribal identities, retaining only the second element, which produced their modern form.

The evidence of place-names in the south suggests that the ancient Ligurian language persisted for some time in the inaccessible Alpine region (see Bonnaud 1981: I, 89, 257). Greek survives in a few place-names as we have seen, and apparently continued to be spoken in Marseille, but it has left few traces in the subsequent Romance speech of the area (see Cohen 1987: 60). More significant perhaps is the dearth of Celtic place-names. Much of the Narbonensis appears in fact to have been Latin-speaking by the time Caesar launched his invasion of the north in 55 BC. He did not consider the province to be a part of Gaul at all (see Berschin et al. 1978: 159). Likewise, Pliny the Elder (first century AD) saw it merely as an extension of Italy (see Whatmough 1970: 55). Early latinisation, strong links with Rome, a sizeable educated urban population were to ensure the maintenance of the linguistic norms of the Capital and the western Mediterranean.

Latinisation of the western province of *Aquitania* was slower (see Rouche 1979: 150–60). Its principal movement appears to have followed the road from Toulouse to Bordeaux (see Dudley 1975: 229). During the fourth century, Bordeaux, with its university, was to become one of the most important centres of Roman culture in the western Empire and a bastion of Roman power during the fifth-century invasions. On either side of this great axis, the progress of latinisation was slow, particularly in the area situated south of the Garonne, in the marshy lands and the isolated area of the western Pyrenees. Here the pre-Indo-European Aquitanian language (the presumed ancestor of Basque) persisted strongly. The administrative detachment of this area from the rest of Aquitania in the late third century – under the name of *Novempopulania* ('land of the nine peoples') – suggests that the ethnic and no doubt linguistic specificity of the region was still very strong. Indeed, the Aquitanian language seems to have survived throughout the Imperial period:

> Tout porte à croire que l'ancienne langue parlée en Aquitaine a résisté à la romanisation et qu'elle est conti-nuée par le basque actuel. L'examen de la diffusion des noms de lieux terminés en -*an*, -*ac* et -*os* nous a permis en même temps de conclure que le domaine de la langue basque s'étendait autrefois bien au-delà de la limite linguis-tique actuelle. Tandis que le latin, avec la civilisation romaine, pénétrait assez facilement dans les régions de la plaine, la langue indigène semble avoir opposé aux con-quérants romains une résistance prolongée dans l'extrême Sud-Ouest et dans les hautes vallées pyrénéennes.

> (Everything leads to the belief that the ancient language spoken in Aquitaine resisted romanisation and that it finds its continuation in present-day Basque. Study of place-names in -*an*, -*ac* and -*os* allowed us to conclude at the same time that the Basque-speaking area extended far beyond the modern linguistic boundary. While Latin and Roman civilisation penetrated the low-lying regions quite easily, the indigenous language seems to have offered a pro-longed resistance to the Romans in the extreme south-west and in the valleys of the Pyrenees.)

> (Rohlfs 1970: 36)

To the north-east of the Garonne lie the Massif Central and Auvergne. Here Gaulish continued in widespread use in the third and fourth centuries. Sidonius Apollinaris (430–89) remarks that even the aristocracy of Auvergne in his day had only recently learnt Latin (see Falc'hun 1963: 33–4). In the more inaccessible parts, Gaulish appears to have remained the mother tongue until at least the sixth century (see Fournier 1955; Rouche 1979: 150–1). P. Bonnaud (1981: 38) finds evidence of its survival as late as the ninth century.

Latinisation of the *Lugdunensis* and *Belgica* radiated from a focal area centred on Lyon and Vienne. Lyon was the hub of a system of five major roads leading respectively to the mouth of the Garonne, the Channel coast, the Rhine frontier, the Po valley and the mouth of the Rhône. Whereas in the Narbonensis and Aquitania Latin-speaking migrants moved principally from the Mediterranean coast, in the Lugdunensis and Belgica, some came from the coast up the Rhône, but many came directly across the Alps from the strongly celticised north of Italy (see Gardette 1983c). It is quite likely, therefore, that the Latin diffused (at a somewhat later date) in the Lugdunensis and Belgica was a different variety from that disseminated in the south.

In the Lugdunensis, romanisation proceeded north-west to Autun, the valley of the Saône, and towards the Channel coast. As one continues on this axis, Roman influence diminishes. In the fifth century the area between the Loire and the Seine was still only superficially romanised (see Rouche 1979: 24). B. Müller (1971, 1974) has shown that latinisation of the north-west received little impetus from Aquitania given the presence in western Poitou, between the Loire and the Garonne, of extensive marshland and forest inhibiting contacts between the two zones. In the Armorican peninsula (subsequently renamed 'Brittany') the diffusion of Latin was even weaker. It is therefore not improbable that when Celtic speakers from Britain migrated there in the fifth century they found sections of the indigenous population still using the related Gaulish tongue (see Fleuriot 1982: 77).

In Gallia Belgica romanisation was particularly intense in the territory of the Remi (around the modern Reims) and (for strategic reasons) along the valley of the Moselle and Rhine from Trier to Cologne. Indeed, in the third century (AD 286) the capital of Gaul was transferred from Lyon to Trier in order to control the frontier (the *limes*) more directly. The penetration of Latin into Gallia Belgica probably took place in different conditions from elsewhere. Latin was the language of officialdom and of the political and social elite, but it is clear that as in

Lugdunensis a proportion of the indigenous population remained for a long time Celtic-speaking (see Lévy 1929: I, 57–62). Indeed, St Jerome remarks that Celtic speech was still very prevalent in the region of Trier in the latter half of the fourth century and that it was more or less the same language as that spoken by another group of Celtic speakers in Galatia (Asia Minor) (see Falc'hun 1963: 33). The survival of Celtic speech in what is now German-speaking Switzerland is attested in the fifth century (see Polomé 1983: 530) and perhaps as late as the eighth century (see Falc'hun 1977: 55). However, in the east of the province, sizeable numbers of German speakers were also to be found (see Polomé 1983: 531–2). Since the first century AD, various groups of Germans had been settled in a peaceful way within the Rhine frontier of Gaul, particularly as mercenaries in the frontier army. L. Guinet (1982: 10) is of the opinion that

les contacts permanents entre Germains, Celtes romanisés et Romains créèrent en Rhénanie un bilinguisme et même un trilinguisme qui autorise à parler d'une véritable symbiose Germano-gallo-romaine.

(Permanent contacts between Germans, romanised Celts and Romans created in the Rhineland a state of bilingualism and even trilingualism which allows us to speak of a real Germano-Gallo-Roman symbiosis).

The numbers of German speakers were swelled considerably during the so-called 'third-century crisis' when the invading Franks and Alamans were pacified only by concessions of land within the Empire, thereby becoming *foederati* ('allied peoples'), with a vested interest in defending the frontier against further incursions. Franks moved into what we now call Lorraine and Flanders. A drip-feed of peaceful Germanic penetration followed. Sizeable numbers of German civilians were periodically admitted as *laeti* (foreign serfs holding and cultivating land within the Empire) to various parts of Gaul, the purpose being to make up for the loss of the indigenous rural population at the time of the 'third-century crisis'. Subsequently the north-eastern part of Gallia Belgica was split off administratively from the rest, and renamed 'Germania'. The sociolinguistic profile of this part of Gaul must have looked significantly different from that of the other provinces of Gaul from an early date, and even more so after the end of the third century.

VARIABILITY IN THE LATIN OF GAUL

Although it is safe to say that by the fifth century AD the process of latinisation was in most areas very advanced – after all, Latin survived as a spoken language in Gaul after the barbarian invasions in a way not possible in neighbouring Britain (see Price 1984: 158–69) – it is clear that the sociolinguistic situation in Roman Gaul was more variable than has traditionally been allowed (see Polomé 1983: 529–30). It is most doubtful that the language shift to Latin in Gaul could have taken place without engendering significant regional and social variation in the invading language. It is quite likely – to take an extreme case – that in certain areas pidginised forms of Latin developed for practical purposes of communication between Latin and Celtic speakers, and indeed a mixed Latino-Celtic is found in inscriptions of the fourth century AD (see Polomé 1983: 21–3). 'It is, however, unwarranted to use the scanty evidence available to build far-reaching theories of pidginisation and creolisation to account for the Romance languages' (Polomé 1980: 193, referring to Schlieben-Lange 1976). Without going so far as to postulate widespread pidginisation, it is clear that the sociolinguistic pressures in favour of spatial and social variation in the Latin of Gaul were too strong not to have any effect.

It is one thing to point to the likelihood of regional differences in the Latin of Gaul, but it is quite another to come up with hard evidence to show that this was indeed the case. Evidence of regional variation is very difficult to find in the written documents surviving from Imperial times: written Latin retained a remarkable degree of homogeneity across the Roman world for the duration of the Empire and beyond. A small amount of direct supporting evidence seems to be emerging from the work of Herman (see 1978 and 1985: 45–50) who is conducting a detailed quantitative analysis of non-standard features found in Latin inscriptions from across the Empire. By and large, however, students of Romance origins still have to make a choice: either they take the (in general) negative written evidence at face-value and argue that dialectalisation of Latin did not occur

51

until shortly before the production of the first Romance texts in the ninth century (see Muller 1929), or alternatively they play down the evidence of the written texts and hypothesise *a posteriori* about regional variability in Latin speech (see Hall 1950). Some scholars see the regional fragmentation of Latin in Gaul beginning with the latinisation of Gaul itself (see Krepinsky 1958); others see it commencing at various subsequent points according to the aspect of the process of language shift which they choose to highlight. Most scholars nowadays, however, seem prepared to accept that some degree of regional variation in Latin did exist before the break-up of the Empire (see Väänänen 1983). Of course, the profundity of the differences between the various forms of Latin spoken in different parts of Gaul is likely to remain unknown to us.

Confirmation of the existence of regional variation in the Latin spoken in Gaul comes from comments on the linguistic situation made by contemporaries. Sulpicius Severus (fifth century AD) refers to people speaking the distinctive form of Latin heard in central Gaul as 'Celtice/Gallice loqui' ('speaking in a Celtic or Gallic way') (see Polomé 1983: 528). Elsewhere he points explicitly to north–south differences in the Latin of Gaul: he reports a man from Gallia Lugdunensis apologising for his uncouth speech in the presence of Aquitanians: 'When I remember that I am a Gaul and that I am going to hold forth in front of Aquitanians, I am much afraid that my rather rustic speech may offend your over-civilised ears' (quoted by James 1982: 14). This is not at variance with conclusions arrived at through a lexical analysis of the Latin of Gaul by C. Schmidt (1974). He examined the regional distribution across the modern French dialects of a number of Latin lexical items and showed that certain regions fairly systematically adopted more 'modern' Latin words than other regions, according to their period of romanisation. This led B. Müller (1974: 22) to propose a division of the linguistic map of Roman Gaul into the three following zones:

(1) Gallo-Romance south of the Loire;
(2) Gallo-Romance along the axis Rhône valley/Belgica/Rhine, with the Rhône valley acting as a contact region with the south;
(3) Gallo-Romance of central France.

CONCLUSION

In Chapters 2 and 3 of this book, as we attempt to understand the process of dialectalisation of the Latin of Gaul, it is obviously important to look in the first instance, as we have done here, at the differential effects upon Latin of the various substrate languages – Aquitanian in the south-west, Celtic in the centre and north-west, Celto-Germanic in the north-east (see Delattre 1970). Although evidence of direct linguistic interference from these languages upon the surviving dialects of Latin is not easy to find, nevertheless the critical importance of contact between languages as an initiator of change has to be recognised (see Weinreich 1968). That said, the effects of such interference in Gaul are not automatically distinguishable from changes in Latin which may have occurred locally simply as a result of the particular sociolinguistic situation obtaining in the region concerned – this obviously varied, for instance, with the type of community involved and with the social networks existing both within it and between it and neighbouring communities. Certain areas, notably those easily accessible from the Mediterranean seaboard, maintained traditional Latin norms more firmly than elsewhere, no doubt through prolonged and intense contact with Rome and through tight integration with the economic system of the western Mediterranean. Other areas, particularly those located north of the Loire, were less closely bound in with the Mediterranean economy and were latinised later and less profoundly. Furthermore, they clearly maintained their ancient Celtic social structures longer: we saw earlier how the Roman administrative divisions of Gaul had in general shadowed those of the existing tribal territories, and how the 'third century crisis' led to a reaffirmation of ancient tribal identities, particularly in the north. It is easy to see how traditional Latin norms were weaker here than in the south, permitting more rapid linguistic change, even before the disruptive effects of the Germanic invasions of the fifth century began to be felt.

3

THE DIALECTALISATION OF GALLO-ROMANCE

If the sociolinguistic situation in Gaul was already marked by variation during the years of political and social stability afforded by the Roman Empire, the upheavals provoked by the great migrations of the fifth century triggered in the Latin language a process of wholesale dialectalisation. In peripheral areas of the western Empire (shaded on Map 5) – in north Africa, Britain, Brittany, parts of Belgium and Alsace-Lorraine and south Germany – Latin speech was eliminated completely. Elsewhere, two centuries of socioeconomic disintegration produced a fragmentation of Latin speech from which there ultimately emerged the Romance languages.

The central theme of this chapter will be the spatial diversification of the Latin of Gaul after the collapse of the Empire in the fifth century AD. (For a detailed examination of this topic, see Wüest 1979.) We shall see that in the succeeding centuries Gallo-Romance polarised between dialects of a northern type and those of a southern type, giving rise, in the Middle Ages, to two embryonic standard languages (the *langue d'oïl* and the *langue d'oc*). As is always the case with the early stages of 'new languages', the linguist has little or no direct evidence either about the structure of spoken Latin or about the diverse conditions in which the language was used during this period traditionally referred to as 'the Dark Ages'. Much that we shall say will then be highly speculative – many of the basic facts about this period are simply not known. However, what the linguist does know is that that by the year AD 900 the relative linguistic uniformity of the Latin world had been broken. How and why had this come about?

Traditionally linguists have explained the fragmentation of

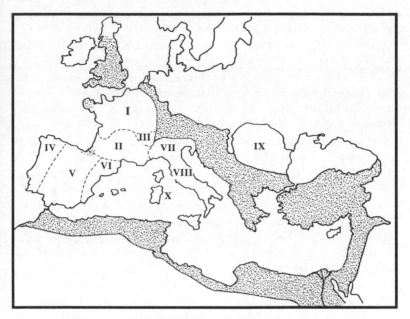

Map 5   The Romance languages

I   French
II   Occitan
III   Franco-Provençal
IV   Portuguese
V   Castilian
VI   Catalan
VII   Rheto–Romance
VIII   Italian
IX   Rumanian
X   Sardinian

Latin principally in terms of the interference it underwent from
the languages with which it came in contact. The central debate
has tended to focus on whether it was the *substratum* language
(essentially Gaulish) which had the more determining influence
on the fragmentation of Gallo-Romance, or whether this role
was performed by the Germanic *superstratum*. While not under-
estimating the role of interference phenomena in language
change, in this chapter we shall not only examine the differential effects of the Germanic migrations, but we shall also look at
the importance of the spread (or diffusion) of language changes.
Linguistic innovations from whatever source tend not to remain

static. Linguistic variability generally results from different groups of speakers adopting new linguistic forms at different rates: we will have then to look at factors which made certain regions more receptive of linguistic innovations than others. It should be borne in mind throughout our discussion of the social disruption implicit in the collapse of the Roman Empire that continuity with the Roman past was by no means completely broken. Indeed, much of Roman culture and many Roman institutions survived the barbarian invasions more or less intact – especially in Italy, Spain and southern Gaul. In many spheres of activity the Pope and the Church hierarchy simply assumed the political and administrative mantle discarded by the Roman Emperor: in many areas the boundaries of the ecclesiastical dioceses perpetuated the old Imperial divisions (which in their turn had often followed earlier Celtic tribal boundaries, as we have seen). In the face of the turbulence reigning in the political and military spheres, the Church secured for western Europe a significant degree of social and ideological continuity. The language of the Church continued of course to be Latin, and this was to remain the principal language of writing, the only language with real prestige in western Europe, for the next 1,000 years.

THE BARBARIAN MIGRATIONS

As the Roman Empire collapsed, western Europe was subjected to a succession of migrations which continued from the fourth to the tenth centuries and which had a devastating impact on the social structures of Roman Gaul as elsewhere. The migrants in question came principally from the Germanic world, but others followed – Britons, Arabs, Vikings. The impact of these incursions on the society and language of Gaul was uneven, not only between one immigrant group and another, but also from one region of Gaul to another. In this chapter our attention will focus principally upon the Germanic invaders, though the others will be mentioned. The three main Germanic groups which settled in Gaul were the Franks, the Visigoths and the Burgundians. They appear to have spoken significantly divergent Germanic dialects (see Keller 1964b) and their patterns of settlement and influence were by no means all the same. For this reason a unitary approach in this chapter aimed at the whole of Gaul will not be possible. We will have to examine the topic region by region. Map 6 on p. 58 is based on Gamillscheg (1938: Karte 14) and is intended to give an overall view of the distribution of Germanic settlements in fifth- and sixth-century Gaul, based on archaeological evidence assembled by Petri (1937). The deeper the shading, the more intense the settlement.

The north

Located as it was against the German frontier of the Empire, the north of Gaul was the region most affected by the barbarian invasions. During the fifth century the north-west was overrun by Britons (in Armorica) and Saxons (along the Channel coast), and the north-east by Alamans (in Alsace), but it was the Franks in the north who were to emerge as the dominant group. It was their name which was eventually imposed as the new name for the whole of Gaul (*Francia*).

The Britons who migrated to Armorica from Britain in the fifth century were semi-romanised and so, technically speaking, were not barbarians. They were in the main refugees who had been forced to flee from their homeland by the Saxon invasion of Britain after the withdrawal of the Roman legions. They appear to have come in sufficient numbers not only to change the name of the region – henceforth it became known as 'Little Britain' as opposed to the 'Great Britain' they had left behind – but also to displace Gallo-Romance as its principal language. The Celtic speech of the invaders was closely related to the Gaulish spoken by the pre-Roman population of Gaul, and, indeed, it is now becoming accepted that this continental variety of Celtic was still spoken in the west of the Armorican peninsula (the Vannetais) when the British migrants arrived (see above, p. 49). The Breton language is still widely used in this region even today, though the frontier between Breton and French has not been stable over the centuries and has moved markedly to the west since medieval times. The Breton-speaking area is divided into four dialectal zones – *Cornouaillais, Léonnais, Trégorrois* and *Vannetais*. It is the speech of this last area which is considered to have been the most influenced by earlier Gaulish speech, as distinct from the Celtic speech imported from Britain (see Falc'hun 1977, 1981).

The Franks were a loose amalgamation of Germanic peoples living near the mouth of the Rhine. It is possible to distinguish

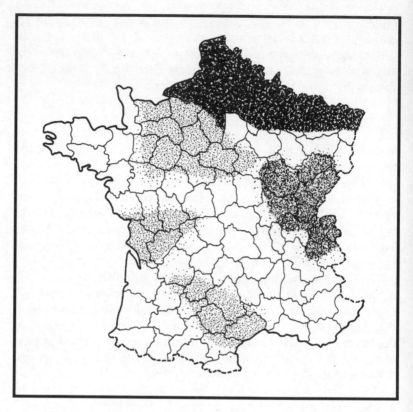

Map 6 Germanic settlement in Gaul (from Gamillscheg 1937)

 Slight

 Moderate

 Intense

slightly between the Salian Franks living in what is now Holland, and the pagan, less romanised Rhineland Franks living in what is now part of west Germany. The Franks had long provided mercenaries for the Roman army and numbers of them had been settled as *laeti* in various parts of Roman Gaul. However, after the 'third-century crisis' they began moving in significant numbers across the frontier. In the wake of this, the Romans adjusted their frontier in the lower reaches of the Rhine. A new system of defences was constructed south of the river along the line of the road leading from Cologne to Tongres, Bavai and Boulogne (see Musset 1975: 73). Salian Franks apparently moved on to the abandoned land as *foederati* in the fourth century and Saxons are known to have settled the Channel coast at the same period (see Keller 1964a).

Unlike the Visigoths and the Burgundians, the Frankish invaders consisted mainly of farmers hungry for land, not marauders hunting for military or political power. They played no part in the spectacular barbarian invasions of Gaul in the early part of the fifth century. However, from about the middle of the century the Alamans moved into Alsace and Salian Franks began migrating south in an uncoordinated way. They established themselves in piecemeal fashion on lands abandoned by the Roman aristocracy as far south as the Loire, but according to Guinet (1982: 5), their numbers were not great until the political and administrative organisation of the territory by Clovis at the beginning of the sixth century.

The political history of the Frankish kingdom between the fifth and the eighth centuries is fairly well documented – the defeat of the Gallo-Roman prince Syagrius and the overrunning of the last area of organised Roman resistance (that situated between the Loire and the Seine) in 486; Clovis's uniting of the disparate groups of Franks under the rule of his Merovingian dynasty; the establishment of the Merovingians in what has subsequently become known as the Ile-de-France; the Franks' defeat of the Visigoths in 507 and of the Burgundians in 534; the extension of Frankish protectorates into south Germany; the development of 'a long rivalry in the seventh century between Neustria in the west where the Franks were only a dominant minority, and Austrasia in the east, which was much more Germanic in character' (James 1982: 30); the triumph in the eighth century of the Carolingian dynasty with its power-base in

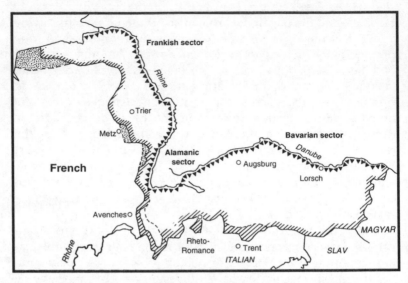

Map 7   The new linguistic frontier (from Musset 1975)

▼▼▼▼   The Roman limes at the beginning of the fifth century

//////   The present-day limits of Germanic speech

⠿⠿⠿   Losses of Germanic since the ninth century

Austrasia. Much more difficult to trace, and much more important from the point of view of linguistic history, are the development of the linguistic frontier between Germanic and Romance, the patterns of Germanic settlement in Gaul, and the chronology of linguistic and cultural assimilation.

In most parts of Gaul invaded by German barbarians, it was the German speakers who ultimately assimilated linguistically to the Romance population. However, in certain areas, particularly those located near the Rhine, the inverse occurred, and it was Romance speech which was displaced. Writing in the fifth century, Sidonius Appolinaris was quite explicit about the areas of Gaul most affected: 'The Roman tongue is long banished from Belgium and the Rhine' (quoted by James 1982: 28).

The modern linguistic frontier in Belgium and along the Rhine coincides with no natural or political boundary – hence no doubt the intense animosity even today between Flemish and Walloon in Belgium (see Genicot *et al.* 1973), and the age-old conflict between France and Germany over Alsace-Lorraine. Explanations for the alignment of the new frontier on the left side of the Rhine have given rise to much controversy (see Verlinden 1956 and Gysseling 1962), fuelled not surprisingly by national prejudices (see Joris 1966). There is no space here to enter into this debate, but it is worth bearing in mind that while the Rhine inhibited contacts across its waters, in an age when rivers provided the most effective means of transport and communication, it also facilitated contacts along its length. Once established on the left bank of the Rhine it is hardly surprising that Germanic speech should have progressed down both sides of that great European thoroughfare.

Petri (1937) argued that Germanic speech in Belgium originally extended much further west than the present border and that the Germanic 'retreat' occurred between the ninth and the fifteenth centuries. (See Map 7.) However, in thinking about this, we have to bear in mind that clear-cut language boundaries, like the ones we have become familiar with since the development of standard languages in association with nation-states, had no reality in earlier periods. Language boundaries were much more blurred, involving wide transition zones of bilingual communities, with linguistic enclaves on either side. It is known that there were enclaves of Romance around Aachen, Prum, Trier and St Trond as late as the eleventh century and in all probability there were Germanic enclaves in areas which are now French-speaking (see James 1988: 119–20). It is likely that in spatial terms pockets of Germanic speech in Gaul were less dense where contacts with areas monolingual in Germanic were looser. Diachronically, the retreat of Germanic in Gaul is likely to have followed the same pattern in reverse. In contrast to this, no transition zone between Germanic and Romance seems to have developed in the east, in the narrow area situated between the Rhine, the Vosges and Switzerland: Alsace. This region was overrun by the Alamans in the fifth century and the descendant of their language (Alsatian) has survived tenaciously in that naturally defined region to the present day. However, the evidence of place-names suggests that Romance enclaves survived in remote parts of Alsace for some time (see Lévy 1929: 1096–108).

What was the impact of the Frankish invasions on the 'interior' of Gaul? There are widely varying estimates as to the numbers of Franks who settled in Gaul. Braudel (1986: II, 93) sets the total population of Gaul in the fifth century in the region of 6 million. Petri (1937: II, 910) saw the Franks in a majority position north of the Seine; others put them at only 3 per cent of the population. Wartburg (1951: 124) estimates their numbers at between 15 and 26 per cent. Such estimates are of doubtful value for they seem based on little more than guesswork, and take insufficient account of the likely regional disparities in the distribution of Franks across the area.

Attempts to identify and locate Frankish settlements in Gaul are likewise fraught with difficulty. Interpretation of the archaeological evidence is by no means straightforward (see James 1988: 109–16), but studies of Germanic-style burials known as row-graves do show a high density of Frankish penetration in the north and north-east of Gaul (see Petri 1973: 123). Wartburg (1939: 105–10) uses the place-names ending in -*anges*, -*court*, -*ville*, -*villier* as indicators of Frankish settlements (see also Johnson 1946 and Walter 1987), for, as the new dominant class in certain areas, it was normal for the Franks to impose their own place-names. While replacement of indigenous place-names does not automatically imply replacement of the indigenous population, nevertheless the varying proportions of Frankish and Latin names in particular regions gives us an idea of the *relative* density of Frankish settlement. Thus, north of the Somme some 70 per cent of place names are Germanic, whereas in the Ile-de-France they account for only 50 per cent (see Berschin *et al.* 1978: 173). What emerges, then, is that while Frankish settlements in Gaul were dense in Flanders and Lorraine, they became progressively more sporadic as the invaders moved away from their German-speaking homeland: north of the Somme their numbers were considerable, north of the Seine they were noticeable, between the Seine and the Loire they were small, and south of the Loire almost negligible. The evidence provided by the modern dialects of Picardy and Wallonia suggests that the area showing the strongest influence from Germanic falls north of a line between Abbeville, Versailles and Nancy (see Pfister 1973a).

The most obvious point of difference between the sociolinguistic development of the 'interior' and that of the area located at the linguistic frontier was that in the former the Frankish invaders assimilated culturally and linguistically to the Romance-speaking population. Lack of evidence makes it exceptionally difficult to trace the process of language shift. We have to project back from cases of change observable in modern societies to reconstruct what may have happened in the past. In the case of the Franks in Gaul it is no doubt safe to say that the process of language shift was spread over several generations and that during that time pidgin-type contact forms and inter-languages must often have been used. The length of time involved, however, no doubt varied with social class, urban–rural residence and, of course, proximity to the German-speaking heartlands.

It appears that from the first the aristocracy (Frankish and Roman) had to be bilingual if they wished to hold office in the Merovingian state. For a while, Romans and Franks were ruled by Roman law and Salic law respectively, but there was no policy of ethnic segregation and gradually the legal distinction between Roman and Frank was lost: in the sixth century the word 'Frank' referred to a member of the German-speaking community; by the eighth century it meant no more than 'an inhabitant of northern Gaul'. Thus the word 'Frank' shifts from an ethnic sense to a territorial sense in the course of the seventh century (see James 1982: 31). It seems reasonable to infer that it was at this time that the aristocracy of Neustria became monolingual in Romance. Much play has been made of the fact that the Carolingian royal family still had Frankish as their first language in the tenth century and that Hugh Capet (941–96) was the first King of France to have had French as his mother tongue. The evidence of the linguistic usage of royal families is singularly untypical of language use in other strata of society. In the case of the Carolingians it should be borne in mind that they were of Austrasian, not Neustrian, descent, and that their homeland was the Germanic region of Aachen. If the Carolingian aristocracy of northern Gaul sent their sons to the Frankish-speaking area in the ninth century to learn the language (see Berschin et al. 1978: 172), this does not automatically demonstrate the widespread use of Frankish in Gaul. Quite the reverse! One could surmise that they sent them because noble tradition demanded it, and because they could no longer acquire Frankish in Gaul.

We have almost no information about the speech of Franks situated further down the social scale. It is known that the towns of northern Gaul, while being reduced in size during the fifth century, nevertheless remained Latin-speaking. Franks settling in them are likely to have shifted to Latin fairly quickly: it is widely attested that 'people who live in urban, industrial or commercial centres, if they speak a small-groups language, are more likely than others to shift to a language of wider currency' (Fasold 1984: 241). The majority of Franks migrated to Gaul as farmers, not as merchants or artisans, hence they settled principally in the countryside, alongside the Gallo-Romans. In so doing they introduced a number of loan-words into Gallo-Romance relating to rural life, e.g. *haie* ('hedge'), *halle* ('covered market'), *jardin* ('garden'), *loge* ('hut'), *hêtre* ('beech tree'). In most areas, varying obviously with the density of Frankish settlement, bilingualism will have become widespread fairly rapidly, but how long it took to reach the final stage of shift when bilingual parents passed on only Gallo-Romance to their children is a matter of conjecture. Separate burials for Frank and Roman ceased by the seventh century. This could give us an approximate date for the fusion of the two groups, though the maintenance of rural enclaves of Germanic speakers beyond that date cannot be ruled out, varying no doubt with the strength of network ties with the more strongly Germanic regions.

A final, but important, aspect of the language shift made by the Franks concerns *why* the conquering Franks abandoned their language in Gaul where the conquering Romans had succeeded in imposing theirs several centuries earlier. Obviously many factors were at work, particularly demographic ones, but among them is the element of motivation: language shift will only occur to the extent that a community desires to give up its identity in favour of an identity as part of some other community (see Fasold 1984: 240). One is thrust back to the conclusion that the Franks, like the Gauls before them, felt that Latin culture was still in important respects superior to their own. In those areas of life where they felt this was not the case, they modified the Latin language accordingly by bringing over substantial numbers of Frankish loan-words. This would explain how large parts of the vocabulary of feudalism (e.g. *baron*, *franc*, *lige*, *fief*, *marquis*, *ban*, etc.) and medieval warfare (e.g. *bouclier* ('shield'),

heaume ('helmet'), *guetter* ('look out'), *adouber* ('prepare'), etc.)
are of Germanic origin.

Before leaving northern Gaul to consider some of the other
regions, mention should perhaps be made of an area in the
north whose sociolinguistic history was somewhat distinctive –
Normandy. The last of the great barbarian incursions into the
Christian west came in the ninth century in the form of the
Vikings. They settled densely in northern England, and terror-
ised Gaul for several decades. In Gaul their densest settlement
was in the lower reaches of the Seine and around its mouth.
After the cession to them in 911 of that part of Gaul now called
Normandy, the Norse invaders went on to establish a remarkable dukedom based on Rouen. They assimilated rapidly to the
Romance population and there is no trace of their language
being spoken after 940 (see Vial 1983: 213). It would appear that
Norse culture and language survived longest in the area of
Bayeux, for the Dukes of Normandy continued to send their
sons there to learn the ancestral language until at least the
middle of the tenth century. Although (surprisingly perhaps)
the number of Norse elements left in the Norman dialects is
small (see Gorog 1958 and Loriot 1967: 127–8), the dynamic and
well-integrated community which grew up in this region developed its own variety of Gallo-Romance. The Dukes of
Normandy for a while posed a great challenge to the King of
France and were able to set up colonial kingdoms of their own in
England and Sicily in the eleventh century. The Anglo-Norman
dialect spoken in England in the Middle Ages had a major role
to play in the development of English (see Price 1984: 217–31).

The south-west

The western part of Gaul from the Loire to the Pyrenees was the
region which suffered least disruption from the Germanic invaders. The Visigoths who invaded Gaul at the beginning of the
fifth century were absorbed quite peaceably as *foederati* in
Aquitania in 413 AD. In return for food and land, they provided
military assistance to the Gallo-Romans in repelling attacks from
other barbarians from Armorica (see Rouche 1979: 152). As the
central power of Rome weakened to extinction during the years
which followed, the Visigoths used their military pre-eminence

to establish a semi-independent but pro-Roman kingdom based on Toulouse, and for a while the Visigoth kings controlled a vast area of Gaul from the Loire to the Rhône and the Mediterranean. They even extended their power beyond the Pyrenees. Place-name evidence shows Visigoth settlements across a wide area of Aquitaine between the Loire and the Garonne. They concentrated most densely around the city of Toulouse.

Their numbers, however, were small. On the basis of the annual quantities of food promised to them by the treaty of 416, M. Rouche (1979: 167) estimates the Visigothic population at that time to have been between 50,000 and 100,000. Moreover, the Visigoths seem to have consciously remained aloof from the Gallo-Roman natives: they adhered rigorously to the Arian brand of Christianity regarded as heretical by Rome; the Visigothic code of law forbade intermarriage with the Gallo-Romans (see Rouche 1979: 171). It is not surprising therefore that when there came the inevitable conflict with the Franks from the north (507), the Visigothic warlords were uprooted with relative ease. They established a kingdom in Spain based on Toledo, but retained control over the littoral from the Rhône to the Pyrenees, known in those days as Septimania. This strengthening of the links across the Pyrenees between Languedoc and Catalonia no doubt had repercussions upon the linguistic geography of that area, but the direct contribution of the Visigoths to the linguistic development of Aquitaine seems virtually nil.

> The destruction of the Visigothic kingdom of Toulouse by the Franks in 507 did not lead to any great changes in Roman society south of the Loire. Few Franks settled in the area, and Roman landowners continued to dominate through their social position and control of the Church. The Merovingian kings were, for the most part, content to exploit Aquitaine from a distance. Thanks to its own cultural and historical traditions, and those of its social elite, Aquitanians too preserved, or more probably found, some kind of ethnic identity during the Merovingian period.
>
> (James 1982: 19)

Thus, for more than two centuries after the nominal attachment of Aquitaine to the Frankish kingdom in 507, the vast region south of the Loire was able to continue with its Roman ways (see

James 1988: 107), turn its back on the Germanic world to the north, and enjoy almost complete autonomy.

While much of Europe in the sixth and seventh centuries was plunged in economic recession, Aquitaine experienced a period of relative prosperity. This is attested in the development of the great towns of the region – Bordeaux, Poitiers, Bourges, Clermont, Rodez, Toulouse. Far from declining, as was the fate of many Roman towns elsewhere, these cities actually expanded, constituting major poles of attraction for the surrounding region in the economic, administrative and religious spheres. The simultaneous presence of a bishop and Roman fortifications appeared to have been an important determining factor (see Rouche 1979: 298). In this way much of Aquitaine saw a continuity of Roman social structures, patterns of life and no doubt language as late as the eighth century.

The great exception to this was the region situated between the Garonne and the Pyrenees – Novempopulania. This area had been only superficially romanised, and in the late sixth century the Basques ('Vascones') broke out of their Pyrenean enclave and invaded it. Attempts to dislodge them proved ineffective until the ninth century, during which time the name Vasconia (Gascony) was extended to the whole region: 'Garonnam fluvium, Aquitanorum et Wasconorum conterminem' ('the land of the Aquitanians and Basques bounded by the river Garonne') (Rouche 1979: 156; see also 87–98). Although the Basques did not cause the Latin-speaking population of this area to shift languages, the modern dialect boundary between the Romance dialects of Gascony and those of the rest of Aquitaine is still coterminous with the Garonne.

It was not until the eighth century that the real if not official autonomy from the Frankish kingdom enjoyed by Aquitaine was seriously interrupted. When the Arabs overran the Visigothic kingdom in Spain in 711 and subsequently began using Septimania as a base for raids into Gaul, the Franks under Charles Martel from Austrasia moved south to check their advance. They used the opportunity to try to bring the south of Gaul more effectively under northern control. The destruction wreaked by Charles Martel during his campaign caused economic decline in the south and finally broke the power of the Roman senatorial families. Despite this, the region bounded by Bordeaux, Poitiers, Clermont and Toulouse remained remote from northern influence, and its cultural and linguistic development was to reflect this.

The development of Latin in this area was on the whole a good deal less rapid than in areas further north. The relative stability of the old social structures in the region, the stronger survival of traditional norms in the towns, the greater contacts with the Mediterranean world no doubt ensured a certain conservatism in the Languedocian dialects (see Map 8 on p. 72). The explanation of the highly distinctive features characterising the Gascon dialect has been much debated. It appears that numerous factors are responsible – the pre-Latin Aquitanian *substratum*, the post-Latin Basque *superstratum*, and close communication networks with Romance speakers south of the Pyrenees, all had a role to play (see Rohlfs 1970). The dialects of north Aquitania (Limousin and Auvergnat) merge into a broad band of transitional Gallo-Romance varieties known as the 'Croissant' and sharing a number of features with northern French dialects – as one would expect in a situation of dialect continuum.

The south-east

The south-eastern part of Gaul from the Jura to the Mediterranean did not enjoy the same insulation from the social and demographic changes of the time as was enjoyed by Aquitaine. Geographically it was located closer to the Germanic world, and it was traversed by one of the major thoroughfares of western Europe – the Rhône valley. As the Roman Empire collapsed, this region of Gaul, like the rest, was overrun by Germanic barbarians.

The part of south-eastern Gaul least touched by invasion was Provence. This area provided a place of refuge for numerous senatorial families fleeing the insecurity of the northern provinces. For some years during the fifth century, Arles became the residence of the Roman Emperor himself. Provence was the last redoubt of the Roman presence in Gaul, just as it had been the first. Political domination of Provence fell successively to Visigoths (482), Ostrogoths (507) and Franks (536), but six centuries of romanisation buttressed by the power of the old landowning families and the Church were not to be effaced by the limited injections of German-speaking population in this period.

Frankish power in Provence remained weak and remote. Like much of Aquitaine, this region continued to live according to the old patterns of life with its Mediterranean trading links for almost three centuries after the collapse of the Empire. It continued to be called Provincia alongside Aquitania, Burgundia and Austrasia (see Busquet *et al.* 1976: 29), until the Arab raids of the eighth century and Charles Martel's devastation of the south. Not surprisingly, therefore, the Latin of the Mediterranean part of Gaul (particularly Provence) differentiated itself only very slightly from the rest of Romance speech current in the western Mediterranean.

Further north, however, the barbarian invasions of the fifth century had a more disruptive effect. The area between Lyon and Geneva was taken over by the Burgundians (see Perrin 1968). Like the Visigoths, the Burgundians had been settled in Gaul as part of deliberate Roman policy in the early part of the fifth century. They installed themselves as *foederati* in the area between Lyon and Geneva, and it is clear that the strategic reason for this was to plug the gap between the Jura and the Alps, thus protecting the prosperous towns of the Rhône valley from the Alamans poised on the eastern bank of the southern Rhine.

> The Burgundian settlements, which are mainly betrayed by the place-names ending in *-ingos* (French *-ans* or *-ens*), are concentrated in the French-speaking part of modern Switzerland, the Jura and the plain of the Saône; they are rarer in Savoy and Burgundy, and almost non-existent south of the River Isère. The archaeological finds of Burgundian type for the period before 534 have a more or less similar distribution pattern.
>
> (Musset 1975: 64)

(See also Perrenot 1942.)

Like the Visigoths, the Burgundians remained faithful allies of Rome so long as the Empire lasted, but as Imperial power disintegrated they set up their own autonomous kingdom based on Lyon. This did not mean an end to the power of the local Roman senatorial families, who continued to have great influence as civilian officials in the Burgundian kingdom, and who, of course, supplied the majority of the bishops. As in Aquitaine, the senatorial aristocracy continued to hold positions of authority until the Carolingian era. A remarkable example of this is to be found in the Syagrius family, the last known member of which was abbot of Nantua in 759 (see Musset 1975: 127). Schools of Latin rhetoric were apparently still flourishing in Lyon and probably in Vienne at the beginning of the sixth century (see Musset 1975: 65). The Burgundians for their part did not remain aloof from the Romans. Instead, they worked closely with them, Romans and Burgundians ruling their respective communities side by side. The Burgundian code of law, while being basically Germanic, was strongly influenced by Roman law. It permitted intermarriage. Bilingualism between Latin and Burgundian was normal in the ruling elite in the fifth century, and not simply among the ethnic Burgundians: Sidonius Apollinaris reports that the senator Syagrius was so fluent in Burgundian that he used to correct the grammatical errors of his Burgundian friends (see James 1982: 23). Gradually, the Burgundian kingdom adapted itself fully to urban life and to Latin civilisation. All the indications are that at the higher echelons at least, the Burgundians assimilated to Roman culture early and thoroughly. How true this is of Burgundians lower down the social scale and how long Burgundians continued to use their own language are matters for conjecture. According to Musset (1975: 64), the Burgundian language was still spoken in Gaul early in the seventh century – he quotes the evidence of the runic texts discovered at Arguel (Doubs) and Charnay (Saône-et-Loire) which date from this time. However, the changing reference of the name 'Burgundian' implies that the separate linguistic and ethnic identity of the Germanic Burgundians had been lost by the end of the seventh century: Gregory of Tours, writing in the sixth century, still distinguished between the Germanic and Gallo-Roman sections of the population, but people writing at the end of the seventh century used the term *Burgundiones* to mean 'all the inhabitants of south-east Gaul' (James 1982: 24).

Burgundy was drawn politically into the Frankish kingdom of which it formed the third major part alongside Neustria and Austrasia. The Burgundians retained a separate legal identity in the Frankish kingdom until the ninth century. Burgundian law was one of the last barbarian law codes to yield to Frankish law. But was this ethnic identity essentially Germanic in character, or did it result from the absorption into the Roman culture of the

Lyonnais of certain relatively superficial Burgundian elements? As a social and geographical unit, Burgundy had little cohesion and permanence – as can be seen from the numerous partitions and reallocations of the territory in later centuries (see James 1982: 25).

THE LINGUISTIC MAP OF FRANCE

After this (admittedly cursory) overview of population movements within Gaul in the centuries following the collapse of the Roman Empire, let us now turn to the new linguistic map of Gaul which was probably emerging in the ninth and tenth centuries, before addressing the general question of why Latin changed more substantially in certain areas than in others.

It is reasonably safe to assume that by the tenth century the everyday speech of Gaul had become quite strongly diversified along regional lines. Some of the evidence justifying this assumption will be discussed at the beginning of the next chapter. The dialectal divisions in question appear in the main to be the ones which have persisted into modern times: a comparison of the geographical distribution of regional forms found in medieval texts with their distribution charted on to modern dialect atlases shows a remarkable degree of stability (see Dees 1985: 112). Map 8 on p. 72 gives an overview of the chief dialectal divisions of rural speech in modern France. In what follows we will begin by looking in general at the notion of dialect boundaries, then we will look at the major cleavage between the *langue d'oc* (often referred to by earlier scholars as 'Provençal') and the *langue d'oïl*, and thirdly at the problem of Franco-Provençal.

Linguistic geographers draw lines on a map (known as 'isoglosses') marking the boundaries where particular linguistic features are to be found. Normally the isogloss derived from the observation of one linguistic feature does not coincide along the whole of its length with the isogloss derived from another. Consequently, in order to establish the boundaries of a given dialect, linguistic geographers take an aggregate of features judged to be criterial. It is no doubt on the basis of this sort of evaluation that the dialect boundaries indicated on Map 8 were established. It needs to be emphasised, however, that, convenient as they are for reference, such lines represent a

71

Map 8   The Gallo-Romance dialects (from Offord 1990)

considerable distortion of the sociolinguistic reality 'on the ground'. For a start, the dialects in question are unlikely ever to have existed in a 'pure' form, that is they were never uniform across the space concerned, but like all vernaculars were characterised by inherent variability (see Gauchat 1903). Second, the boundaries between dialects are in fact largely artificial divisions in a continuum. This latter point has in fact been the subject of bitter dispute between dialectologists, some of whom we can label the 'separatists' and others the 'continuators'. 'Separatists' are particularly anxious to see clear lines around the dialect(s) they are studying (often, one suspects, for non-scientific reasons, like the promotion of a regional identity, or even regional autonomy). 'Continuators' prefer to see dialects as a continuum, one merging imperceptibly into the next, an

72

approach which, it too, is not automatically free from political *parti pris*.

The most significant cleavage within Gallo-Romance is that between the linguistically conservative dialects in the south and the more innovative dialects in the north. Medieval observers gave them the labels *langue d'oc* and *langue d'oïl* after the words for 'yes' in the two languages. In order to get a slight 'feel' for the differences between them, let us contrast a southern dialect of the *langue d'oc* (Languedocian) with the standard variety of northern French. This has the virtue of clarity and simplicity, but the great drawback of ignoring all the regional diversity of Occitan (for this language exists principally as a highly diversified collection of dialects) and all the spatial and social variability present in northern French.

Spatial variation came to affect Gallo-Romance at all levels of the linguistic system (lexical, morpho-syntactic and phonological), but the reader should obtain an impression of the extent of diversification by looking at some of the principal phonological variables:

Evolution of stressed vowels

Latin	Occitan	French
ō	/o/	/œ/
e.g. *florem*	*flor*	*fleur*
ē	/ɛj/	/wa/
e.g. *peram*	*peira*	*poire*
a	/a/	/c/
e.g. *amare*	*amar*	*aimer*

Palatalisation

Latin	Occitan	French
ca-	/ka/	/ʃə/,/ʃa/
e.g. *capillos*	*capels*	*cheveux*
cantare	*cantar*	*chanter*

Medial consonants

Latin	Occitan	French
c	/g/	–
e.g. *securum*	*segur*	*sûr*
p	/b/	/v/
e.g. *sapere*	*saber*	*savoir*
t	/d/	–
e.g. *maturum*	*madur*	*mûr*

A fuller idea of the difference between the *langue d'oïl* and the *langue d'oc* may be had from comparing the following two versions of part of the Parable of the Prodigal Son:

Un òme aviá pas que dos dròlles. Lo plus jove diguèt a son paire: 'Es ora pèr ièu de me governar sol e d'aver d'argent: me cal poder partir e véser de païs. Despartissètz lo vostre ben e donatz-me çò que devi aver.' – 'O mon filh,' diguèt lo paire, 'coma voldràs tu; siás un marrit e seras castigat.' Apuèi dubriguèt una tireta, despartiguèt lo sieu ben e ne faguèt doas parts. [Languedocian]

Un homme n'avait que deux fils. Le plus jeune dit à son père: 'Il est temps que je sois mon maître et que j'aie de l'argent; il faut que je puisse m'en aller et que je voie du pays. Partagez votre bien et donnez-moi ce que je dois avoir.' – 'O mon fils,' dit le père, 'comme tu voudras; tu es un méchant et tu seras puni.' Et ensuite il ouvrit un tiroir, il partagea son bien et en fit deux parts. [Standard French]

(Bec 1967: 114)

It should not be assumed that within either of these linguistic zones there exists a high degree of homogeneity. As is normal with oral vernaculars, each of them is characterised by extreme variability, along regional lines. Within the *langue d'oïl* area the Picard zone, for instance, manifests strongly marked characteristics, setting it apart from the speech of other regions: e.g. *chanter* (French); *canter* (Picard). Normandy, Champagne and the rest present similarly diversified features.

Likewise, within the *langue d'oc* area, the speech of Gascony has strongly marked regional features of its own: e.g. *farina* (Occitan); *haria* (Gascon). Northern Occitan (Auvergnat and Limousin) and other dialects all have their own characteristics, distinguishing them from Southern Occitan (Languedocian and Provençal).

What is the nature of the major division within Gallo-Romance, namely that between the *langue d'oïl* and the *langue d'oc*? It is undoubtedly the case that several important isoglosses follow a closely parallel trajectory across the French *patois* surviving into the twentieth century: there does seem to be a significant bunching of isoglosses as one moves north–south through the Gallo-Romance dialect continuum. See Map 9. The resulting line runs east–west from Bordeaux to Geneva, fanning out into a confused transitional zone at its eastern end. What is intriguing is that it follows no long-standing political frontier and that there is no obvious natural barrier to communication along much of its length. Actually, the sharpness of the line may in the past have been unduly emphasised by scholars. The great philologist Gaston Paris, writing a century ago, was seeking to minimise its importance when he declared:

> La science . . . nous apprend qu'il n'y a pas deux Frances, qu'aucune limite réelle ne sépare les Français du nord de ceux du Midi, et que du bout à l'autre du sol national nos parlers populaires étendent une vaste tapisserie dont les couleurs variées se fondent sur tous les points en nuances insensiblement dégradées.

> (Science teaches us that there are not two Frances, and that no real boundary separates French people in the north from French people in the south, and that from one end of our national territory to the other, our popular dialects make up a vast tapestry whose varied colours merge into one another at all points in imperceptible nuances.)
>
> (Paris 1888: 3)

Paris was undoubtedly influenced in this view by his own 'one-nation' political attitudes – if there is a Romance dialect continuum, why stop at the Spanish and Italian frontiers? However, by and large it is true to say that clear-cut dialect boundaries tend to occur only where there are serious barriers to communication, like mountains, forests, marshes, etc., and such barriers to communication between the north and the south of France are less dramatic than those offered by the Alps and the Pyrenees.

There is indeed a significant blurring of the boundaries between the *langue d'oc* and the *langue d'oïl*. It is widely accepted that during the Middle Ages there existed a mixed transitional

75

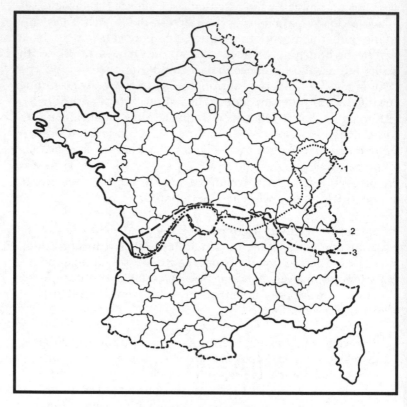

Map 9   Oc–Oïl isoglosses

1 ⋯⋯   Southern limit of *mener* (cp Occitan *mina*)

2 ‒⌐‒   Southern limit of *heure* (cp Occitan *ora*)

3 ⌐·‒·⌐.   Southern limit of *chanter* (cp Occitan *cantar*)

zone between *Oc* and *Oïl* in Poitou – Occitan features were current as far north as the western reaches of the Loire (see Millardet 1922: (61) 125–9; Pignon 1960; Gossen 1969; Wüest 1969). A similar zone is attested today across the north of Limousin and Auvergne and has been labelled the 'Croissant' (the 'Crescent'), because of its shape (see Bec 1967: 9 and Brun-Trigaud 1990). However, the most significant transition zone is the one located in the east and labelled 'Franco-Provençal'.

The term 'Franco-Provençal' was introduced over a century ago by the Italian dialectologist G. T. Ascoli (1873, republished 1878) who attempted to see the dialects spoken between the Lyonnais and Geneva, around the confluence of the Rhône and Saône, between the Jura, the Alps and the Massif Central, as a coherent group, distinct from both the *langue d'oc* and the *langue d'oïl*. On analysis the distinctiveness of Franco-Provençal lies perhaps less in its possession of its own peculiar linguistic traits than in its own peculiar combination of linguistic traits, some drawn from the *langue d'oïl*, others from the *langue d'oc*. Here is a simple example of the sort of feature mixing which can occur:

chanter (French); *chantar* (Franco-Provençal); *cantar* (Occitan).

No part of the Gallo-Romance area poses the problem of the delimitation of a dialect/language more acutely than Franco-Provençal.

The dialectal situation in the region has been closely analysed by P. Gardette and his collaborators, and they seem firmly convinced of the specific linguistic reality of Franco-Provençal (see Gardette 1983b). This view was shared by W. von Wartburg who attempted to correlate the boundaries of Franco-Provençal with the area of greatest Burgundian settlement. This suggestion raises a number of difficulties: firstly, no one can be sure of the exact location and density of the Burgundian settlements in question; secondly, apart from a number of lexical items, it is hard to see precisely in what ways the dialects of the area were influenced by Burgundian speech; thirdly, it is exceptionally difficult to draw the line separating Franco-Provençal from Burgundian to the north, from Auvergnat to the west and from Provençal to the south.

R. A. Hall (1949) called into question the whole linguistic reality of Franco-Provençal, echoing P. Meyer's view, expressed in his review of Ascoli that

aucun groupe de dialectes . . . ne saurait constituer une famille naturelle, par la raison que le dialecte (qui repré-sente l'espèce) n'est lui-même qu'une conception assez arbitraire de notre esprit. . . . C'est que les phénomènes linguistiques que nous observons en un pays ne s'accor-dent point entre eux pour couvrir la même superficie géographique. Ils s'enchevêtrent et s'entrecoupent à ce point qu'on n'arriverait jamais à déterminer une circons-cription dialectale, si on ne prenait le parti de le fixer arbitrairement.

(No group of dialects can constitute a natural family, for the reason that the dialect (which represents the whole group) is itself only a somewhat arbitrary conception of our mind. . . . The problem is that the linguistic phenomena which we observe in a particular area do not coincide in their coverage of the same geographical area. They overlap and intersect one another to such an extent that we can never succeed in determining the boundaries of a dialect without fixing them arbitrarily.)

(Meyer 1875: 294)

It is not impossible that part of the motivation for seeking to fix and ennoble the dialects of the region sprang rather arbitrarily from the desire of inhabitants of Lyon (France's second city) to assert their own regional identity.

Situated at the crossroads of Gaul, the Franco-Provençal area received cultural and linguistic influences from all directions, not least from across the Alps. It is not really surprising, there-fore, that the region shows dialectal features of both north and south. More disconcerting is the bewildering complexity with which these heterogeneous elements are distributed across the area. Part of the explanation for this no doubt lies in the fact that the mountainous terrain in the east of the region isolated from each other the communities living there. Another factor worth bearing in mind, however, is the fact that the focusing influence of the city of Lyon does not appear to have been strong between the collapse of the Empire and the later Middle Ages (see Gardette 1983a).

CAUSATION

So far in this chapter we have looked first at the settlement of large numbers of non-Latin-speaking migrants on the territory of Roman Gaul, particularly in the fifth and sixth centuries AD, then at the dialectalised state of spoken Latin which we can assume to have emerged by the ninth or tenth century. In the latter part of this chapter we will explore the nature of the link between these two orders of events. For all the gradations existing between the *langue d'oc* and the *langue d'oïl*, it is evident that particular language changes happened to the Latin spoken in certain areas but not in others, and it is important to ask ourselves why.

Traditional explanations of the origins of spatial variation rely heavily upon interference from other languages – in our case languages which came into contact with Latin either as a *substratum* or as a *superstratum*. We saw in the last chapter how the contact of Latin with the various indigenous (substrate) languages of Gaul, coupled with differential rates of romanisation, almost certainly meant that even before the Germanic invasions the Latin spoken in Gaul was not uniform. Certain scholars see this as the most decisive element in the dialectalisation process. However, these scholars are probably not the majority. The explanation of the dialectalisation of Gallo-Romance which still predominates is that proposed by W. von Wartburg – the differential impact on Latin of the speech of the Germanic invaders. He sees the Franks as having exerted the determining influence on the Latin spoken in Gaul north of the Loire, with the Burgundians having a similar, though weaker effect in the east. According to Wartburg, the boundary between the *langue d'oïl* and the *langue d'oc* 'coincide assez exactement avec une limite ethnique et politique qui s'est formée vers 500, grâce aux invasions germaniques' ('coincides pretty exactly with the ethnic and political boundary estblished around 500 AD as a result of the Germanic invasions') (Wartburg 1962: 64). He sees Frankish *superstratum* influence as profoundly and directly affecting not only the lexicon, but also phonology and syntax.

The difficulties which arise from the hypothesis of direct *superstratum* influence as the principal factor in the dialectalisation of Gallo-Romance are considerable. Firstly, as we have seen, no one is very sure about the precise limits and intensity of

Frankish settlement in Gaul, but support seems to be growing for the idea that it was a good deal more restricted than that required by Wartburg's explanation. Secondly, given that it was the invaders who abandoned their first language in favour of Romance, it is not easy to see how the indigenous population, who were in most places in the majority after all, were induced to adopt the 'foreign accent' and simplified morphosyntax of the invaders as their normal mode of speech. Such a scenario is plausible in those areas where Germanic settlement was dense and where Germanic speakers occupied positions not only at the top of society, but also half-way down, between the dominant elite and the low-status mass of the population. Such speakers could have acted as vehicles for the downward spread of Germanic-oriented innovations. Evidence either way on the existence of such a bridging group is not available. However, it seems unlikely that the necessary conditions for this obtained outside the northern region, let us say beyond the line running between Abbeville, Versailles and Nancy which we considered earlier (see above, p. 62).

We are left then with the conclusion that both the *substratum* and the *superstratum* theory in their simple form provide an inadequate explanation for the dialectalisation of Gallo-Romance. Let us now look at other factors.

It is important to distinguish between the *origins* of a linguistic innovation and its *diffusion*. By no means all linguistic changes have their origins in 'other languages': changes commonly occur spontaneously in certain styles or within particular social groups without necessarily being triggered by outside influence. However, as far as the origins of the linguistic changes which occurred at this time are concerned, it is quite possible that a fair proportion of them arose through interference from Germanic, for example the tendency to diphthongise stressed vowels in northern Gallo-Romance (see Pope 1952: 102). Even so, this does not necessarily mean that wherever we find diphthongisation, Germanic speakers had settled in abundance: linguistic items like goods and ideas can travel outside the areas of settlement of their originators.

Dialectal fragmentation can perhaps best be seen as the product of differential rates of change, that is to say that, for whatever reason, a language may evolve more quickly in certain areas than others, creating variation between the speech of one region and that of the next. It is arguable that the origins of particular innovations and indeed the rate of speaker innovation in fact matter little: the rate of linguistic change in a given area is determined above all by the speed of diffusion. What factors inhibit or facilitate the diffusion of language changes through the speech community?

The importance of the diffusion or 'spread' of innovations as a factor in language change has long been acknowledged in what is called 'wave theory': changes initiated in one area spread to other areas like ripples in a pond (see Bynon 1977: 192–5). Linguistic innovations can be shown to have focal areas and to engender transitional zones and relic areas as they spread. The diffusion of a particular innovation will be related to the level of communication between groups: it will be checked by a high degree of communicative isolation between groups. The most obvious barriers to communication are natural ones (mountains, forests, marshes, etc.). The most important channels of communication in the pre-modern age were river valleys. In this way, the Alps, the Pyrenees and the sea present clear boundaries around much of the Gallo-Romance zone, while across the middle, as Müller observed (see above, p. 49), the Massif Central, and the forests and marshes of Poitou, presented important obstacles to communication in earlier times. Conversely, the major channels of communication provided by the great rivers of France, notably the Rhône and the Loire, ensured considerable contact between north and south, at least in the east of the country. According to 'wave theory', innovations initiated in the contact zones between Germanic and Romance would have spread south and west until checked by natural barriers in the centre and west and would have mingled with conservative, southern features in the contact corridor located at the head of the Rhône valley, i.e. in the area now referred to as Franco-Provençal. 'Natural' constraints on north–south communication seem to have brought it about that southern Gaul remained predominantly within the economic and cultural system of the Mediterranean, while northern Gaul was drawn more closely into the markets offered by the Germanic north. It is significant that the isoglosses running across France correspond to an extent with cultural boundaries involving such things as roof styles, field patterns and legal systems (see Map 10).

The rate of diffusion of innovations is not determined solely

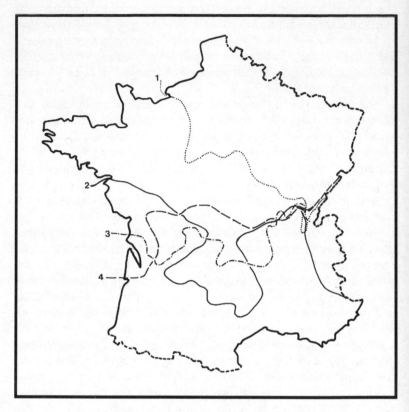

Map 10 Cultural boundaries within France

1 ····· Southern limit of open-field farming

2 ⌣ Northern limit of round roof-tiles

3 ∼·⌒∖ Southern limit of the langue d'oïl

4 ∼⌣⁄ Boundary between customary law and Roman law

by geographical factors, however. It is determined also by social factors like the structure of social networks within the population concerned: 'a close-knit network has an intrinsic capacity to function as a norm-enforcement mechanism' (Milroy and Milroy l985b: 359); 'social and geographical mobility is conducive to the formation of weak ties' (p. 366); 'innovations flow from one group to another through weak network links' (pp. 343–4); 'linguistic change is slow to the extent that the relevant populations are well-established and bound by strong ties; whereas it is rapid to the extent that weak ties exist in populations' (p. 375). Transposing these ideas to Gallo-Romance, we can see that so long as the Roman world was bound together at macro-level by strong ties, the Latin language was subject to relatively slow rates of change. Once the ties became weaker, the rate of change accelerated. Social networks were loosened at different rates in different parts of the Gallo-Romance area and in consequence we find differential rates of linguistic change. We have seen how the Mediterranean area and much of Aquitaine suffered relatively little social disruption during the Merovingian period: Roman patterns of life were able to survive for several centuries longer than in northern Gaul. The relatively strong ties there acted as something of a brake on linguistic change. Northern Gaul in contrast suffered substantially more social disruption: in the first place the old Roman structures were not so firmly established (particularly in the north-west), and secondly the area was much more affected by the Germanic migrations. The resultant weak ties triggered more rapid linguistic change in northern Romance. The north-east of Gaul along the line of the Rhône and the Saône to the Moselle was intensively romanised, but in the north at least suffered very severe social disruption and loosening of the Roman social networks. Predictably the rate of language change here was rapid. The south-eastern region (Merovingian Burgundy) saw its Roman structures less violently disrupted and was in more permanent contact with the conservative south. Not surprisingly, therefore, it maintained a lower rate of linguistic change. Müller (1974: 22) plausibly argues that Franco-Provençal is 'le dernier témoin de la latinité de l'axe Rhône–Belgica/Rhin' ('the last survival of the Latin once spoken along the axis Rhône–Belgica/Rhine'). As the old Roman world economy was replaced by small autarkic communities, strong local ties developed, giving rise to local cohesion, but paradoxically also to the overall fragmentation. This was to characterise rural speech in France until the nineteenth century.

CONCLUSION

In this chapter we have continued the discussion begun in Chapter 2 concerning the dialectalisation of the Latin of Gaul. We have seen that, in order to explain this process, it is not sufficient simply to consider direct interference from other languages upon the Latin of Gaul (*substratum* and *superstratum* influences). We have had to consider how important sociolinguistic factors affected different regions of Gaul in different ways: the variable strengths of Latin norms, the variable stability of Roman social structures, the diverse types of social network and the different patterns of communication within and between particular social groups.

4

SELECTION OF NORMS

In the last chapter we looked at the progressive dialectalisation of the Latin of Gaul in the centuries following the collapse of the Roman Empire. Now we shall examine the beginnings of the long process whereby French passed from 'dialect' to 'language', from 'vernacular' to 'standard'. In Haugen's analysis (see above, pp. 25–6), the first phase of standardisation involves the 'selection' from among the dialects spoken over a given geographical area of one which is to form the basis of the future standard language. The 'selection' of vernacular norms is a 'social' process entailing modifications to the status of the varieties concerned.

The social aims of language standardisation involve ultimately the wider acceptance of a particular set of supraregional linguistic norms. As with standardisation of the coinage, weights and measures, etc., the suppression of variation in language makes for greater functional efficiency and the ability to communicate over longer distances (of space and time): pressure for shared norms comes importantly from the economic needs of the community (the development of wider markets etc.). It comes also, however, from the universal tendency for human groups to use language as a symbol of their identity (serving to bond members of the group together and to differentiate them from members of other groups). The development of linguistic norms shadows the structure and evolution of social groups. The most constraining linguistic norms tend to be found in communities which Le Page and Tabouret-Keller (1985) refer to as 'highly focused societies' (groups whose members interact frequently with one another on a number of levels, who have a strong focal point and feel themselves to be under some sort of outside threat). Such groups most often occur either at the bottom of society (e.g. minorities like the Bretons who feel oppressed, marginal groups like the criminal fraternity of *ancien régime* Paris with its *argot*) or at the top (e.g. dominant elites like the products of the British public schools). However, similar principles seem to operate at the level of whole 'nations' too: as the examples of present-day Belgium and Canada show, the symbolic power of language and feelings of language loyalty can be extremely strong.

The notion of a linguistic standard or 'norm' is not a simple one and the term is given a wide variety of applications (see Bédard and Maurais 1983 and Müller 1985: 263–94). We shall have to return to it later (see below, pp. 154–7). However, a preliminary discussion of certain aspects of the word's meaning might be helpful here. It is important to distinguish two possible meanings of the term: (a) norm as a descriptive, statistical fact, as in the sense of the adjective 'normal'; and (b) norm as a prescriptive yardstick of socially acceptable behaviour, as in the sense of the adjective 'normative'. In this chapter, and indeed in most of this book, we shall be using the word 'norm' with the sense (b). We shall need also to establish a distinction between two sorts of linguistic norm in sense (b) – spoken norms and written norms – and to treat them separately, not because they were not connected in the history of French, but because they developed at different rates.

For very obvious reasons writing is more easily standardised than speech. As a consequence of this, written standards can emerge without the prior existence of a spoken standard. In Middle English, for instance, West Saxon was used as a written standard when no spoken one existed. In early medieval France, as we shall see, writing and speaking were conducted in quite 'separate languages' – Latin and the Gallo-Romance vernaculars. Conversely, all speech communities (by definition) possess shared spoken norms, of varying degrees of localisation (local, supralocal, regional, supraregional, etc.). The norms of writing only become important for speech when it is a question of diffusing local speech-norms over a wider area, i.e. of transforming them into supralocal or even supraregional norms:

> Once a standard variety has been selected, writing is a
> powerful agent for its dissemination especially as literacy

spreads and printing makes written materials more readily available. As the written forms acquire prestige, and are considered to be 'correct', they increasingly exert a pressure on speech. The written standard acts as a norm, a yardstick and a guide.

(Leith 1983: 34)

However, we shall see that there is no real evidence to demonstrate that a single spoken standard had been 'selected' in France before the end of the twelfth century and, moreover, that little writing was conducted in the vernacular before that date. It is difficult therefore to conceive of the norms of writing significantly affecting those of speech before the greater spread of literacy in the sixteenth century.

In exploring the development of norms in Gallo-Romance, we will begin with a discussion of the vexed question of the delimitation of French and Latin, i.e. the 'beginnings' of French. We will then see how prestige varieties were 'selected', one in the north and one in the south of the Gallo-Romance area. We will conclude with a survey of the emergence of Romance writing systems and the beginnings of a written standard.

DELIMITATION OF LATIN AND FRENCH

When did the people of Gaul stop speaking Latin and start talking French? The question has frequently been asked (see Muller 1921; Lot 1931; Norberg 1966; Richter 1983) and all the scholars who ask it begin by giving the same obvious answer: they never did. French, like Italian, Spanish, etc., stands in the same unbroken line of descent from Latin as does modern Greek from Ancient Greek. Despite this, it is still legitimate to ask when it is more appropriate to label the language of a particular period as 'Late Latin', 'Proto-Romance', or 'Early Old French'. On the problems associated with labelling languages, see Lloyd (1991: 9–18).

The delimitation of genetically related languages on purely linguistic grounds is very often impossible: just as spatial dialects merge into one another in continua which commonly ignore political frontiers (or did until the imposition of standard languages from the centre), so different diachronic stages of a language form an unbroken temporal continuum. The only

87

valid internal criterion would appear to be loss of mutual intelligibility, but mutual intelligibility is itself a matter of degree (see Hudson 1980: 34–7), and it is highly unlikely that during the formative period of Gallo-Romance there was any significant break in communication between one generation of speakers and the next. We must assume that language change proceeded as usual by imperceptible gradations over the years, different dialects and styles evolving at different rates. While accepting this principle, various scholars have nevertheless made attempts to identify a period in the evolution of Proto-Romance when linguistic change may have accelerated, producing, to justify a temporal boundary between Latin and French, a diachronic equivalent of the bunching of spatial isoglosses we find in linguistic geography (see Banniard 1980). The difficulty here is that in Proto-Romance the evidence for linguistic change in speech is very scanty indeed.

Much detailed work has been done on the written Latin of the period to wring from it information about what was happening in the speech of Gaul: the writings of Gregory of Tours (see Bonnet 1890), the *Appendix Probi* (see Robson 1963), Merovingian charters and legal documents (see Vielliard 1927), the Reichenau Glossary (see Elcock 1960: 312–17) have all been minutely analysed with this purpose in mind (see Pei 1932; Hall 1950; Straka 1956). In the light of this work Norberg (1966: 355) felt able to claim that it was in the seventh century that a significant acceleration of linguistic change can be detected in Gallo-Romance. However, the fact that the different scholars who have engaged in this exercise have tended to produce different estimates (see Uytfanghe 1976) suggests that the effort is probably not worth it. Although it is clear that a great deal happened to spoken Latin between even an 'advanced' text like *A Pilgrimage to the Holy Places* (fifth century) and the 'Strasbourg Oaths' (842) – the earliest text to survive which is written in what is recognisably French rather than Latin – the evidence available is simply not strong enough to allow anyone to affirm with confidence when the rate of change may have accelerated so significantly as to permit us to draw a neat chronological boundary between one language (Latin) and another language (French), especially since, as we have seen, there developed considerable regional variation in the way Latin was spoken.

Analogous problems of dividing up continua have been

encountered by scholars trying to define the boundary between Latin and Romance in stylistic or sociolinguistic terms: when did the Latin of the uneducated in Gaul diverge sufficiently from that of the educated to create a situation of mutual unintelligibility? The traditional answer has been labelled the 'two-norm theory' (see Wright 1982) and postulates the early establishment of a diglossic situation in Gaul with 'Low Latin' (Post classical Latin distinct from the highly literary 'Classical' variety associated with the prestigious authors of the Augustan period) fulfilling the High functions in society (writing, religion, education, formal speaking, government, etc.), and 'Proto-Romance' the Low. H and L varieties of Latin, allegedly already very distinct in the fifth century, steadily diverged until the end of the eighth century when we find explicit evidence of problems of mutual intelligibility in the Reichenau Glossary, and official recognition of the separate existence of the Gallo-Romance vernacular at the Council of Tours (813). At this synod priests were enjoined to preach their sermons not in Latin but in the local vernacular if they felt that this would facilitate communication.

Aspects of this 'two-norm theory' have been challenged in an interesting way by Wright (1982) who sees in the hypothesis of an early binary split between educated and colloquial Latin a thinly disguised continuation of the now discredited opposition between Classical and Vulgar Latin, and a reluctance endemic in traditional scholars to see Latin as a language subject to

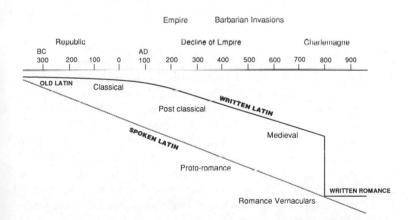

Figure 3 The 'two-norm' theory (from Pulgram 1950)

variation just like any other. For Wright, Latin and Proto-Romance constituted not two discrete varieties with little in between, but, for a good deal longer than was previously thought, a single stylistic continuum embracing the language of formal, educated usage at one end and uneducated informal speech at the other (the 'one-norm theory'): mutual intelligibility between speakers of this amalgam of varieties continued to be possible (according to Wright) for much longer than is allowed for in the 'two-norm theory' through normal processes of linguistic accommodation (see Trudgill 1986: 1–38) and through the application of 'automatic conversion rules' (Weinreich 1968:2), just as it can be maintained across the diverse varieties of English currently in use in various parts of the world. Incidentally, we need to remember when thinking about mutual intelligibility that the ability to understand a particular variety need not entail an ability to produce it actively, for our capacity to understand what we hear is always greater than our capacity to speak (see Richter 1983: 445).

Written Latin of the seventh to eighth centuries may then 'look' very different from what we assume to have been Romance speech, but this should not blind us to the fact that writing systems are abstractions capable of multiple concrete realisations in speech. Wright quotes the example of some of the ways in which the word *virginem* may have been pronounced at this time:

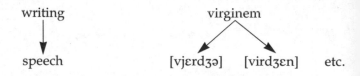

The only way Romance speech could be recorded at this time was with written Latin, and, conversely, the only way written Latin could be read (and throughout Antiquity and the Middle Ages reading meant reading *aloud*) was with the accents of Romance speech. Thus, according to Wright, the 'crisis' in Latin, when it eventually came, was precipitated not by an over-rapid evolution of colloquial speech, but rather by artificial modifications to the pronunciation of written Latin introduced by educational reforms in the Carolingian period. What *were* these reforms?

When the Carolingian dynasty displaced the Merovingians as

rulers of Gaul in the middle of the eighth century, a series of dynamic Austrasian princes – Martel, Pippin and Charlemagne – extended their power over the greater part of western Europe: Gaul, the Low Countries, Switzerland, much of Germany and parts of Spain and Italy. The only institution capable of endowing this 'new Roman Empire' with a degree of ideological and administrative cohesion was the Church, through the medium of Latin. Although written Latin had remained homogeneous, the pronunciation of spoken Latin had come to vary considerably from one part of Europe to another. How was spoken Latin to be unified as part of the movement to promote the cohesion of the Carolingian state? It was decided that Latin pronunciation should be firmly anchored to spelling and that when Latin was read out it should be pronounced *litteraliter*, 'sounding every letter', without accommodating the speaker's pronunciation to local phonology as had traditionally happened in Romance-speaking regions. The 'letter by letter' pronunciation of Latin had long been the practice in Germanic-speaking England where no amount of phonetic accommodation could have made Latin comprehensible to monolingual speakers of Anglo-Saxon. An English scholar, Alcuin, was therefore brought to Gaul from York to reform the pronunciation of Latin in the newly established schools of Tours, Orléans, Corbie, Metz and Lyon.

This move may have brought a greater semblance of uniformity to the Roman Church, but at the same time it broke the last threads of mutual intelligibility between a Latinate clergy and monolingual speakers of Proto-Romance – in northern Gaul at any rate. It precipitated a crisis of communication between clergy and laity, and led eventually to the development of new writing systems designed specifically for the various vernaculars. Wright goes on to show that the effects of the introduction of the 'new Latin' were felt later in some parts of the Latin world than in others – he compares in particular the situation in northern Gaul with that found in Spain where (presumably) even the 'new Latin' continued to be comprehensible, and consequently the need for vernacular writing systems was not perceived until a good deal later.

It is legitimate to ask why the clergy should have persisted with the 'new Latin' if it led to serious communication problems with their flock. It is indeed hard to believe that the 'new Latin' could have been widely adopted in liturgical use if the clergy had seen it primarily as a more efficient means of communicating information or ideas to the unlettered laity (i.e. of admitting the laity into full knowledge of the faith). Its adoption by the clergy can be understood, however, if we consider two factors: firstly, the Church's strong desire to combat heresy through identical performance of its liturgy throughout western Christendom, and secondly the idea that the 'new Latin' was intended not essentially as a more efficient instrument of communication with the laity but as a symbol of identity within an exclusive group. There is, in fact, strong evidence to show that the Church of the period wanted to see Latin (and with it the mysteries of the faith) retained as the monopoly of the priestly elite, conformity with a minimum of comprehension being all that the laity required for its salvation (see Richter 1975: 70). This sort of linguistic attitude is common in most societies:

> Les locuteurs sont poussés à réduire les barrières linguistiques lorsque domine le désir de communiquer avec autrui ou, au contraire, d'en dresser pour exclure ou s'en démarquer.

> (Speakers are induced to reduce linguistic barriers when the desire to communicate with other people is dominant, and, in contrast, to raise them in order to exclude people and set onself apart from them.)

> (Valdman in Vermes 1988: I, 10)

The difference between the 'two-norm theory' and the 'one-norm theory' is perhaps mainly one of chronology: during the course of the centuries being discussed here, there eventually developed in Gaul a situation of diglossia. This situation came about earlier according to the first theory than it did according to the second. From what we have just seen, it is pointless to look for a historical moment when there occurred a clear break between the linguistic structures of Latin and those of French. If we still wish to impose a boundary between French and Latin, the safest way is probably to link it to the time when speakers themselves became conscious of the gulf separating the two systems, i.e. when there developed 'a social consensus that Romance [was] to be considered a different language from Latin' (Lloyd 1991: 15). This comes at the beginning of the ninth century. The linguistic problems which inevitably resulted from the changes in clerical practice regarding the pronunciation of Latin were discussed at synods of the Church assembled in 813 in five episcopal centres in Gaul and Germany – Mainz, Reims, Tours, Chalon-sur-Saône and Arles. At these synods it was decided that, whereas the liturgy of the Mass proper should be conducted everywhere in the canonical linguistic forms (with the new pronunciation), in the sermon or homily priests were given latitude to use the language variety most conducive to comprehension by the local congregation.

> Il s'agit, à l'époque carolingienne, de préserver le latin écrit de tout contact avec les bas langages, et simultanément d'utiliser l'existence des parlers locaux pour le gouvernement des fidèles.
>
> (In the Carolingian period it was a question of protecting written Latin from all contact with lower speech varieties, and at the same time of using these same varieties for the control of the faithful.)
>
> (Balibar 1985: 38)

An analysis of the decisions taken at each of the five synods mentioned above enabled Richter (1983) to demonstrate how the newly purified Latin created varying degrees of intelligibility problem in different regions. In Mainz priests were permitted to preach in the language which the congregations would understand (German). In Reims (northern Gaul) they were authorised to preach 'secundum proprietatem linguae' ('according to the appropriateness of the language'), and in Tours (western Gaul) they were enjoined to 'transferre [= 'translate' or 'transpose'?] in rusticam romanam linguam aut thiotiscam, quo facilius cuncti possint intellegere quae dicuntur' ('translate/transpose into the rural Romance tongue or into German, so that everyone may understand what is being said more easily'). No such linguistic guidance was felt necessary in the synods held at Chalon (east-central France) and Arles (Provence). It would not be unreasonable to conclude from this disparity that the linguistic distance between reformed Latin and the Romance varieties was significantly greater in the north and west than it was in the south.

If a cut-off point between Latin and French is required for purposes of exposition, the year 813 is perhaps the most suitable, for purely symbolic reasons – it marks the first occasion when official recognition is given to the existence of a Romance vernacular. The decisions of the Church councils of 813 make it clear that by that time the sociolinguistic situation of northern Gaul (like that of Germanic Europe) was diglossic: the new Latin performed the H functions in society and the numerous local vernaculars the L. Latin indeed possessed all the characteristics generally recognised in H languages (see Ferguson 1959: 235–45; and above, pp. 13–14):

Function: Latin alone was used for writing and for the conduct of important matters like religion, the law and government. Latin continued to be the common language of the educated elite of Europe throughout the Middle Ages.

Prestige: Latin was the only language which possessed any prestige in western Europe, the oral vernaculars being regarded as mere 'idioms'.

Literary heritage: Since all writing was conducted in Latin, only Latin possessed a literary tradition. The oral traditions of the vernaculars had no standing beside the great authors of Ancient Rome.

Acquisition: Latin had to be specially taught at school. The vernaculars learnt at one's mother's knee were indeed referred to as *linguas maternas*. To speak in the vernacular was *maternaliter loqui* (see Decrosse 1987).

Standardisation: Only Latin had a strongly codified grammar and was perceived as invariable beside the ever-changing vernaculars.

Grammar: The grammatical structure of any given L variety is 'simpler' than that of its corresponding H. Latin has grammatical categories not present in L and has an inflectional system of nouns and verbs which is much reduced or totally absent in Gallo-Romance.

Lexicon: Latin included in its lexicon learned expressions which had no Gallo-Romance equivalents, and likewise Gallo-Romance can be assumed to have included in its total lexicon popular expressions and the names of very homely objects or objects of very localised distribution which had no Latin equivalents.

The sociolinguistic history of France between the ninth and the sixteenth centuries traces the gradual breakdown of this diglossic situation and the leakage of function from H to L, from Latin to French. This process began with the emergence of prestige forms among the vernaculars and the adaptation of the vernaculars to writing.

THE SELECTION OF SPOKEN NORMS

The defining characteristic of non-standardised languages is not the absence of norms but their proliferation in response to the local needs of the loosely networked social groups which make up the speech community. It is reasonable to suppose the existence of local norms, supralocal (regional) norms and eventually supraregional norms. Standardisation involves the progressive elimination of alternative norms through the selection of one norm which is superimposed on the rest. Frequent attempts have been made to trace the beginnings of the process whereby the spoken norm of Paris was 'selected' and subsequently diffused into the French provinces, evidence for spoken usage being sought in the written texts of the period. While this written evidence clearly cannot be discounted in tracing the history of French speech, the partial autonomy of written and spoken norms we discussed earlier makes writing an unreliable guide to the development of spoken standards.

Labov (1973: 120) argues that

> the speech community is not defined by any marked agreement in the use of language elements, so much as by participation in a set of shared norms; these norms may be observed in most types of evaluative behavior, and by the uniformity of abstract patterns of variation which are invariant in respect to particular levels of usage.

It is this attitudinal approach which we shall adopt in this section: how did contemporaries feel about the different Gallo-Romance varieties present in the early Middle Ages? When did the Parisian French of the King's court begin to be more highly valued than other varieties?

Let us look at some of the terms used to label vernacular language in medieval France and at metalinguistic statements indicative of attitudes towards particular varieties. In order to distinguish the Romance vernaculars from Latin, the general term *lingua romana* (in French *roman*, in Spanish *romans*) was used from an early date (813). Within the *lingua romana* spoken in Gaul, what terms were used to distinguish the speech of the south from that of the north? A distinction appears for the first time on the occasion of the First Crusade (1095) when speakers from the south are designated as *Provinciales, Proensals, Provensals* and those from the north *Francinae*. In the thirteenth century the Latin term for northern French is *lingua gallica*, and it is commonly used by Occitan speakers to differentiate the speech of the north from their own speech, which they label *noster idioma* (see Brun 1923: 15) or *romancium* (see Lusignan 1987: 38). We have to wait till the end of that century, however, before we find the first attestations of the terms *lingua d'oc* and *lingua d'oïl*: they appear in 1291 (see Meyer 1889: 11), and are taken up in the following century by Dante in his *De Volgari Eloquentia* I, viii and ix, and *Vita nuova* XXV (see Danesi 1991: 248–58). It is very likely that the designations *langue d'oc* and *langue d'oïl* had been current a good while before that, for from 1271 the King's chancellery regularly refers to the domains of the Count of Toulouse as *partes linguae occitaniae*. The name *Occitania* appears to be a blend of *oc* + *Aquitania*. The widespread use of these terms to differentiate the two broad types of Gallo-Romance comes surprisingly late. We must suppose that such differentiation became necessary only when the northern conquest of the south in the thirteenth century brought speakers from distant ends of Gallo-Romance into regular contact with one another, in circumstances by all accounts of mutual unintelligibility (see Monfrin 1972: 756–7). What is absent from this bipartite division of Gallo-Romance is any term referring to Franco-Provençal: was this variety subsumed under the label *lingua d'oc* or was it felt to be part of *langue d'oïl*? One suspects that the term *bourguignon* is often used to refer to the speech of part of this area, but usage is far from clear.

Within the *langue d'oc*, we find two terms specifically designating the literary variety cultivated by the troubadours: *lemosi* (= the dialect of the Limousin) and *mondin* (= the language cultivated at the courts of the Raimondins in Toulouse). The only southern regional variety felt to be clearly distinguished from the rest is Gascon, referred to as *lengatge estranh* on a par with the *langue d'oïl* and with Italian (see Monfrin 1972: 761).

The *langue d'oïl* was referred to in Latin as *lingua gallica/gallicana* and in French as *françois*. This term, like the name *France* from which it was derived, was frequently ambiguous. In the twelfth to thirteenth centuries, just as *France* is sometimes a geographical term designating the Ile-de-France (see above: p. 63), sometimes a political term designating the area over which the kings of France exercised feudal suzerainty, so the term *françois* designates sometimes the dialect of the Ile-de-France, sometimes the northern French dialects in general. Nineteenth-century linguists coined the term 'Francian' to cover the former meaning and remove ambiguity (see Chaurand 1983).

Within the *lingua gallicana* Roger Bacon, writing in the 1260s, distinguished four main dialects (*idiomata*) which, though distinct, were mutually intelligible:

> ut Picardum et Normanicum, Burgundicum, Parisiense et Gallicum: una enim lingua, est omnium, scilicet Gallicana sed tamen in diversis partibus diversificatur accidentaliter; quae diversitas facit idiomata non linguas diversas.

> (Picard, Norman, Burgundian, Parisian and French: they are all the same language, namely French, but they vary accidentally in different regions; this variability makes for different dialects but not different languages.)
> *(Compendium studii philosophiae*, VI, 478–9)

It is not clear from this whether Bacon sees 'Parisian' and 'French' as denoting the same thing or as designating separate entities. His usage elsewhere inclines us to the former interpretation. Thomas Aquinas and Nicolas de Lyre writing at approximately the same time give a similar quadripartite description of the dialectal situation in northern France (see Lusignan 1987: 61–2). Elsewhere Bacon talks about the negative attitudes felt by speakers of one French dialect towards those of a neighbouring one:

> Nam et idiomata ejusdem linguae variantur apud diversos, sicut patet de lingua gallicana, quae apud Gallicos et Picardos et Normannos et Burgundos et caeteros multiplici idiomate variatur. Et quod proprie et intelligibiliter dicitur in idiomate Picardorum horrescit apud Burgundos, immo apud Gallicos viciniores quanto magis igitur accidet hoc apud linguas diversas?

> (For dialects of the same language vary between different speakers, as can be seen in the French language which varies in numerous dialects among the French, the Picards,

97

the Normans and Burgundians and others. What is correctly and intelligibly expressed in the Picard dialect is unpleasant to Burgundians and indeed to their closer neighbours in the Ile-de-France. How much more likely is this to happen between people speaking different languages?)

(*Opus Majus*, II, 80–1)

Between speakers of the different *oïl* dialects there clearly existed a degree of linguistic xenophobia, but the level of mutual intelligibility seems to have been high. Monfrin (1972: 762) quotes a revealing incident which took place in 1388 and which apparently degenerated and ended in a brawl and a knifing. Two workmen met in a Paris street, a Parisian named Jean de Chastillon and a Picard named Thomas Castel:

> Ledit de Chastillon cognut au parler que icellui Thomas estoit Picard, et pour ce, par esbatement, se prist a parler le langage de Picardie; et ledit Thomas qui estoit Picard, se prist a contrefaire le langage de France, et parlerent ainsi longement.

> (The aforesaid person from Chastillon recognised from his accent that the aforementioned Thomas was a Picard, and on account of this, for a joke he began talking with a Picard accent himself; and the aforesaid Thomas who was a Picard started mimicking the accent of Ile-de-France, and they went on like this for quite a while.)

It is quite likely that several regional variations acquired relatively high levels of prestige during the twelfth century, associated with regional centres of power and wealth. This is certainly the case with the language of the court in Toulouse, but the sociolinguistic history of the south was obviously quite separate at this time. It may well have been true of linguistic usage in the Plantagenet courts in the west (Angers, Rouen) and the great towns of the north (e.g. Arras), but this is only conjecture. However, it is clear that the variety used at the King's court in Paris emerged in the second half of the twelfth century as the most prestigious of the northern Gallo-Romance vernaculars. Various writers in the twelfth and thirteenth centuries refer to its pre-eminence: 'Mis lenguages est bons car en France fui nez' ('My language is good because I was born in the Ile-de-France')

(Guernes de Pont Sainte-Maxence, *La Vie de Saint Thomas Becket*, 1. 6165, *c.* 1175)

Conon de Béthune (in Picardy) reproves the Queen for picking him up on linguistic features used by him which do not conform with the Parisian norm:

> La Roine n'a pas fait ke cortoise
> Ki me reprist, ele et ses fueis li Rois;
> Encoir ne soit ma parole franchoise,
> Si la puet on bien conprendre en franchois
> Ne chil ne sont bien apris ne cortois
> S'il m'ont repris se j'ai dit mos d'Artois,
> Car je ne fui pas norris a Pontoise

(The Queen, along with her son the King, acted discourteously when she criticised me: although my speech is not that of Ile-de-France, one can still undertand me in French. And those who criticised me for using words from Artois are not courteous or polite, for I was not born in Pontoise.)
(Conon de Béthune, *Chansons*, III.8–14, *c.* 1180)

The value set on politeness and refinement in the courtly code quite naturally generated a notion of good (and bad) usage in language – referred to at the time as *bel parler*. The speech of Paris clearly formed the basis of this upper-class norm: 'Mainte bele dame cortoise/Bien parlant an langue françoise' ('Many a beautiful lady conversing elegantly in the French language') (Chrétien de Troyes, *Chevalier de la Charette*, ll. 41–2, *c.* 1175).

Aimon de Varennes says of his poem:

> Il ne fu mie fait en France
> Maix en la langue de fransois
> Le prist Aymes en Loenois.
> Aymes i mist s'entension,
> Le romant fit a Chastillon.

(It was not written in Ile-de-France, but Aimon put it into French in the Lyonnais. Aimon set his mind to it and wrote the romance in Chastillon.)
(*Florimont*, ll. 14–18, *c.* 1188)

Chastillon has been identified (somewhat surprisingly) with Châtillon-sur-Azergue near Lyon (see Pfister 1973b: 218–19). Later in his poem Aimon declares:

As Fransois wel de tant servir
Que ma langue lor est salvaige;
Car ju ai dit en mon langaige
Az muels que ju ai seu dire,
Se ma langue la lor empire,
Por ce ne m'en dient anui.

(I want to serve the French even though my language
sounds barbarous to them. For I have expressed myself as
best I could in my language. If my language is hurtful to
them, let them not criticise me for it.)

(ll. 13614–19)

In the last quarter of the twelfth century the growing sense of a
prestige norm is visible in the attempts by various French
writers to represent the speech of foreigners. The most notable
examples are to be found in the *Roman de Renart* where the
authors mimic speech of Italians and Englishmen as they
attempt, rather unsuccessfully, to speak French (see Reid 1958:
102–3, Lodge and Varty 1989: 70–3).

The thirteenth century brings more explicit statements about
the emergence of Parisian French as a dialect with special status.
Roger Bacon's use of the word *puros* to refer to Parisian French
indicates that, for him at least, it served as a spoken norm: 'in
Francia apud Picardos, et Normannos et puros Gallicos, et
Burgundos, et alios' ('In France [there exist several dialects]
among the Picards, the Normans, the pure French, the
Burgunds and others') (*Compendium studii philosophiae*, VII, 467).

Likewise, the Anonymous of Meung, writing later (*c.* 1325,
according to Van de Vyver (1939: 257–8)), extols the special
merits of the French of Paris at the expense of his home dialect:

Si m'escuse de mon langage
Rude, malostru et sauvage
Car nes ne sui pas de Paris
Ne si cointes com fut Paris;
Mais me raporte et me compere
Au parler que m'aprist ma mere
A Meun quand je l'alaitoie,
Dont mes parlers ne s'en devoye,
Ne n'ay nul parler plus habile
Que celui qui keurt a no vile.

100

(I apologise for my rough, uncouth and barbarous language, for I was not born in Paris, nor am I as elegant as was Paris; but I hark back and compare myself to the speech my mother taught me when I took milk from her breasts. My speech does not stray from this, and I consider no speech more subtle than the one which is current in our town [presumably Paris].)

The growing ambiguity in the notion of *langue maternelle* is here expressed quite explicitly: in the past (as we saw above, p. 94), to speak *maternaliter* meant to speak the vernacular acquired at home as opposed to the Latin learned at school. Now we find the Anonymous of Meung's home dialect being treated as his *langue maternelle* to distinguish it from a new prestige variety – the speech of Paris (see Batany 1982). The traditional Latin–vernacular hierarchy is being superseded by a standard–dialect hierarchy. As the power of the King was extended beyond the Ile-de-France in the thirteenth century, so his language set the norms among influential people in the subjugated provinces. *François* gradually ceased to be the name for the dialect of the Ile-de-France as the King's French became the administrative language of a vastly extended kingdom.

The prestige of the King's French did not stop at the borders of the kingdom: the aristocracies of neighbouring countries (especially England and Germany) felt impelled to follow Parisian fashions not least in matters of language. Particularly through the Crusades, the King's French had come to play a vehicular role across Europe's aristocracy. Writing in the 1270s Adenet le Roy alludes to the contemporary aristocratic practice in Germany of learning Parisian French:

> Tout droit a celui tans que je ci vous devis
> Avoit une coustume ens el tiois paÿs,
> Que tout li grant seignor, li conte et li marchis
> Avoient entour aus gent françoise tous dis
> Pour aprendre françois lor filles et leur fis.
> Li rois et la roÿne et Berte o le cler vis
> Sorent pres d'aussi bien le françois de Paris,
> Com se il fussent né ou bourc a Saint Denis.

(At the very time I am talking about it was the custom in Germany that all the great lords, earls and marquesses

101

surrounded themselves with French people to teach
French to their sons and daughters. The King and Queen
and Berthe with her radiant face knew French almost as
well as if they had been born in the town of Saint Denis.)
(Berte aus grand piés, ll. 148–55)

During the twelfth century and into the thirteenth, the royal
court was generally held in the Abbey of Saint-Denis, 11 km
north of Paris, for it was here that the royal household could be
sure to find clerks with the necessary writing and chancery
skills. The kings of England used the Abbey of Westminster in a
similar way.

It is clear that by the thirteenth century the speech of Paris
had become the most highly valued of the northern French
vernaculars, but disagreement exists over the period at which
social attitudes first began to view the speech of Paris in such a
special light. Basing their argument on an analysis of the
earliest written texts, some scholars see it as having acquired
special status as early as the ninth century (see Hilty 1973).
Others see the process of selection happening only in the late
twelfth century (see Delbouille 1962). The former position
becomes difficult to sustain when we consider the early history
of Paris.

Roman *Lutetia Parisiorum* had been a city of some importance,
but it belonged firmly in the second rank of Roman towns in
Gaul after Lyon, Trier, Autun, Arles, Bordeaux, etc. It achieved
greater prominence under the Merovingians, for Clovis established his headquarters there in the sixth century, but this was
by no means his dynasty's principal residence – of the 195
surviving Merovingian charters, only nine originate from Paris
(see Rauhut 1963: 269). It is true that Dagobert founded the
famous abbey at Saint-Denis in the seventh century, but the
significance of this foundation did not become great until the
twelfth century. Indeed, under the Carolingians, Paris lost all
importance as a political centre – of the 700 surviving
Carolingian charters, none originates from Paris (see Rauhut
1963: 269), and Petit-Dutaillis (1950: 220) feels compelled to
describe Paris at this time as a 'bourg rural'. Its vulnerability to
water-borne Viking attacks no doubt inhibited its development
during the early years of the Capetians (late tenth century), who
based themselves primarily in Orléans. It is only at the end of

the eleventh century that we begin to see a growth in the demographic, economic and political importance of Paris.

Factors which fostered the growth of Paris at this time are primarily economic: its location at the centre of the rich agricultural area of the northern plain; the navigability of the Seine connecting the depots of the Ile de la Cité with the sea and with the markets of Champagne. During the twelfth century Paris mushroomed into the largest urban community of northern Europe. Accurate estimates of population at this time are impossible to make, but a figure in excess of 50,000 seems likely (see Dollinger 1956: 35–44; Duby 1980: II, 401; Braudel 1986: I, ii, 135). The Church played an important role in the development of the city through its great abbeys at Saint-Denis, Saint-Germain, Saint-Victor and Sainte-Geneviève and through its schools, soon to become the University of Paris. It comes as no surprise, therefore, to find the Capetian kings in the eleventh century seeking to gain control of this expanding city. During the first third of the twelfth century they transferred their principal residence from Orléans to Saint-Denis, extending the boundaries of the royal domain (see Pernoud 1966: 28) and forging a close bond with the Church which of course provided the technical expertise required by the royal bureaucracy – as well as spiritual legitimisation of the Capetian dynasty.

The evidence suggests then that the pre-eminence of Paris as a social and economic centre should not be dated before the beginning of the twelfth century, that is not long before contemporary observers begin to remark upon its linguistic prestige. From the end of that century onwards, the notion that the King's French constituted the spoken standard slowly came to gain acceptance across the *langue d'oïl* area, though participation in Parisian norms was of course much slower in the *langue d'oc*. The contrast between Occitan prestige variety – to be found in the courts of the counts of Toulouse – and the King's French is revealing. The speech of the ruling elite in Toulouse never achieved the same prestige in the Occitan area as the King's French achieved in the *langue d'oïl* – partly because the counts of Toulouse failed to achieve the same political and economic supremacy in their domain as did the Capetian kings in theirs, partly because the independence of the county of Toulouse was broken by the superior resources of the kings of France in the early years of the thirteenth century. Occitan remains to this day a language with no spoken standard shared by a majority of its dwindling number of speakers.

It is sometimes implied, if not openly asserted, that the French of Paris was 'selected' to form the basis of the future standard on the grounds of its inherent structural superiority over the other Gallo-Romance dialects. While it would be rash to assume that linguistic factors had no bearing on the matter at all – it has been argued, for instance, that the central geographical location of the Ile-de-France within the *langue d'oïl* area meant that it represented the lowest common factor among the *oïl* dialects (see Wartburg 1962: 89–90) – nevertheless, social, demographic and economic factors were undoubtedly the decisive ones. As political and economic power came to be concentrated in Paris in the twelfth century, making Paris the crossroads of France with its markets, law courts and schools, so the language of the rich and powerful in Paris came to be accorded greater status and respect.

THE DEVELOPMENT OF VERNACULAR WRITING SYSTEMS

There is a widespread belief in communities with a long-established standard language and long traditions of literacy that the written language represents the 'real' language while the spoken forms constitute derivative if not degenerate varieties. The fleeting and variable nature of speech is commonly compared unfavourably with the stability and uniformity of writing. In literate societies the written language enjoys particular prestige: reading and writing are essential if an individual is to have access to education and knowledge, and in consequence the ability to write, or more particularly to spell, is often taken to be an unmistakable sign of intelligence (and *vice versa*). Now, to expose the myth of the primacy of the written word, we need only look at the history of natural languages: the development of writing always comes chronologically after the development of speech. There are still languages in the modern world which do not have a written form. One of the cornerstones of modern linguistic science is then quite rightly the affirmation of the primacy of speech. Having said that, however, we must not fall into the opposite trap. Writing does not simply reproduce speech visually; rather it involves the creation of a separate and distinct performance adapted to different conditions of use (i.e. where the sender and receiver of the message are separated in time and space). Writing and speaking have different domains of use, and 'graphisation' adds to the language a new variety (see Ferguson 1968: 34). Historically speaking, writing is derived from speech and it is the case that in most languages it retains a close correlation with speech. However, it is not uncommon to find communities where speaking and writing are conducted in separate languages, it being in these instances more convenient to use the writing system of a foreign language than to develop a new one based on one of the oral vernaculars. This was the case in much of Europe in the early Middle Ages.

The two most widely used types of writing system are logographic (e.g. Chinese script where the smallest units are characters representing whole words) and graphemic/phonemic (e.g. Roman, Greek, Cyrillic, where the smallest units are letters representing (in theory) individual sounds) (see Cohen 1953). In a graphemic/phonemic system the visual sequence of characters on the page is to an extent motivated by corresponding sounds in speech. However, the graphemic/phonemic systems operating in different languages embody differing degrees of correspondence between letters and sounds: that is, they involve differing degrees of arbitrariness. Letters, like phonemes, are generalisations: firstly they are made to represent an often wide range of positional variants (e.g. the three *os* in *monopoly* represent in fact three different sounds varying with their position in the word). Secondly, spellings often represent wide ranges of regional and social variation in pronunciation (e.g. in British English the three forms *Mary*, *marry*, *merry* are written and pronounced differently; in the American Mid-West they are written differently but all pronounced the same). Thirdly, because writing operates in the medium of sight not sound, it can operate a system of visual distinctions which do not necessarily replicate the aural distinctions of speech (e.g. French spelling maintains a visual distinction between homophones like *pin*, *pain* and *peint*).

Acceptance of a high degree of arbitrariness in the letter–sound relationship allows for a degree of uniformisation in spelling which far exceeds what can be achieved in pronunciation: 'spelling is the most uniform level of language use and contrasts in this respect with the variability of its counterpart in speech – pronunciation' (Milroy and Milroy 1985a: 66). In societies like Britain and France where respect for the standard language is deeply engrained, any deviance in the area of spelling is severely stigmatised. While acceptance of a high degree of arbitrariness in the spelling system facilitates its uniformity, the converse is also true: the maintenance of stability and uniformity in spelling progressively increases the arbitrariness of the system. The modern spelling systems of English and French represent the fossilisation of a disparate collection of medieval systems which have become progressively divorced from pronunciation as sound change has proceeded (e.g. *thought, plough, through* in English and *chat, vieux, beaux* in French). Thus, in their initial stages graphemic/phonemic systems aim at a one-to-one correspondence between letter and sound, but the more successful they are in being adopted for long-term and widespread use, the less this one-to-one correspondence becomes attainable. Extension and prolongation of their use tends to make them more and more logographic and less and less graphemic/phonemic.

In early medieval Europe Latin played a role whose importance it is difficult for us 1,000 years on to appreciate: whatever the vernacular one used for speaking, Latin was the normal language of writing. Learning to *write* meant essentially learning to write *Latin*. Vernacular writing systems developed at quite an early date in Germanic-speaking Europe (e.g. in England from as early as the eighth century), but they were used much less commonly than Latin. In Romance-speaking Europe they took longer to emerge, no doubt because written Latin read aloud remained vaguely intelligible for longer. It is significant that the first attempts to record the Gallo-Romance vernacular in writing were made in north-east Gaul where Germanic practice was familiar and where existed no doubt the greatest problems of intelligibility between Gallo-Romance and Latin (see Wright 1991: 105).

The first specimen of writing which has survived in the *langue d'oïl* is the celebrated 'Strasbourg Oaths' of 842 (conserved in a manuscript copied in Soissons *c.* 1000), followed at half-century intervals by the *Sequence of Saint Eulalia* of *c.* 900, the *Sermon sur Jonas* of *c.* 950 (both copied near Valenciennes), the *Passion* and the *Life of Saint Leger* of *c.* 1000 (both copied in or near Clermont-

Ferrand). A century later we find the *Epreuve judiciaire* and the *Cantique des Cantiques* (both copied in the north-west, Normandy or Brittany). On all these texts see Poerck (1963). In the twelfth century, writing in the *langue d'oïl* becomes more common (though only a handful of twelfth-century manuscripts have survived) and the texts involved are literary and in verse. Only in the thirteenth century is French used in written prose and in non-literary as well as literary texts. The first surviving non-literary texts written in French are charters from Tournai (1197) and Douai (1204) (see Brunot 1966: I, 359 and Gossen 1967).

In the *langue d'oc* the development of writing takes slightly longer (see Bec 1967), the first specimen being a translation of Boethius's 'Consolation of Philosophy' (the *Boecis*) copied *c.* 1000, followed by *Sainte Foy c.* 1050). However, once the practice of vernacular writing started in the south, it appears to have spread quite quickly. The eleventh century sees the use of the *langue d'oc* in numerous legal texts, beginning in 1034 and 1053 in Foix and Narbonne respectively (see Brunel 1922, 1926, 1952). Thereafter the use of Occitan in writing becomes very frequent, in both literary texts and in administrative documents.

Why did the practice of writing in the Gallo-Romance vernaculars take so long to develop? Of course, it could be that the low numbers of vernacular manuscripts surviving from the tenth and eleventh centuries, compared with the substantially larger numbers surviving from the twelfth, reflect a greater loss of vernacular documents in the earlier centuries. It would be unwise, however, to maintain that the survival rate of these documents bears no relation to their rate of production. The explanations for the slow start are partly economic, partly technical and partly 'political'. Firstly there was the economic problem – the production of parchment, ink and pens in the subsistence economy of the early Middle Ages was an expensive business, particularly in a primitive rural and oral culture where the demand for writing was not great. In the early centuries very little writing happened at all. From a technical viewpoint devising a writing system for a vernacular with no previous written tradition was a formidable undertaking: the only letters available were those designating Latin sounds – how was the divergent phonology of Romance to be accurately represented? Moreover, the phonology of Romance varied from region to region – a writing system devised for one area could not be

107

easily reused in another area. In this way lack of a vernacular standard almost certainly discouraged people from committing matters important enough for written record to such a variable and low-prestige medium. Finally there was the 'political' problem.

We have already seen that at this time learning to write traditionally meant learning to write Latin. The acquisition of this expertise was long and arduous, and only a select few were successful. As a result, the few who could write (the clergy) enjoyed a special status in society, which they were not eager to surrender. All words associated with writing converged in the popular mind with the meaning 'Latin'. For example, *letré* (< *litteratus*) designated a man acquainted with Latin; a *clerc* (< *clericus*) was a man who could read and write Latin, and his language – *le clergeois* – was Latin. *Gramaire* normally meant Latin grammar, sometimes simply 'Latin' and occasionally 'magic'. The tiny priestly elite who possessed the ability to write were regarded by the unlettered populace (the *lai* people) with superstitious awe. This monopoly, which bestowed on the clergy immense political and social power, was jealously guarded: the clergy were under no pressure to devise new and more widely available systems of writing (see Richter 1975: 70). We shall see that the development of vernacular writing systems went hand in hand with the growth of groups in society (the secular aristocracy and the merchant class in the towns) which stood somewhat outside the traditional value-system of the Church.

In these circumstances it is legitimate to ask what made clerks break with their Latin habits in a few sporadic cases between the ninth and eleventh centuries and try their hand at writing the vernacular. The fact that so many of the early texts are in verse offers us a clue – such texts, along with the 'Strasbourg Oaths', were written exclusively for oral performance. We saw earlier how prior to the Carolingian reforms it had been possible to read a Latin text aloud in such a way (by operating certain 'automatic conversion formulae') as to render it comprehensible to Romance speakers. We saw too how the Carolingian reforms had discouraged this practice (in church at least) and readers learned to pronounce every letter (*litteraliter*). It seems reasonable to suppose that the initial pressure to write in the vernacular sprang from the need to specify as precisely as possible the sounds, metre and rhyme which the vernacular text demanded in oral performance. A vernacular performance required a vernacular script.

However, despite the presence of such texts as *Saint Eulalia*, *Jonas*, the *Passion* and the *Saint Leger*, use of vernacular writing systems in Gallo-Romance did not become widespread until the twelfth century. Why should there have been an acceleration of the process then? To answer this we will have to look at the wider social and cultural changes which were taking place at the time. Once the threat posed by external enemies (Arabs and Vikings) receded, major economic and demographic changes began to transform the whole tenor of life in western Europe. Slavery virtually disappeared in the tenth century (see Braudel 1986: II, 122); technological changes followed (e.g. the introduction of watermills and the development of the harness to replace yokes) and engendered a cycle of increased agricultural production, growth in population and the clearing of new lands for cultivation. The Church was closely involved with this economic revival through its monasteries which came to be the centres of great agricultural enterprises. However, growth was not restricted to rural areas: existing towns increased in size and new towns (*villes neuves*) were created. Urban development in western Europe got under way earliest in northern Italy (Pisa, Genoa, Venice) and in Flanders (Ghent, Bruges, Ypres), but Gaul did not lag far behind (see Map 11).

The cultural implications of these socioeconomic changes were far-reaching: the narrow confines of a subsistence economy presided over ideologically and culturally by the Church began to be broken down. The aristocracy began to enjoy a life of greater well-being and comfort. They found in the courtly literature which originated in the *langue d'oc* an expression in the vernacular language of the earthly values of chivalric fame and physical pleasure they were beginning to adopt. A new class of town-dwellers came into being – the word *burgensem* (= 'burgess') is first attested at the very end of the tenth century (see Duby 1980: II, 103). They stood somewhat outside the traditional social framework encompassed by the Church and developed their own money-making values. They had strong commercial reasons for wanting a convenient (i.e. vernacular) writing system. Meanwhile, the Church itself was not inactive in the face of change: it contrived to use the fruits of prosperity

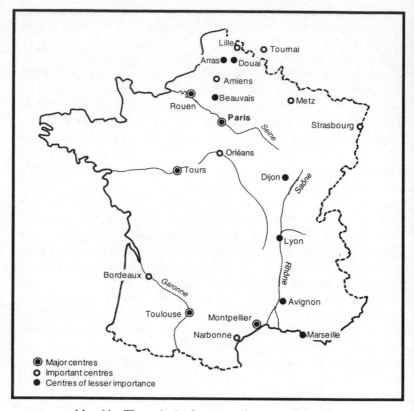

Map 11 The principal towns of medieval France.

to encourage the Crusades, build the great cathedrals of Europe, develop schools for the defence of orthodoxy (Tours, Orléans, Chartres, Reims, Paris) and to produce vernacular literature of its own to combat the subversive ideas it saw developing in many parts of society (see Zinc 1976). It was the conjunction of all these cultural and social changes which stimulated the great development in the case of vernacular writing systems in the twelfth and more particularly in the thirteenth century. Now let us look a little more closely at what happened firstly in the south and then in the north of the country.

At the end of the eleventh century, it is in the *langue d'oc* that we first see a marked increase in the use of the vernacular in writing, in both literary and administrative texts. What is striking about the writing system we find here is its high degree of uniformity. We are dealing with what has been termed a *koine*, that is a language variety shared by people of different vernaculars. Concerning the literary *koine* of the troubadours which appears in the late eleventh century, P. Bec has this to say:

> Du point de vue linguistique, ce qui frappe dans l'occitan des troubadours, c'est qu'il présente, dès ses premières manifestations, c'est à dire dès le XIe siècle, une assez grande unité: les différences dialectales y sont en effet minimes et sans aucun rapport en général avec la provenance dialectale du troubadour: l'idiome est sensiblement le même du limousin jusqu'à la Méditerranée.

> (From the linguistic point of view what is striking in the Occitan of the troubadours is that it presents a reasonable degree of unity from its earliest manifestations onwards, that is from the eleventh century; dialectal differences are in fact minimal and bear no relationship with the dialectal origin of the troubadour; the language is perceptibly the same from the Limousin to the Mediterranean.)

> (Bec 1967: 69)

It would be misleading to suggest that all variability had been suppressed in this poetic language: deviations from the norm do occur but in an apparently unsystematic way, uncorrelated with the place of origin of the composer of the lyric in question.

The origins of this *koine*, like that of the lyric itself, are obscure. It seems to have crystallised first at the court of the counts of Poitiers and to have been subsequently taken over by the counts of Toulouse. Its uniformity was maintained in the twelfth century by a notable series of works of codification – e.g. *Razos de Trobar* of Raimon Vidal de Besalu (1160–1210). This highly codified variety was used by non-natives – Italians, Catalans – as the vehicle for their own lyric poems. The Occitan *koine* was then a specially cultivated variety restricted to a small aristocratic elite and to specific literary genres. The notion of singing in a language other than the one which one speaks has nothing to surprise us – Italian was for long the language of European opera and the use of an interregional dialect for the popular ballad is well attested in English (see Leith 1983: 39). Raimon Vidal du Besalu – a Catalan – explains in the preface to his *Razos*

111

de Trobar which of the Gallo-Romance languages is appropriate for which literary genre:

> la parladura francesca val mais
> e es plus avinens a far romanz
> retrousas et pasturellas mas
> cella de Lemosin val mais per
> far vers et cansos et sirventes.

(The French language is more worthy and more appropriate for writing romances, refrains and pasturelles, but the Limousin language is better for composing songs and *sirventes.*)

(quoted by Chaytor 1945: 23)

The development of the medieval *lingua franca*, based on Italian-Provençal speech and used on the Crusades, dates from about this time (see Hall 1974: 33).

A similar degree of uniformity is to be found in the Occitan writing system used in the large number of charters and administrative documents surviving from the twelfth century. C. Brunel (1926, 1952) has located and published 540 such documents written before 1200. It is clear that the heavy concentration of vernacular documents in the region of Toulouse and the southern slopes of the Massif Central is not simply the result of the chance survival of medieval archives (see Wolff 1971: 147). The development was spearheaded by a small group of towns (Toulouse, Moissac, Villefranche, Rodez, Millau, Castres), with an important outpost in the Limousin, and the trail was blazed by the military orders (Hospitalers and Templars) and by municipal organisations; predictably the clergy (secular and regular) clung more tenaciously to their Latin tradition. The linguistic homogeneity of these documents is quite striking and it springs no doubt from the fact that they originate in almost 90 per cent of cases from the four departments of Aveyron, Tarn, Tarn-et-Garonne and Haute-Garonne. The use of Occitan as an administrative language soon spread to other areas of the south. It became very extensive in the thirteenth and fourteenth centuries (see Armengaud and Lafont 1979: 398) and began to disappear in the face of French only in the fifteenth century. However, the spellings of documents written outside the original focal area showed early signs of regional variation (see Grafström 1958: 252–8 and Lodge 1985: 50–8).

In the *langue d'oïl*, if we disregard the French used in England after the Norman conquest (see Clanchy 1979 and Price 1984: 217–31), the vernacular began to be used extensively in literary manuscripts from the middle of the twelfth century, and in administrative texts during the thirteenth century. Unlike the literary texts of southern provenance, those composed in the north of France were characterised from the start by a significant degree of regional variation. The earliest twelfth-century texts contain numerous Norman or western features (reflecting the literary influence of the Plantagenet court). The famous romances of Chrétien de Troyes (*c.* 1180) contain Champenois features. Many literary texts composed in the thirteenth century reflect the linguistic usage of the great Picard towns. Interestingly, it is only in the thirteenth century that we begin to find vernacular texts written in the Paris region. However, what is striking about the writing systems of all these early texts is their variability.

Vernacular texts from the twelfth and thirteenth centuries were clearly written by people who had nothing like the modern conception of linguistic uniformity. Not only was there no obvious supraregional norm, but even regional norms allowed much scope for variability: any one text normally contained a proportion of features 'belonging' to regions different from the one in which it was composed. This is particularly the case with literary texts where poets commonly 'borrowed' forms from other dialects for purposes of rhyme and metre. Moreover, literary texts (unlike administrative documents) were perambulatory (see Poerck 1963: 2), so they usually acquired layers of linguistic features from regions other than the place of composition, as each new scribe brought to each new copying of the text his own regional and personal spelling. However, even 'static' texts (charters and administrative documents which survive in very great numbers from the thirteenth century) contain a considerable mixture of forms (see Monfrin 1968).

Over the past 100 years the linguistic variability of medieval French texts has greatly exercised the minds of scholars concerned with the development of the written language. In the latter part of the nineteenth century the approach was dominated by Neogrammarian thinking which held that 'the sound-laws admit of no exceptions', i.e. that in a particular dialect (a) the direction in which a sound changes is the same for all the members of the speech community in question, and (b) all the words in which the sound undergoing the change occurs in the same phonetic environment are affected by the change in the same way (see Bynon 1977: 25). To this was added the view that medieval vernacular spelling systems represent naïve attempts at a phonetic alphabet. So where a text contained features belonging to more than one region, the variation was typically explained as the result of the writer working in a border-zone between two or even three dialects, or of his having lived in more than one dialectal area. The myth of 'pure dialect' was very much alive. Twentieth-century scholars have questioned this approach. The Romantic assumption that medieval culture was 'naïve' and 'spontaneous' was replaced by one which saw it as extensively governed by implicit conventions: medieval writers were seen as tacitly recognising a common written language (a *koine*) based on the speech of the Ile-de-France. Certain conventional dialectalisms were admitted to this *koine*, but genuine regionalisms were rare (see Wacker 1916). These ideas were developed further by Remacle (1948) and Gossen (1967) who originated the notion of *scripta* (a conventional supra-dialectal writing system). All writers in the *langue d'oïl*, regardless of their region of origin, allegedly wrote basically in the same central dialect. The number of Walloonisms, Picardisms, Normanisms, etc. which are present in the texts they produced is variable, but nevertheless strictly limited. Opinions are divided as regards the nature of the supra-dialectal norm: some see it as the dialect of Paris, some as the form of Gallo-Romance current everywhere in the *langue d'oïl* area prior to dialectal fragmentation, some as an artificial, neutralised variety representing the 'lowest common denominator' of the northern dialects (see Delbouille 1970; Cohen 1987: 77). Opinions are divided too on the date at which the central dialect is supposed to have begun to have its unifying influence. Hilty (1968, 1973: 271) dates it in the eighth century, Pfister (1973b: 253) maintains that Paris at least could not have exercised any such influence before the end of the twelfth century. Whatever the origins of the *koine*, however, in *scripta* theory the writing systems found in twelfth- and

Map 12   Distribution of the -s/-z spelling variables (from Dees 1980)

thirteenth-century texts are not fundamentally regional, but attempt to conform, implicitly and with varying degrees of success, to a supraregional written norm.

The *scripta* theory seems to retain the support of most contemporary scholars, but it has recently been seriously challenged by a Dutch researcher, A. Dees (1980, 1985, 1987). Working on the basis of a quantitative analysis of orthographic and morphological variables attested in texts clearly dated and located, and drawn from the whole *langue d'oïl* area, Dees is led to deny the influence of a supraregional norm in northern French before the fourteenth century. In Map 12, taken from Dees (1980: 282), we find an illustration of the final *-s* ~ *-z* variable in Old French past participles. The plural past participles of verbs like *dire*, *douer*, *avoir* could be written either *dis* or *diz*, *doués* or *douez*, *eus* or *euz*. The charters analysed by Dees more often than not admit both spellings, but in proportions which vary from *département* to *département*. The percentages indicate the proportion of final *-s* spellings in each *département*.

Dees argues persuasively that northern French writing systems were fundamentally variable, as was vernacular speech, and that the nature, extent and distribution of spelling variation in the thirteenth-century texts he analysed can be fairly reliably correlated with variation in the underlying spoken language as evidenced by the dialect atlases compiled in modern times (see Dees 1985). It may well be wrong to see writers in this period as consciously seeking to replicate in writing all the variability of local speech, but equally it is vain to look for some tacit spelling convention uniting in secret accord all the writers of northern France. Dees goes on to argue plausibly that it is not until the advent of printing in the late fifteenth century that the French spelling system is effectively standardised on the basis of Parisian usage.

CONCLUSION

We saw in Chapter 3 how a diglossic situation had arisen in Gaul by the ninth century through the development of numerous oral vernaculars and the restriction of Latin to only the H functions in society. This situation was to remain in place for most of the Middle Ages and, indeed, Latin has continued to occupy a dominant position in European culture right down to our own day. This pre-eminence led to what has been called 'la superstition du latin': not only was Latin the essential language of writing, the key to culture, learning and power, it was also believed to be the very model of what a language should be, possessed of those qualities of uniformity and permanence whose absence prevented the vernaculars from being considered as languages at all. In this chapter, however, we have also seen the first small signs of cracks appearing in this diglossic edifice dominated by Latin. Firstly we saw the beginnings of a change in attitudes towards the different varieties of Gallo-Romance – they started to be viewed as different languages from Latin. Next we looked at 'selection of norms' and saw how, among the northern French vernaculars, one variety in particular began to disengage itself from the others and to be endowed with greater prestige: the French of the rich and powerful in Paris. Finally, we observed the beginnings of a reallocation of functions between Latin and the vernaculars – the vernaculars began to be used in writing, giving birth to written norms in French. A new linguistic 'superstition' was in the making.

5

ELABORATION OF FUNCTION

In Haugen's analysis of standardisation, the 'selection of norms' (whereby one variety is singled out to serve eventually as the linguistic standard across wider geographical and social space) is essentially a *social* process, bringing enhanced status for one dialect and consequential disparagement for its neighbours. 'Elaboration of function', which we shall consider next, is in contrast a *linguistic* process bearing upon the 'corpus' of the variety involved, and transforming it from an 'undeveloped' oral vernacular into a 'developed' language. As a vernacular assumes functions over and above those of everyday conversation (for example in writing, government, learning, etc.), it has to graft on to itself new linguistic mechanisms to enable it to perform its new functions. During the early period of the history of French the only 'developed' language in use in western Europe (with the notable exception of Irish, and, up to a point, Anglo-Saxon) was Latin; it was uniquely equipped to perform the H functions in society. Gradually, however, leakage of function occurred between the H language (Latin) and the vernaculars, obliging French to make significant additions to its lexicon and syntax to cope with its new role in society. The period in the history of French when developments like this were particularly in evidence was between the thirteenth and seventeenth centuries, but, of course, the process of 'elaboration of function' is an on-going one, for, even in our own day, the language is constantly adapting itself to new conditions of use (e.g. on radio and television and on the telephone). As Haugen says, 'there are no limits to the elaboration of language except those set by the ingenuity of man' (1966: 108).

In this chapter we shall first of all examine how during the later Middle Ages in France, as in the rest of western Europe, vernacular languages came to be used in a greatly extended range of social functions at the expense of Latin, and how in so doing the King's French in particular acquired all the functional characteristics generally associated with H languages. Then we shall look at the more properly linguistic consequences of this, that is at how new varieties were added to the language through lexical and syntactic expansion and through the development of social and stylistic variation. In a concluding section we shall review the changes which occurred in the medieval situation of diglossia, observing not only how French displaced Latin as the H language, but also how, as time went on, the 'rules of the game' were changed: the evolution from a predominantly agrarian society towards a mercantile one necessitated an overall increase in literacy and the diffusion of a more readily available system of writing than had traditionally been provided by Latin. We shall observe too that in many parts of France this process involved for many people merely the substitution of one incomprehensible H language (Latin) for another (the King's French).

THE DEVELOPMENT OF FRENCH AS AN H LANGUAGE

The sociolinguistic situation of twelfth-century France was, in comparison with the situation today, exceedingly complex. Language was firmly divided into two, with Latin performing the H functions in society and numerous local vernaculars the L. It is true, as we saw in the last chapter, that this diglossic situation had altered somewhat since the tenth century – the vernacular had now come to be used to an extent in literature and in legal documents, and certain vernacular varieties had acquired prestige compared with the rest. The vast geographical area over which Gallo-Romance was spoken had seen the emergence of two potential vernacular standards – *lemosi* in the south and *françois* in the north. However, Latin was still the only language used for 'serious' purposes, the only language which did not vary over space and time, the only pan-European language (see Calvet 1981: 85), the only language deemed worthy of the name 'language'. The learned in society had then to be at least bilingual (see Lusignan 1987: 9). H culture, the preserve of a small ecclesiastical elite, was Latin and written; L culture, the

119

property of the mass of the population, was vernacular and predominantly oral. Between the thirteenth and the seventeenth centuries, this sociolinguistic situation changed radically: the two principal Gallo-Romance vernaculars underwent major developments in their social functions. Slowly but unremittingly they displaced Latin from most of the H functions in society. As time went on, the northern vernacular ('the King's French') ousted Occitan from these functions in the south of the country. In so doing it acquired all the essential characteristics associated with H languages (see above, pp. 13–14, 94). Let us look at three of the main ones here: (1) functions in government, writing and higher thought; (2) high prestige; (3) a literary heritage. We will see how French acquired the others (particularly 'codification') in the next chapter.

Sociolinguistic function

Between the thirteenth and sixteenth centuries French acquired a wide range of official and public functions, not only as the language of government and the law but also as a language of learning.

Between the thirteenth and sixteenth centuries, the King's French effectively replaced Latin as *the language of government and the law*. The penetration of the vernacular into these areas had begun in the south in the late eleventh century, but the process had to await the thirteenth century in the north. The replacement of Latin took place in two stages: in the first instance each of the regions introduced its own vernacular writing system into the administrative and legal domains; in the second instance the writing system of Paris gradually spread throughout the kingdom (and beyond), eliminating not only Latin but also regional vernaculars, notably the *langue d'oc*. The diffusion of French in the administration clearly follows the extension of the power of the kings of France.

The expansion of the power of the kings from Paris has been charted many times (see Pernoud 1966). It is graphically expressed in Map 13. The first wave of expansion took place in the thirteenth century with the conquest of the Plantagenet west – Normandy, Maine, Anjou, Touraine and Poitou (1205). This was followed by conquests in the south – Auvergne (1211) and the county of Toulouse (1272). The pretext for the attack on the

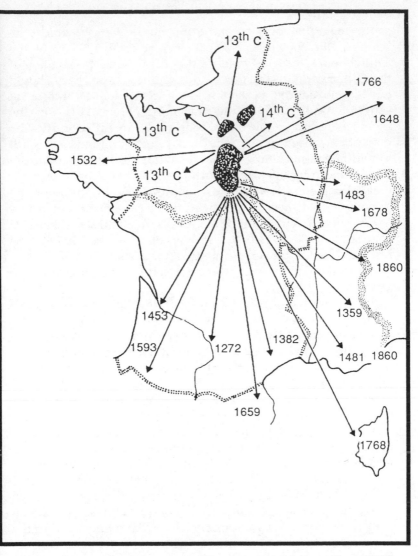

Map 13 Expansion of the power of the French kings (from Citron 1987)

Capetian domains *c.* AD 987

Boundaries of the western Carolingian Kingdom
c. AD 987

Eastern boundary of the Burgundian Kingdom and northern
boundary of the Duchy of Aquitaine in the tenth century

121

south took the form of the Albigensian heresy which the Parisian King opted to extirpate ostensibly on behalf of the Church, but it is no coincidence that the ensuing persecution of the Cathars and destruction of the southern aristocracy should have removed the possibility of a rival political power in southern Gaul. Champagne was annexed in 1284, and the Lyonnais and Dauphiné followed in the fourteenth century. The disruption caused by the Hundred Years War (mid-fourteenth to mid-fifteenth centuries), the demographic and economic decline induced by the Black Death (1348–9) and subsequent outbreaks of plague (between one-eighth and two-thirds of the population perished according to the area) slowed down this royal progress, but in the fifteenth century Parisian expansion continued into Gascony, Provence, Franche-Comté and Brittany. As the power of the kings was extended, the denotation of the name *France* was extended in tandem (see Lugge 1960).

The diffusion of the King's French as the language of government and administration in the provinces has been the subject of detailed studies by Brun (1923, 1935) and Gossen (1957, 1962, 1967). On Map 14, the pairs of dates in northern France indicate the beginning and end of the process whereby Parisian spellings replaced regional ones in administrative documents. The single dates in southern France indicate the time when Occitan was replaced by French. In the northern Gallo-Romance area, regional writing systems came into use in the domain of government alongside Latin in the thirteenth century, initially in areas of contact with non-*langue d'oïl* varieties – Picardy, Lorraine and Poitou (see Gossen 1967: 72). By the end of the thirteenth century, vernacular documents outnumbered those written in Latin, and during the fourteenth century Latin became somewhat exceptional. As the dominance of Paris grew during the fourteenth century, regional forms gradually disappeared from administrative writing, variation being suppressed at different rates in the different regions involved. The beginning of the extension of Parisian forms is evident in Champagne in the mid-thirteenth century, but in the north only at the end of the fifteenth century. In some areas regional variation was suppressed over a period of about fifty years (Orléanais); in others it took two and a half centuries (Burgundy). Strongest resistance to 'Parisianisation' took place in Picardy, Wallonia and Lorraine,

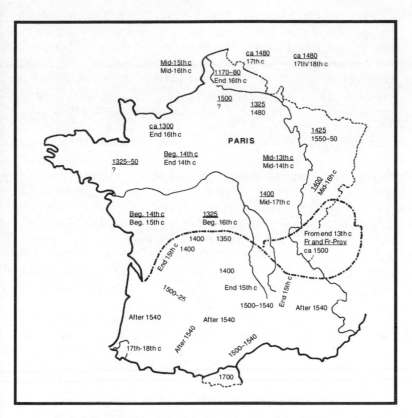

Map 14   Spread of the Parisian writing system

~~~~   French border at the death of Francis I (1547)

------   French border in 1792

-·-·-   Modern linguistic boundary

Northern France: The date above the line indicates the
approximate beginning of the process of decline of the
regional scripta; the date below the line indicates the
approximate end of this process, i.e. from this time on
the local scripta is the same as the standard

Southern France: The italicised dates indicate the
replacement of an Occitan writing system by the French one
(Gossen 1957: 429)

123

and is to be explained not simply with reference to any political independence they may have had (Wallonia was never absorbed into France, and Lorraine was not annexed until 1766), but also with reference to the degree of establishment of their local writing traditions (that of the Picard towns was particularly well established). A similar diffusion of the King's French by convergence seems to have occurred in the Franco-Provençal area (see Marchello-Nizia 1979: 29–30).

In the southern Gallo-Romance area, the transition between the use of Occitan and the use of French was more abrupt. Occitan had been in widespread use as an administrative language for rather longer than had French in the north, and its position remained very solid until the end of the fourteenth century. The departmental archives in the south of France contain sizeable collections of administrative documents written in various regional forms of Occitan in the thirteenth and fourteenth centuries. The Parisian overlords at first made no attempt to disturb the tradition (see Brunot 1966: I, 869–70), but during the fifteenth century the use of French gradually increased. The chronological and geographical dimensions to the infiltration of French into administrative functions in the south are indicated in Map 14. On this topic Brun (1923: 106) points out, interestingly, that the language shift which occurred essentially between 1450 and 1550 was 'moins une évolution qu'une mutation brusque' ('less an evolution than a sharp switch'). The relative ease of this transition suggests the superficiality and indeed the artificiality of the change – only the written language and the language of official business were affected, and in a society whose population was overwhelmingly rural and whose culture was fundamentally oral it is unlikely that the shift had major implications for everyday speech.

The case of the municipal records of Montferrand (Puy-de-Dôme) is revealing in this respect (see Lodge 1985). Montferrand was founded as a 'new town' in the twelfth century, and was endowed by the local lord with the usual municipal privileges. Its account books record the detailed expenditure of its town council of eight consuls from 1259 until 1630 (in not uninterrupted sequence). Although Auvergne was annexed to the Crown in 1211, the local variety of the *langue d'oc* was used on an increasing scale as the thirteenth century proceeded and, alongside Latin, continued as the only language of record until 1390.

Far from becoming contaminated with French as the period proceeds, the language of the Montferrand documents actually shed some of its regional features and conformed more closely to general Occitan norms. The transition from Occitan to French in the Montferrand archives, when it eventually came in 1390, is abrupt and is clearly politically inspired – the representative of royal power in the area (the Duc de Berry) felt he could no longer rely on the inhabitants of Montferrand to defend their town adequately against the English in the Hundred Years War, so he installed his own men as consuls. They naturally enough used the King's French in their administrative documents. However, it took a further three centuries for even the 'best families' of the town and surrounding countryside to adopt the King's French in everyday speech (see below, pp. 196–7).

What was it that impelled the kings to seek to unify the language used by their administration? During the thirteenth and most of the fourteenth centuries the kings conducted their business with the Occitan south in Latin, with explanations and translations in Occitan where necessary. The factor which changed this policy appears to have been the political and social transformation brought about by the Hundred Years War. The end of this war led the Crown to seek to consolidate its power in the southern provinces by establishing parliaments (law courts) in Toulouse (1444), Grenoble (1453), Bordeaux (1462) and Aix (1501). The King's power was no longer to rely on the fidelity of his vassals in distant provinces. It was to be solidly based on the presence in the provinces of the King's own functionaries who constrained obedience. At first the only language which the Crown sought to eliminate from its administration was Latin, not Occitan. The working language of officialdom in the south was no longer to be Latin – it was to be the vernacular (Occitan or the King's French). This policy is stated explicitly in several royal edicts of the later part of the fifteenth century and the early sixteenth century. In 1490 the Ordinance of Moulins specifies 'langage françois *ou* maternel' for all court interrogations and verbatim reports. In 1510 Louis XII requires 'vulgaire *et* langage du pays' for all procedural documents. This is repeated with the suggestion of a change in prospect in 1535 in the Ordinance of Is-sur-Tille: 'en françoys *ou a tout le moins* en vulgaire dudict pays'. The emphasis is mine.

Finally, in 1539 François I emits his famous Ordinance of Villers-Cotterêts whereby

> tous arrestz ensemble toutes aultres procedures, soit des cours souveraines ou aultres subalternes et inferieures, soit de registres, enquetes, contrats, commissions, sentences, testaments ou aultres quelquonques actes ou exploits de justice ou qui en dependent . . . soient prononcez enregistrez et deliverez aux parties en langage maternel françois et non aultrement.

> (all legal decisions and all procedures pertaining either to the highest courts or to the lower or inferior ones, whether they concern records, inquests, contracts, commissions, wills or whatever other legal acts or instruments or whatever is dependent thereon . . . should be pronounced, registered and delivered to the litigants in the French vernacular language and in no other way).

Like the edicts of 1490, 1510 and 1535, Villers-Cotterêts was directed primarily against the use of Latin as the judicial/administrative language. However, there has been much debate among historians about what language or languages are stipulated for use instead: what is the meaning of 'langage maternel françois'? Previous edicts had contrasted 'françois' with 'langage maternel/vulgaire du pays'. This one conflates the terms in the same noun phrase. Peyre (1933) and Fiorelli (1950) argue that the edict merely reiterated previous ones – French and the local vernacular were both acceptable replacements of Latin. Brun (1951), however, maintains his earlier position that Villers-Cotterêts is innovatory: only the King's French is now permissible. He takes 'langage maternel' as having its traditional meaning of vernacular as opposed to Latin (see above, pp. 94, 101). 'Langage françois' was one vernacular among others. Villers-Cotterêts stipulates for the first time that only the northern ('françois') vernacular ('langage maternel') may now be used.

The chief target for the 1539 edict, as for the preceding ones, was Latin: the numerous reiterations which this aspect of the edict received right down to the end of the *ancien régime* testify to the resistance offered in favour of Latin by the legal fraternity (see Peyre 1933: 92–101). As far as the regional vernaculars were concerned, no such reiterations were necessary, strongly suggesting that Brun's interpretation of the ordinance is correct. By 1539 in fact most regional languages had already been replaced in legal documents by the King's French – not only in provinces under the political control of the King, but in neighbouring provinces too (Wallonia, Lorraine, Franche-Comté, Vaud, Provence, Savoy, Bigorre, Foix – see Brun 1923: 423). Exceptions to this pattern are Navarre and Roussillon which continued with the official use of Gascon and Catalan for substantially longer (see Bec 1967: 83). It is probably anachronistic to suppose that the Crown, in issuing this edict, had any thought of propagating the use of the French language outside the law court at the expense of the vernaculars (see Trudeau 1983). What was at stake was political control through administrative efficiency – the use of three languages (French, Latin, Occitan) in legal documents made administration cumbersome. Linguistic uniformity was simpler for the King's officers, provided the language used was that of the King. The dominant elite surrounding the King were undoubtedly aware of the social power which accrued for them simply by being bearers of the linguistic norm.

In the later medieval period, French developed not only as the language of government, but also as *the language of learning*. Throughout the Middle Ages, Latin was the jealously guarded prerogative of the educated class, composed essentially of *clercs* (the Church and the University) but embracing also doctors and lawyers. Latin fulfilled specific religious and scientific functions at a formal level, it served as a *lingua franca* between *clercs* of different linguistic backgrounds, and it conferred on those who possessed it considerable status and social power. In the University of Paris French had probably always been the language of informal discourse between *clercs*, but it was not until the foundation of the Collège de France in 1530 that French was admitted for the first time to the class-room. That said, from the fourteenth century onwards French was used more and more in the world of learning as a written language. In the south of the country Bec (1967: 79) notes a similar extension in the use of Occitan at this time. The areas first penetrated by the vernacular were history, science and philosophy. The penetration occurred initially through translations from Latin (see Monfrin 1963, 1964; Rickard 1976: 7–10; Lusignan 1987: 129–71). While it is probably the case that in the fourteenth century French was being used mainly to vulgarise knowledge long since current in Latin, the level of vulgarisation rose gradually so that by the end of the fifteenth century French was well established as a vehicle for higher thought.

Rising prosperity, particularly in the towns, led to strong pressure to break the monopoly of knowledge (enshrined in Latin) held by a small priestly caste. The development of printing gave it added momentum (see Eisenstein 1979). Writing in the vernacular meant lower prestige for the writer in the eyes of some, but it promised a wider readership and hence greater revenue for the printer. Lefèvre and Martin (quoted by Huchon 1988: 23) show the following progression in the number of books published in French on the Paris presses in the sixteenth century:

	1501	1528	1549	1575
Total	80	269	332	445
No. in French	8	38	70	245
Percentage	10%	14%	21%	55%

In one field after another, authors began to compose original works of scholarship in French rather than in Latin. Brunot (1966: II, 36–79) traces the extension of French into medicine, mathematics, philosophy and history during the sixteenth century. The areas most resistant to the encroachments of the vernacular were certain branches of medicine and Catholic theology. On the other hand, surgery and pharmacy – traditionally the non-learned branches of medicine (practised as they were by barbers and *épiciers*) – saw the production of original treatises in French by writers like Ambroise Paré, and Calvin's Protestant ideas were disseminated in France largely through the medium of French (see Brun 1923: 426). France, like the rest of Europe, had begun the long progress from a state of restricted literacy to one of mass literacy, from a largely oral, public, collective culture to a written, private, individual culture.

However, the displacement of Latin by French as the language of writing and learning was by no means complete by the end of the sixteenth century. Scientific and philosophical works continued to be composed in or translated into Latin throughout the seventeenth century (see Brunot 1966: V, 21–4). Latin was to remain the principal language of the Catholic Church until the twentieth century. Despite developments such as the foundation of the Collège de France in 1529 which permitted the limited use of French in lectures (see Monfrin 1972: 765), Latin was to remain the principal language of formal education in France until the nineteenth century. It was only in 1905 that the rule requiring theses presented to the Sorbonne to be written in Latin was rescinded. Learning to read and write in the sixteenth century still meant essentially learning to read and write Latin. The fact that this was often achieved through the medium of French was of secondary importance. Montaigne opted to write his *Essais* in French but he was in no doubt as to which was the most suitable language for *real* learning:

> J'escris mon livre a peu d'homes et a peu d'annees. Si c'eust esté une matiere de duree, il l'eust fallu commettre a un langage plus ferme. Selon la variation continuelle qui a suivy le nostre jusques a cette heure, qui peut esperer que sa forme presente soit en usage, d'icy a cinquante ans? Il escoule tous les jours de nos mains et depuis que je vis s'est alteré de moitié. Nous disons qu'il est a ceste heure parfaict. Autan en dict du sien chaque siecle.

> (I am writing my book for a limited number of people and for a limited number of years. If it had been a subject destined to last, I would have had to commit it to a more stable language [i.e. Latin]. Given the continual variation which our language has undergone up to the present time, who can expect its present form to be still in use in fifty years time? It slips away from our hands day by day and in the course of my lifetime it has changed by half. We say that it is perfect at the present time. Each century says the same thing about its own.)

> (Montaigne 1967: 397)

It is paradoxical that expansion in the use of the vernacular as a language of learning should have gained such impetus at the time of the Renaissance (or 'rebirth') of Latin and Greek studies in Europe. We noted analogous developments in the use of the vernacular at the time of the Carolingian and twelfth-century renaissances (see above, pp. 91, 110). It is sometimes alleged that it was the 'purification' of Latin carried out by sixteenth-century scholars such as Erasmus (with the hope of restoring it to Ciceronian norms) which finally excluded it from all but formal functions and left the way open for the development of the vernacular. One could also argue the converse: that the wider diffusion of learning through the vernacular stimulated the scholarly elite to cultivate their Latin in order to maintain their prestigious status. More probably, however, the development of the vernacular and the refinement of Latin were both products of the general increase in intellectual activity which took place in the late fifteenth and sixteenth centuries. Now, however, the Latin monopoly of written culture was finally broken. The Reformation required that the means of salvation (the Bible) be made available to all believers: the Word could no longer be the exclusive property of the Priest. The development of a mercantile economy required that the tool of literacy be made available to a wider section of the population than previously had access to it.

Prestige

A second important characteristic of H languages stems from the first: the language of power in the community is usually perceived to be a superior, more elegant, more beautiful, more logical language than the other varieties: it has greater prestige. The growth in prestige of the King's French appears to have accelerated in the fifteenth and the sixteenth centuries, no doubt in association with the development, in the minds of the ruling elite at any rate, of a new sense of national identity. In this section we shall look at this growth in prestige of the King's French, in comparison with on the one hand Latin, on the other with the vernaculars (those spoken in France, particularly Occitan, and those spoken outside the country, particularly Italian).

In the diglossic situation obtaining in thirteenth-century France, Latin as the H language was obviously the more highly valued. The oral vernaculars had lower prestige, and were associated with home, mother and the place of one's birth (see above, p. 101). To this extent they were associated with one's 'nation' (< Latin *nasci* 'to be born'). However, the thirteenth-century idea of 'nation' was very remote from that of the centralised 'nation-state' which in France and England began to crystallise in the late fifteenth century (see Beaune 1985, 1987). The feudal state was a loose association of 'nations', knowing no language loyalty to the state embodied by the suzerain, affairs between the 'nations' of the realm being theoretically conducted in the H language (Latin) (see Chaytor 1945: 22–47). The gulf separating medieval and modern assumptions about the relationship between language and nation is clearly illustrated in the following quotation from the Italian Brunetto Latini, writing in the 1260s:

> Et se aucuns demandoit pour quoi cis livre est escris en romanc selonc la raison de France, puis ke nous somes italien, je diroie que c'est pour .ii. raisons, l'une que nous somes en France, l'autre pour cou que la parleure est plus delitable e plus commune a tous langages.

> (And if anyone were to ask me why this book is written in Romance after the French manner, given that we are Italian, I would say that it is for two reasons, firstly because we are in France, secondly because [French] speech is the most pleasant and the most widely spoken among all languages.)

(quoted by François 1959: I, 103)

By the fifteenth century this relationship between language and 'nation' had altered. The French 'nation' (i.e. the Paris region) had come to dominate many of the other 'nations' of Gaul. The centralising of power led to the assimilation of the dominated provinces to the French 'nation' and in this process the dominant group began to see their language as a symbol of a new national identity. The displacement of Latin from its function as *lingua franca* (the medium for conducting political, legal and administrative business between the 'nations') inevitably led to some transfer of prestige from Latin to the King's French.

Lusignan (1987: 47) notes that as early as the thirteenth to fourteenth centuries intellectuals were not altogether at one on the relative statuses of Latin and the vernaculars: the traditional clerical position placed Latin on a plane of excellence quite unattainable by the vernaculars. Dante on the other hand saw no intrinsic qualities which might justify Latin's special status. This higher status, he felt, came simply from the fact that it had been elaborated and codified – processes which the vernaculars could themselves undergo. During the sixteenth century in France, the traditional clerical thesis came under strong attack. Intellectuals began overtly affirming the equality of status

131

between French and Latin. In 1529 Tory asserts that the French language 'est aussi belle et bonne qu'une autre, quant elle est couchee par escript' ('is just as fine and good as any other when it is set in writing') (quoted by Rickard 1968: 3). The most famous affirmation of the new prestige of French comes from du Bellay in his *Defense et Illustration de la langue françoise* (1549). The French language became for the first time a worthy object of study in itself – serious metalinguistic attention was given to the lexicon (see Quemada 1968), to the grammar of French (see Padley 1983) and to the origins of the language (see Fauchet 1581; Huchon 1988: 16–20). French was acquiring dignity through the acquisition of an illustrious past or 'historicity'. Thus, although Latin remained the supremely dignified, unchanging language chiefly associated with the Church, the Renaissance saw the progress of secular values and inevitably altered the status of Latin – Latin was to an extent marginalised or 'pushed upstairs'.

At the same time as French was gaining prestige at the expense of Latin, the King's French was raising itself above the level of the Gallo-Romance vernaculars. As we saw in a previous chapter (p. 98), the status connotations of the King's French were acknowledged relatively early in the north of France. This is reflected in the language considered suitable for literary texts. 'Western' linguistic features associated with the Plantagenets were effaced from the 'noble' genres (courtly literature) soon after the Annexation of Normandy and Anjou in the early thirteenth century (see Lodge 1979: 58; Nezirovic 1980: 183–5). Picard forms in literary works survived strongly throughout the thirteenth century, for the rich northern towns possessed a prestige not yet very much lower than that of Paris. The fourteenth century, however, witnessed the economic decline of these northern towns and, no doubt in consequence, gradually only Parisian linguistic norms become the acceptable ones in literary texts. The last literary author of some standing in noble circles who used regional forms to a substantial degree in his writing was Froissart (second half of the fourteenth century). It has been noted even in his work, however, that the incidence of Picardisms is higher in direct speech than in the narrative proper.

In the south, recognition of the prestige of the King's French was slower. The Albigensian Crusade (1209–44) broke the independence of the southern aristocracy, but it is hard to discern

any significant linguistic impact before the end of the fourteenth century. Literary production in Occitan continued to
flourish in the fourteenth and fifteenth centuries, and Bec
(1967: 82) notes that in the sixteenth century it still retained a
good deal of its earlier prestige. Numerous Occitan grammars
were produced in the later Middle Ages. We can note in particular the *Regles de Trobar* of Jofre de Foixa, the *Donat Proensal*
of Hugues Faidit (thirteenth century) and the celebrated *Leys
d'Amor* (fourteenth century). In 1323 the leading burgesses of
Toulouse set up the Consistori del Gai Saber to encourage
literary activity in Occitan. During the fifteenth century, however, the prestige of Paris literary fashions gradually pushed
Occitan production into second rank. H. Lewicka (1971) studied
the theatre in France in the fifteenth and sixteenth centuries,
and observed that in the south mystery and morality plays
were written in French, and the lower genres in the southern
dialects. The date 1513 is of symbolical importance: the
Consistori del Gai Saber changed its name to Collège de
Rhétorique and ceased to consider literary works composed in
Occitan (see Bec 1967: 79).

By this time it is clear that the King's French was perceived
throughout the Gallo-Romance area as a 'superior, and more
elegant' variety than any of the others. Sixteenth-century
writers whose mother tongue was Occitan chose to publish in
French – Montaigne, Brantôme and Du Bartas are perhaps the
most celebrated examples. However, this did not prevent an
Occitan Renaissance in the sixteenth century paralleling that of
the north, with similar expressions of language loyalty. The
Toulousain poet P. Goudouli (1580–1649) declared:

Noirigat de Tolosa, me plai de mantenir son lengatge bel, e
capable de derrambulhar tota sorta de concepcions; e per
aquo digne de se carrar amb un plumachon de pretz e
d'estima.

(A child of Toulouse, it gives me pleasure to uphold her
elegant language, capable of unravelling all sorts of ideas;
and for that reason worthy to sport a great plume of value
and esteem.)

(quoted in Bec 1967: 88)

133

As the people of France, particularly those at the top of society, developed a sense of common government, their language became a vehicle and symbol of their common identity, particularly in contradistinction to rival groups outside the country. Discussions about the status and prestige of the French language were given added focus in the sixteenth century through considerable cultural contact with Italian. During the fourteenth and fifteenth centuries, the Italian city states (particularly Venice, Milan, Genoa and Florence) had become spectacularly prosperous and populous. Trade with Italy developed accordingly and stimulated the growth of Lyon as the second largest conurbation in France. Italian prosperity naturally excited the cupidity of the kings of France, three of whom crossed the Alps with plundering armies between 1494 and 1525. Dynastic marriages were arranged which brought to the French court not only Italian courtiers, artists and hangers-on, but an Italian Queen – Catherine de Medici. Throughout the sixteenth century and well into the seventeenth, the feeling of the cultural inferiority of France to Italy ran very deep in the minds of the ruling elite. François I (1515–47) ardently desired to emulate the splendour of life enjoyed by the great Italian princes. Much of the metalinguistic activity of the period sprang from a similar motivation (see Dubois 1970, 1972). Jean Lemaire des Belges's *Concorde des deux langaiges* (1511) was an attempt to demonstrate the equal worth of French and Italian. Du Bellay's *Defense et illustration de la langue françoise* (1549) was an adaptation to French of an Italian text on Italian (see Brunot 1966: 87); the Académie Française set up a century later (in 1635) was modelled on the Florentine Accademia della Crusca. Contact with this more advanced culture led to a large amount of word borrowing (see Hope 1971: I, 148–248).

Things Italian were not greeted with enthusiasm by everyone, however. H. Estienne (a Protestant) had religious as well as nationalistic reasons for his hostility to Italian, but the titles of the polemical works written by him illustrate the new role of French as a symbol of national identity:

1565 *Traicté de la conformité du langage françois avec le grec*
(Italian was by common admission related to Latin; French, according to Estienne, was related to Greek, an even more prestigious language)

1578 *Deux dialogues du nouveau françois italianizé*
1579 *La Précellence du langage françois*

These frantic expressions of language loyalty were to have very close parallels in the twentieth century with French campaigns against anglicisms (see Hagège 1987: 17–23). Word borrowing from Italian was seen by some as a betrayal, and the sight of such 'betrayals' invariably causes resentment among the more steadfast members of the dominated group, a resentment which brings with it unswerving language loyalty (see Weinreich 1968: 101).

Despite the metalinguistic activity engaged in the defence of a language, its prestige is inevitably tied to the perceived wealth and power of its speakers. The international status of French developed progressively in the seventeenth century until it achieved a prestige no vernacular language had ever possessed. It is hard to substantiate the claim frequently made that the basis of this prestige lay in the language's inherent properties ('clarity', 'logic', 'elegance', etc.). It is quite easy to show, on the other hand, how this prestige coincides with the growth of the power of the Paris monarchy (at the expense of the Habsburgs in the Germanic Empire and of the kings of Spain), culminating in the 'glory' of the 'age of Louis XIV' (1643–1715).

Development of a French literary heritage

A third criterion which for Ferguson (1959: 238) marks off H languages from L is that they are generally the vehicle for a literary tradition much admired by their speech community. The literature in question is usually remote from contemporary society, having its roots in the distant past or in another speech community altogether (see Fasold 1984: 36). This had been the position of Latin literature in Europe since Roman times – before the seventeenth century none of the vernacular literatures of western Europe could rival the prestige of the Latino-Hellenic tradition. Like the renaissances of the ninth and twelfth centuries before it, the fifteenth- to sixteenth-century Renaissance increased its prestige even further. That said, it is possible to see literary developments in French over this period which led to the constitution of a canon of French 'classical' texts which would be regarded by future generations in rather similar ways to those in which the literature of Classical Rome was viewed by scholars of the Middle Ages and Renaissance. This movement indeed reached a culmination in the work of the great 'classical' authors of the seventeenth century.

For all the prestige of Latin, there grew up in the later Middle Ages a much admired literary tradition in French, associated particularly with the Court. Thirteenth-century writers like Jean de Meung, fourteenth- to fifteenth-century poets like Alain Chartier, chroniclers like Froissart and Commines, left a corpus of texts which came to constitute an admired literary heritage (see François 1936: 96–7). Such literature was at first viewed as less serious than that written in Latin, but it provided a tradition for subsequent writers to follow or reject as the case may be. The fifteenth century saw the first attempts to codify French literary models in the 'arts de seconde rhétorique' (see Marchello-Nizia 1979: 48–9), and the sixteenth century saw conscious steps being taken to enhance the status of French literature and bring it to the level of admiration enjoyed by Latin (and Italian) literature (see Fauchet 1581, Huchon 1988: 49–63). Creative writers, especially those in the Pléiade, consciously strove to produce works which would 'illustrate' (i.e. make illustrious) the French language, the 'manifesto' of the movement appearing in the celebrated *Defense et illustration de la langue françoise* (du Bellay 1549). The literary language became a sort of artefact to be cultivated as an object of pride, to be nurtured by the great minds of the community and enriched by poets – 'Plus nous aurons de mots dans nostre langue, plus elle sera parfaicte' ('The more words we have in our language, the more perfect it will be') was one of the chief maxims of the Pléiade.

In certain literary circles during the sixteenth century there emerged for the first time the notion that the French literary language had reached a state of 'perfection' – an idea which aroused some suspicion in the mind of the great relativist Montaigne (see above, p. 129). However, the apogee of this notion was not to come until the seventeenth century. The Court of Louis XIV (1643–1715) had some respect for the literature of the past, but its main interest was reserved for writers of its own day – Corneille, Molière, Racine, Bossuet, Mme de Sévigné, Boileau, etc. It was these who were to be regarded by the eighteenth and nineteenth centuries as constituting the essential literary heritage of France, the 'great classical authors' who would be held up as models for imitation by future generations of schoolchildren.

THE ELABORATION OF NEW LANGUAGE VARIETIES

The increase in the range of functions performed by French automatically entailed a broadening of its stylistic range. This involved not only the development of an elaborated lexis and syntax to handle the new H functions, but also the development of social stratification in the language as the number and diversity of its speakers increased. We shall devote much of the rest of this chapter to a discussion of these problems.

As French passed from the stage of 'oral vernacular' to that of 'developed language', it became 'possible to use the selected variety in all the functions associated with writing – in government, in law courts, in bureaucratic, educational and scientific documents of all kinds, and of course in various forms of literature' (Hudson 1980: 33). The language had to develop new linguistic tools to enable it to perform its new functions: extra linguistic items (lexical and syntactic) had to be added to the variety. Let us consider each of these in turn.

The period between the fourteenth and sixteenth centuries was one of considerable *lexical* creativity. Working on the dates of first attestation of all the root-words listed in Dauzat's *Dictionnaire étymologique*, Guiraud (1966: 50–72) calculates that 43 per cent of the modern French lexicon entered the language between the fourteenth and sixteenth centuries:

?–Twelfth century	15%
Thirteenth century	7%
Fourteenth century	15%
Fifteenth century	8%
Sixteenth century	20%
Seventeenth century	11%
Eighteenth century	11%
Nineteenth century	13%

A half of these neologisms first attested between the fourteenth and sixteenth centuries are borrowings from Latin or Greek and are known as 'learned words' or *mots savants*. Some of these words formed etymological doublets with 'inherited words' or *mots populaires* which had been in continuous use since Roman times, e.g.

Latin	'populaire'	'savant'
hospitalem	hôtel	hôpital
fragilem	frêle	fragile
fabricam	forge	fabrique
liberare	livrer	libérer

Learned words and technical terms exist only in H. At the same time there are words in L for homey objects such as farm implements and some cooking utensils that have no equivalents in H. But the most striking feature of diglossia as far as the lexicon is concerned, is the existence of paired items, one in H and one in L, for commonly referred to objects.

(Fasold 1984: 38)

This duality lies at the heart of the comedy in Rabelais's celebrated evocation of the speech of his 'scholar from Limoges':

Nous transfretons (= traversons) la Sequane (= Seine) au dilucule (= jour naissant) et crepuscule (= soir). Nous deambulons (= promenons) par les compites (= carrefours) et quadriviez (= carrefours) de l'urbe (= ville). Nous dispumons (= dégoisons) la verbocinatio (= langue) latiale (= latine) et comme verisimiles (= vraisemblables) amorabonds (= amoureux) captons (= obtenons) la benevolence (= bienveillance) de l'omnijuge (= qui décide de tout), omniforme (= de toute forme) et omnigene (= de toute espèce) sexe féminin.

(We go across the Seine in the morning and in the evening. We stroll along the streets and crossroads of the town, we trot out a great deal of Latin and like true lovers we obtain the favours of womankind which is the judge of all and which comes in all shapes and sizes.)

(after Rickard 1968: 88)

Obviously, lexical expansion in French did not stop in the nineteenth century, as Guiraud's figures suggest. The lexicon has constantly been restocked as the language has entered new domains of use and as new topic areas have developed.

The fourteenth and fifteenth centuries also saw major changes in the *morphosyntax* of the language in the disappearance of noun flexions, the expansion of determiners and subject pronouns, generalisation of SV word order, etc. These changes, however, merely transformed syntactic items already in existence. They did not add new ones. Other changes affecting essentially syntax added a new dimension to the language. J.-P. Caput (1972: I, 68) contrasts two extracts of French prose, written two centuries apart. Villehardouin, thirteenth century:

> Ainsi s'en alla li cuens et li autre baron en Venice; et furent receu a grant feste et grant joie, et se logierent en l'isle Saint Nicolas avec les autres. Mout fut l'oz bele et de bonnes genz. Oncques de tant de gens nus uem ne vit.

> (In this way the Count and the other barons went off to Venice; and they were received with much joy and feasting, and they lodged on Saint Nicholas Island with the others. The army was very splendid and composed of fine people. Never did any man see so many people.)

Commines, fifteenth century:

> Li roy feist mettre le lit de Contay dedans un grand hostevent et vieil, lequel estoit en sa chambre, et moy avec luy, afin qu'il entindist et peust faire rapport a son maistre des paroles dont usoient ledit connestable et ses gens, dudit duc; et le roy se vint scoir dessus un escabeau rasibus dudit hostevent, afin que nous peussions entendre les paroles que diroit le dit Loys de Geneville; et avec ledit seigneur n'y avoit que ledit seigneur du Bouchage.

> (The King set de Contay's bed inside a large and ancient draughtscreen which was in his bedchamber, and me along with him, in order that he may hear and report to his master the words which were used by the said constable and his followers concerning the aforesaid Duke; and the King came and sat down next to the said screen, in order that we might hear the words which the said Loys de Geneville might say; and with the said lord there was only the said lord of Bouchage.)

The striking syntactic difference between the two texts is the absence of subordination in Villehardouin – the text consists of

139

five simple sentences linked on two occasions by *et* and on two others merely by juxtaposition (parataxis) – compared with the extent of subordination found in Commines, by means either of the relatives *lequel, dont, que* or of the conjunction *afin que.* Whereas Villehardouin's syntax is reminiscent of that of speech, that of Commines is the syntax of writing. The fourteenth and fifteenth centuries see a major increase in the number of subordinating conjunctions available (*alors que, attendu que, afin que, supposé que, excepté que, surtout que,* etc.) and an expansion in the use of relatives, particularly *lequel* etc. (see Guiraud 1966: 112–14). 'Complex sentences with numerous subordinate constructions are appropriate in H, but seem stilted and artificial on the rare occasions when they are attempted in L' (Fasold 1984: 37).

Traditional histories of the language invariably draw attention to these additions to the lexical and syntactic systems of French. They discuss them under such headings as 'L'influence du latin sur le français' or 'Le rôle des traducteurs'. No one can deny that writers were copying Latin on a large scale in these innovations (see Lorian 1967), but where disagreements occur is over the explanations offered. Some maintain that the additions were initiated by a desire to extend and embellish the French language (somewhat gratuitously), as though it were an artefact like a château – the French language needed to be made more sophisticated and dignified (see Rickard 1976: 11; Guiraud 1966: 117). Others personify language and argue that the French language in the fifteenth century was emerging from the infancy of the Middle Ages: as it became more intellectually aware, it required more subtle cohesive devices (see Wartburg 1962: 132). Both of these approaches are basically prescriptive: they assume that as the language evolves to something we are familiar with it 'gets better'. It is preferable simply to see the language adding a new variety to its repertory. As an oral vernacular it had the lexical and syntactic resources for everyday speech. As it developed a written code for use in government, education, science and a literature designed for private reading, it had to develop the new linguistic resources required. This process of adaptation to new uses is a permanent feature of living languages. Since, between the fourteenth and sixteenth centuries, French was stepping into the shoes of Latin, it was inevitable that the lexis and syntax of Latin should have been so extensively copied.

A visible symptom of the dominance of the Latin model in the scholarly mentality of the time is offered by the latinisation of spelling (see Rickard 1976: 20–3 and Catach 1978a). Spellings like *doigt* (*digitum*), *faict* (*factum*), *doubter* (*dubitare*) served to confer on French something of the dignity of their Latin etyma. They may even have helped people to read French, for until as late as the eighteenth century reading skills were acquired first in Latin and only subsequently transferred to French.

THE DEVELOPMENT OF SOCIAL AND STYLISTIC VARIATION

This chapter has so far been concerned with sociolinguistic developments in the realm of the H functions (government, education, literature, etc.). Indeed, many histories of French occupy themselves exclusively with this level of language. However, it is important to bear in mind that vastly more language 'happens' in performing the L functions (i.e. in every-day speech) than in performing the H functions. This principle is fundamental when we try to understand how a language changes, but it raises obvious difficulties for the historian, given the evanescent nature of speech compared to the permanence of writing, and given the shortage of data about informal varieties of French and about the French used by the lower socio-economic groups in the past. Despite this, such data are not totally lacking for the early modern period in France and, as we move nearer our own day, we find progressively more infor-mation to help us build up a picture of what everyday speech used to be like. In this section, therefore, we will look at some of the information which has survived about the speech of 'ordinary people' in France in the later Middle Ages and the gap which developed between it and more cultivated varieties of French.

What characterises everyday speech at all periods is its ex-treme variability, on the axes of geography, social class and style. The most striking feature about the speech to be heard in early modern France was probably its variability from region to region. We shall not explore this point in detail here, but it is important not to lose sight of the fact that France in the Middle Ages, and indeed until modern times, had a predominantly agricultural economy supporting a predominantly rural population.

En gros, entre 1450 et 1500 . . . la population paysanne a représenté au moins les neuf dixièmes, soit l'énorme majorité de la population de la France.

(In general terms between 1450 and 1500 . . . the peasant population made up at least nine-tenths of the French population, that is the vast majority.)

(Braudel 1986: II, 2ᵉ partie, 187)

The mass of the French population continued until well into the nineteenth century to use extremely localised rural vernaculars, and were in most cases quite unaffected by changes in the H language. Acquisition of the standard language and bilingual or bi-dialectal code-switching may well have been necessary for members of the nobility and the legal and merchant class (depending on where they lived), but since time immemorial and until at least the nineteenth century, the peasant population of France had little use for any language variety other than their local *patois*.

The overwhelmingly rural nature of the Gallo-Romance population meant that, until the end of the nineteenth century, the predominant axis for language variation was the geographical one. However, from the thirteenth century onwards, the beginnings of urbanisation and in particular the growth of Paris begin to add a new dimension to language variation in Gallo-Romance – variation reflecting social stratification. Given the sociolinguistic importance of Paris in France, and its role as a diffuser not only of the written language but also of colloquial forms, it will be helpful to devote space to the demography of Paris in the Middle Ages and Renaissance. Estimates of the population of medieval Paris fluctuate wildly: Lot (1929: 297, 300, 305) and Carpentier and Glénisson (1962: 109) put it at 200,000 by the early fourteenth century. Dollinger (1956: 44) pitches his estimate much lower at 80,000. Nevertheless, even if, through caution, we were to accept Dollinger's estimate, medieval Paris was twice the size of its nearest rival in France. Here are Duby's (1980: V, 191) estimations of the populations of the major towns of France in the fourteenth century:

40,000:	20,000:	10,000–20,000
Montpellier	Amiens	Arras
Rouen	Bordeaux	Avignon
	Lille	Beauvais
35,000:	Tournai	Dijon
Toulouse	Metz	Douai
		Reims
25,000:		Lyon
Narbonne		Marseille
Orléans	•	
Strasbourg		

We can see from these figures, approximate as they are, that Paris was by a long way the biggest conurbation in France. Indeed, it was probably the biggest conurbation in northern Europe: Dollinger makes the following population estimates for the early fourteenth century: Ghent = 56,000; London = 40,000; Bruges = 35,000; Cologne = 30,000. Only the great Italian cities outstripped Paris in size – Milan and Venice apparently had 100,000 inhabitants each, and Genoa slightly fewer. Later in the fourteenth century, economic depression, the plague and war reduced the French population catastrophically, but recovery is visible from the mid-fifteenth century and the Parisian population in the mid-sixteenth century has been put as high as 300,000 (see Descimon 1989: 69). By this time, Paris had become Christendom's largest city – 'non urbs sed orbis' ('not a city, but a world'). The population of France is estimated to have been approximately 15 million, and it is easy to see how Paris was now beginning to dominate the economic and sociopolitical life of the country.

The social structure of late medieval towns was pyramidal. In line with this we find that the affairs of Paris were dominated by its great banking and merchant families (*la Ville*), by the hierarchy of the Church and University, and by a powerful body of legal and administrative officials associated with the King's government (*le Palais*). These groups were supplemented in the second quarter of the sixteenth century by the permanent settlement of the Royal Court in the city, and hence the presence of members of the upper nobility (*la Cour*). The mass of the urban population (*le Peuple*) lived in varying degrees of affluence/poverty as artisans (tanners, cloth-weavers, shoe-makers, etc.), as small shopkeepers, as servants of the rich. Their numbers were constantly replenished by immigration from the surrounding countryside. The Paris population

> could be likened to an accordion, expanding when harvest failures or warfare led inhabitants from the surrounding countryside to seek refuge or charity behind city walls, shrinking when plagues sent the rich fleeing to the safety of their country estates or prolonged economic difficulties provoked the emigration of skilled artisans.
>
> (Benedict 1989: 13)

In parallel with the growth in the population of Paris and other towns, it becomes clear from the thirteenth century onwards that language variation along lines other than geographical ones was now developing. The very expression 'the King's French' implies a degree of social variation. We know too that the concept of courtliness involved refinement of language as well as of dress and manners: François (1959: I, 29–31) and Delbouille (1962) argue for the existence of an awareness of *bon usage* as early as the twelfth century. However, whereas aristocratic speech is amply illustrated in literary texts, evidence of the speech of the lower orders is not so easy to find. The best insights come from medieval plays, the earliest examples of which are the tavern scenes in Jean Bodel's *Jeu de St Nicolas* composed in Arras *c*. 1200 (see Foulet and Foulon 1944–5). Richer documentation is to be found in the mystery plays and farces originating in Rouen and Paris in the fifteenth century (see Lewicka 1974: 64–6). Unfortunately it is usually difficult to tell whether the deviant linguistic forms involved here were used as markers of informality or as indicators of social class. The absence of such forms from the speech of high-born characters suggests that the latter is at least sometimes the case.

Uncertainty on this point led A. Dauzat to conclude that:

> Tant que le français fut laissé à son libre développement, il n'existait aucune différence linguistique en raison des milieux sociaux: le grand seigneur parlait comme le manant.
>
> (So long as French was left to develop freely, there existed no linguistic difference related to social class: the great lord spoke like the villager.)
>
> (Dauzat 1930: 112)

It was allegedly the grammatical movement of the seventeenth century which introduced social stratification into the language. It could be that Dauzat was thinking solely about usage in the countryside, but the growth of towns, particularly Paris, means that such social homogeneity is, *prima facie*, unlikely. Indeed, metalinguistic comment in the sixteenth century makes it quite clear that by that time the speech of Paris was strongly characterised by social stratification. Let us look at the information to be gleaned about lower-class Parisian speech in the sixteenth century from the comments made by contemporary grammarians. We shall deal first with vocabulary and then with grammar and pronunciation.

In the medieval period the evidence does not generally allow us to situate 'non-standard' *vocabulary* very securely on the social/stylistic axes of variation: lexical items which in medieval drama appear to be the monopoly of low-status characters (e.g. executioners) could in fact be informal words which medieval rhetoric forbade in the mouths of upper-class characters (see Faral 1924: 86–9). Where we can be more certain of a social correlation is with the esoteric, indeed clandestine vocabulary, used by criminals, brigands, beggars and other marginals, known at the time as *le jargon*. The existence of *jargon* is attested in French as early as the thirteenth century (see Guiraud 1976: 10). We find copious documentation about it in the records of the trial of the Dijon 'Coquillards' (1455), and Villon exploited it to literary effect in his *Ballades en jargon* (*c.* 1450) (see Guiraud 1968). In the sixteenth century, the term *jargon* is extended to include the in-group vocabulary of students, satirised by Rabelais in *Pantagruel*. Users of criminal jargon are roundly criticised by Tory (1529):

> me semble qu'ils ne se montrent pas seulement dediés au gibet, mais qu'il seroit bon qu'ils ne fussent onque nés.

> (it seems to me that they show themselves not only set for the gibbet, but that it would have been a good thing had they never been born.)
>
> (quoted by François 1959: I, 188)

H. Estienne was somewhat more tolerant of lower-class vocabulary than Tory, preferring such words to Italian borrowings. However, he is acutely sensitive to the social hierarchisation of vocabulary. In his *Conformité* (1565) he writes of the way people seek to 'parquer les mots en castes' ('divide up words into castes'): 'Ce mot-là sent sa boulie, ce mot-là sent sa rave, ce mot-là sent sa place Maubert' ('This word reeks of gruel, this one of rapeseed, this one of the Place Maubert') (quoted by Brunot 1966: III, 161). He naturally excludes from 'good usage' 'les expressions propres a la lie du peuple' (*Hypomneses*, 1582), e.g. *tretous* (= *tous*), *tretant* (= *tant*), *illeques* (= *la*), *nani* (= *non*), *c'est mon* (= *oui*).

It is not easy to ascertain how far the *jargon de l'argot* (the esoteric vocabulary of the Paris criminal fraternity) existed as a special lexicon distinct from the rest of lower-class vocabulary. At all events, prescriptive grammarians strove to stigmatise both, and the association of poverty and criminality was constantly present in their minds. A good deal of modern French slang seems to have lived a subterranean life in the colloquial speech of Paris since the Middle Ages, being generally excluded from the respectable written language until the present century.

Aspects of lower-class *morphology and syntax* stigmatised by contemporary grammarians are:

(i) use of the first person plural verb form for the first person singular (e.g. *j'avons*, *je sommes*) (see Brunot 1966: II, 335–6).

(ii) use of the preterite form of the second conjugation for the first (e.g. *donismes*, *enformismes*). 'The perfect of the first conjugation ends in *-ai*, *-as*, *-a*. Some, however, prefer to end in *-i*, *-is*, *-it*. . . . You will hear both pronounced in Paris, but the first approves itself to most people because it is nearer the Latin' (Dubois 1531, quoted by Pope 1952: 375).

Pronunciation features condemned by contemporary grammarians are:

(i) /er/ → /ar/:
'Plebs . . . praesertim parisina hanc litteram *a* pro *e* in multis vocibus pronunciat, dicens *Piarre* pro *Pierre* . . . *guarre* pro *guerre*' ('The Paris populace pronounces the letter *a* as an *e* in many words, saying *Piarre* instead of *Pierre* . . . *guarre* instead of *guerre*') (H. Estienne quoted by Thurot 1881: II, 3).

(ii) /wɛ/ → /wa/:
'Corruptissimi vero Parisiensium vulgus . . . pro *voirre* sive

ut alii scribunt *verre, foirre* . . . scribunt et pronuntiant *voarre* et *foarre*, itidemque pro *trois, troas* et *tras*' ('The most corrupt elements of the Parisian populace write and pronounce *voarre* and *foarre* where others write and pronounce *verre* and *foirre*, likewise *troas* and *tras* instead of *trois*') (Bèze, quoted by Pope 1952: 197).

(iii) /jaw/ → /eo/:

'Vitanda est autum vitiosissima vulgi Parisiensis pronuntiatio in hac triphthongo, nempe l'*iaue* et l'*iau* pro l'*eau*' ('One must also avoid the extremely incorrect pronunciation of the Paris populace in the triphthong *iaue* and *iau* instead of *eau*') (Bèze, quoted by Thurot 1881: I, 439).

(iv) /jẽ/ → /jã/:

'Selon le dialecte des Parisiens, on prononce *an* au lieu de *en*, et quelques poetes en ont usé, mais rarement, et le faut remarquer comme une licence. Exemple, *Je vy monsieur le Doyan Lequel se portoit tres bian*' ('In Parisian dialect, people pronounce *an* instead of *en*, and some poets have used this form but only rarely and it has to be regarded as poetic licence. Example: *I saw Mr Dean and he was keeping very well*') (Tabourot, quoted by Thurot 1881: II, 436).

(v) /ĩ/ → /ẽ/:

'Autres i a qui prononcent à la parisienne *in* comme *ain*. Exemple . . . *vain* . . . *pain*, pour dire . . . *vin* . . . *pin*' ('There are others who pronounce *in* in the Parisian manner as *ain*. Example: . . . *vain* . . . *pain* for . . . *vin* . . . *pin*') (Tabourot, quoted by Thurot 1881: II, 483).

(vi) /r/ → /z/:

'Idem faciunt hodie mulierculae parisinae pro *Maria* sonantes *Masia*, pro *ma mere ma mese*' ('Various little women from Paris do the same thing today, pronouncing *Masia* instead of *Maria*, *ma mese* instead of *ma mère*') (Erasmus, quoted by Pope 1952: 157).

(vii) /rl/ → /l/:

'Infantes et parrhisii . . . *paller* pro *parler* dicunt' ('Children and Parisians . . . say *paller* instead of *parler*') (Tabourot, quoted by Pope 1952: 157).

(viii) Effacement of final consonants:

/r/ 'The people say . . . *plaisi, mestie, papie, resueu*' for *plaisir, mestier, papier, resueur*' (H. Estienne, quoted by Pope 1952: 158).

/s/ *'Tousjours* . . . plebs . . . non solum prius *s*, verum etiam posterius, atque adeo literam *r* sono suo privat: proferens *toujou'* ('The populace deprives of its sound not only the first *s*, but also the second, as well as the letter *r*, pronouncing *toujou'*) (H. Estienne quoted by Thurot 1881: II, 83).

(ix)   Effacement of /h/ aspiré:
    'Many people say *un'onte* . . . *un'arpe* . . . *il m'ait* (for *il me hait*)' (H. Estienne, quoted by Pope 1952: 94).

It is clear from metalinguistic comment in the sixteenth century that social stratification was quite marked in the language of Paris. We should nevertheless exercise some caution when assessing the social attributions made by these commentators. It is well attested that speakers representing the dominant socio-cultural groups use features in their spontaneous style which they attribute to members of less prestigious sociocultural groups. This becomes abundantly clear when we examine the transcriptions made by Jean Héroard of the speech of the young Dauphin (the future King Louis XIII) between 1605 and 1610 (see Ernst 1985). Here we find that many of the stigmatised features listed above were frequently used by the heir to the throne himself, evidently reflecting linguistic usages which were widespread at Court.

Some of the low-status forms gradually diffused upwards and became accepted into the standard language (e.g. /wɛ/ → /wa/). Others appear never to have done so and to have survived only in regional *patois* (e.g. *j'allons*). Yet others continued a subterranean existence in colloquial usage only to resurface in the twentieth century as non-standard French and labelled 'slang' or 'français populaire'. It is indeed currently a matter of some debate to know which vernacular forms in lower-class usage in our own day represent recent innovations and which represent long-standing features which a powerful normative tradition has kept hidden from published view (see Hunnius (1975); Steinmeyer (1979); Hausmann (1979)).

TOWARDS A NEW DIGLOSSIA

In this chapter we have attempted to show how the Gallo-Romance variety which had been 'selected' to form the basis of the future standard language entered new domains of use in the later Middle Ages and developed new linguistic tools to enable it to perform its new functions. This process was labelled by Haugen 'elaboration of function'. As the functions of the King's French were 'elaborated', it acquired many (though not yet all) of the characteristics normally associated with H languages. We have seen in fact how between the thirteenth and sixteenth centuries the diglossic situation of France changed as the King's French gradually replaced Latin in the H functions in society. It could be argued, however, that although Latin had been removed from its pedestal by the end of this period, the sociolinguistic situation obtaining in most of France nevertheless remained diglossic, with H functions now performed by the King's French and the L by the rural vernaculars. (For discussion of the term 'diglossia' see above, pp. 13–14.) This generalisation needs some discussion, for the evolution towards a new situation of diglossia just outlined did not involve a straightforward replacement of Latin by the King's French as the H language. Firstly, Latin retained an important role in international diplomacy, in education and above all in the Church long after the sixteenth century. Secondly, by the end of the period in question here, French was still not explicitly taught in France as a second language, as Latin had been: for a long time yet, the object of language education in schools remained Latin and indeed where the teaching of French did take place it was primarily to facilitate the learning of Latin (see Brun 1923: 441–63). Whereas Latin was an add-on language acquired by memorising rules of grammar, the King's French was learnt in the provinces in largely informal ways. Indeed, the 'vernacular standard' was not fully codified until the eighteenth century, as we shall see in the next chapter. Thirdly, by the sixteenth century the King's French had been diffused as an H language to a far wider section of the community than that represented by the small priestly caste who had had exclusive use of Latin in earlier centuries. One of the prime aims of the humanists and the religious reformers was the vulgarisation of knowledge through the use of the vernacular. The role of printing in stimulating the demand for knowledge should not be played down. Indeed, the whole notion of culture had now changed:

149

Au Moyen Age, même la culture savante est tout pénétrée d'oral; à partir du XVIe siècle, même la culture populaire est dominée par l'écrit.

(In the Middle Ages, even learned culture is shot through with orality; from the sixteenth century onwards, even popular culture is dominated by writing.)

(Furet and Ozouf 1977: 71)

A final and very important qualification to our suggestion that by the sixteenth century a new situation of diglossia had developed in France concerns the fact that, for a sizeable proportion of the population, Parisian French functioned as a colloquial L language in addition to its H role. This obviously applies to the population of Paris, but it may also have affected parts of the provincial population. In this chapter we have treated the diffusion of French into the provinces as something involving the H functions only. Evidence about the diffusion of colloquial Parisian French is inevitably limited, but given the overwhelming importance of Paris as an economic centre, with a population constantly shifting through immigration and emigration, it is not improbable that the colloquial variety of Parisian French was diffused to provincial towns even more pervasively than the H forms adopted by provincial elites.

If the French of Paris was used by sections of the population in the L as well as the H functions, can we properly refer to the sociolinguistic situation in sixteenth-century France as 'diglossic'? Would it not be more appropriate to talk about a 'standard-with-dialects' situation? Can the situation of 'standard-with-dialects' be subsumed under the general heading of 'diglossia', or should the two situations be kept apart? Ferguson (1959: 245) sees parallels between the two, but prefers to keep them distinct.

What is crucial for Ferguson . . . is that no segment of the community uses H in ordinary conversation. . . . In other words, as long as you can find some group in the speech community that uses the putative H in normal conversation, even though there are other groups which do not, we do not have a case of diglossia, but rather a standard-with-dialects.

(Fasold 1984: 43)

In the French case, it was the variety used in the King's Court (in speech as well as in writing) which began to be diffused as the H language. The fact that this variety was used in ordinary conversation by at least one group in society – in this case the upper social groups in the Paris region – prevents us (according to Ferguson) from using the term 'diglossia' to describe the resulting situation. Fasold overcomes this objection by pointing out difficulties with Ferguson's definition of the speech community. While not defining 'speech community' himself, he defines a diglossic community as 'a social unit which shares the same High and Low varieties'. Thus,

> each regional dialect distinguishes a different diglossic community, and within each of them, no one uses the standard for normal conversation. If there is a group within the same country that uses the standard, or something close to it, for all functions, then it is not a sector of any of those diglossic communities. Rather it is a separate community (not necessarily a diglossic one, at least not in the same sense) because it does not share a Low variety with any of them.
>
> (Fasold 1984: 44)

The evidence available to allow us to confirm or invalidate any model of the sociolinguistic situation in sixteenth-century France is pitifully inadequate, but from what information we have, Fasold's definition of the diglossic speech community fits the situation in sixteenth-century France reasonably well. Following Fasold we could tabulate the position thus as shown in Figure 4.

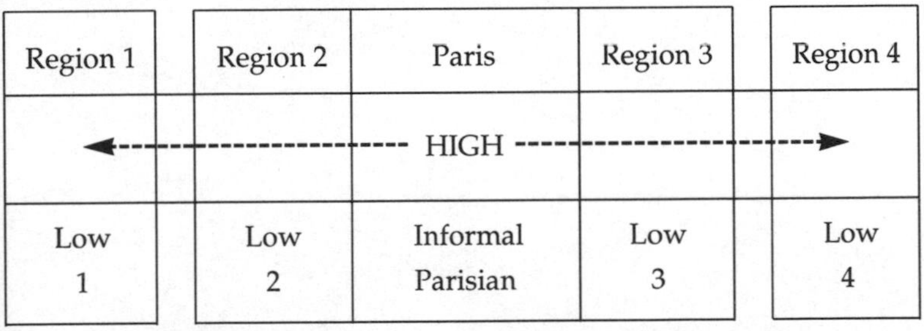

Region 1	Region 2	Paris	Region 3	Region 4
←------------------------ HIGH ------------------------→				
Low 1	Low 2	Informal Parisian	Low 3	Low 4

Figure 4 Diglossia in sixteenth-century France

France cannot be regarded as a single diglossic community at that time – it is doubtful whether a kingdom as large and as diverse as sixteenth-century France could be called a single social unit at all. It is preferable to see it as an amalgam of numerous diglossic communities organised around a monoglot Paris region.

6

CODIFICATION

In our last chapter we discussed the 'elaboration of function' which occurred in French in the later Middle Ages when the language took over the H functions previously carried out by Latin. The process of 'elaboration' did not of course stop then, for it is an on-going one: since the sixteenth century the lexicon has had to expand to cope with the innumerable social, economic and technological changes involved in France's transition from being a simple agricultural economy to an advanced industrial one (e.g. railways, aviation, computing); new varieties of French have been generated over and above traditional writing and interpersonal speech, by the development of new modes of communication like the telegraph, the telephone, radio and television, etc. The ideal goal of the process of 'elaboration' has been summed up as the achievement of 'maximal variation in function' (see Haugen 1966: 107).

What we need to consider next is a process which can be seen as pulling the language in the opposite direction – 'codification'. This process has been a particularly important feature of the history of French, for French is arguably the most highly codified of the European languages and was for a long time considered the model for other standard languages (e.g. English and German). Codification in a general sense involves the production of a systematic and explicit set of rules laying down what is and what is not permissible in a particular area of social life (e.g. the Highway Code). It is a term which is commonly applied to legal systems (e.g. the Visigothic Code and the *Code Napoléon*), but it can also be applied to language. Language codification entails the production of grammars (which lay down prescriptive rules governing spelling, pronunciation, morphology and syntax) and dictionaries (lexical inventories which give legitimacy to certain words but not to others, and which specify their meaning and value). The ideal goal of 'codification' in language has been defined as the achievement of 'minimal variation in form' (Haugen 1966: 107), or, to put it another way, 'the suppression of optional variation in language' (Milroy and Milroy 1985a: 8).

RULES AND LINGUISTIC NORMS

Codification involves then the production of lists of rules, but an important distinction has to be made between two sorts of linguistic rule: *descriptive* rules which make explicit the underlying and usually subconscious patternings of language (in French often referred to as *lois*), and *prescriptive* rules which lay down which one out of two or more competing linguistic items is currently considered by society to be correct and acceptable (in French often referred to as *règles*). It is rules of the latter type which are involved in language codification, although prescriptive grammarians commonly attempt to present their *règles* as though they were *lois*. In this chapter, therefore, we will not be concerned with the development of linguistic theory in France, but with the evolution of prescriptive ideas about language and linguistic norms.

The notion of 'linguistic norm' has already been looked at (see above, p. 86), but a distinction of relevance to our discussion of codification, which parallels that between *loi* and *règle* we have just looked at, is that proposed by Garmadi (1981: 64–72) between *norme* and *sur-norme*. Let us look at this distinction here. The *norme* (for Garmadi) represents the implicit linguistic consensus which permits mutual intelligibility within any speech community – 'la contrainte effective garantissant le fonctionnement satisfaisant de tout système linguistique en tant qu'instrument de communication' ('Constraints which effectively guarantee the satisfactory functioning of any linguistic system as an instrument of communication'). Garmadi's *norme* appears to be not far removed from Saussure's (1915) underlying and collective *langue* and implies a stock of common or overlapping linguistic structures which all members of the speech community participate in to varying degrees. The precise degree of overlap or convergence between individuals or groups with respect to the *norme* determines the level of communication between them, though it does not exclude linguistic variability.

The *sur-norme* appears to be a set of explicit 'instructions' regarding the selection of particular items already admitted by the *norme*, to the exclusion of others:

> C'est un système d'instructions définissant ce qui doit être choisi si on veut se conformer à l'idéal esthétique ou socio-culturel d'un milieu détenant prestige et autorité, et l'existence de ce système d'instructions implique celle d'usages prohibés.

> (It is a set of instructions defining what should be selected if one wishes to conform to the aesthetic or sociocultural ideal of a social group enjoying prestige and authority, and the existence of this set of instructions implies the existence of forms that are banned.)

> (Garmadi 1981: 65)

The consensus rules of the *norme*, by their statistical, probabilistic nature do not exclude variation, but the prescriptive rules of the *sur-norme* are intolerant of variation and demand uniformity. Whereas the rules of the *norme* are implicit and are acquired by dint of acquiring language within the community, those of the *sur-norme* often result from explicit codification, are imposed from above and have to be consciously learnt. Thus, while all speech communities by definition possess consensus *normes* of some sort, with varying degrees of localisation, the *sur-norme* is more strongly present in some communities than others, depending on the social structure of the community concerned (see above, pp. 85–6). We shall see that France is a society in which the *sur-norme* has become particularly powerful.

When we considered the selection of linguistic norms in the medieval period (see Chapter 4), we were able to handle spoken norms and written norms separately. It might be felt desirable to continue to do this in the present chapter, for spoken language and written language are not amenable to the same level of codification. However, we shall find that as time goes on such a separation becomes progressively more difficult to maintain: codification is closely linked to literacy, and as literacy develops, the written language increasingly comes to be regarded as the ultimate reference-point for correctness of speech. Something approaching uniformity is only possible in writing, and it is no doubt this which leads codifiers to regard the written language as the ultimate reference-point in standardisation. The degree of variability permissible in standard languages is a question which creates fundamental disagreement between sociolinguists. Leith (1983: 37) takes the view that a standard language is a variety 'like any linguistic variety' and that it 'has its dimensions of variation, including those of informality–formality, since for many people it must function as the medium of everyday conversation'. Milroy and Milroy (1985a: 22–3), after observing that absolute standardisation of a spoken language is never achieved, prefer to speak more abstractly of standardisation as 'an *ideology*, and a standard language as an idea in the mind rather than a reality – a set of abstract norms to which actual usage may conform to a greater or lesser extent.'

It is clear, when one looks at the histories of English and French, that standardisation goes a good deal further than the selection and diffusion of *normes* (in Garmadi's sense): it commonly involves the superimposition of *sur-normes* and, in the case of France, a strong tradition of purism. The *sur-norme* is legitimised and maintained by a whole edifice of beliefs about the nature of language and what is correct/incorrect in it, dictated inevitably by the dominant social and aesthetic values in the society concerned. This edifice has been labelled by Milroy and Milroy (1985a) the 'ideology of the standard'. What are these beliefs? They can be summarised as follows:

(1) The ideal state of a language is one of *uniformity* – everyone should (ideally) speak (and write) in the same way. Non-standard usage is always to some degree improper, and language change is to be deplored.

(2) The most valid form of the language is to be found in *writing*. Indeed, languages without a written form are deemed not to be languages at all, but *idiomes, patois, parlers*, etc. Although prestige norms for speech do exist, speaking is generally considered to be 'less grammatical' than writing. The purest form of the language is to be found in the work of the community's 'best' authors – as defined by the aesthetic values of the dominant cultural tradition.

(3) This form is *inherently better* than other varieties (i.e. more elegant, clearer, more logical, etc.) – it also happens to be the

156

variety used by persons of the highest status with the greatest potential for exercising power. Other social dialects are *debased* corruptions of the standard, i.e. sloppy, slovenly, uncultivated, failed attempts to express oneself properly – these tend to be used by people of lower status and who exercise little power.

Such hostile attitudes to language variation are not universal – in some communities (e.g. Germany) language variation is treated more generously. In societies like those of Britain and France, however, which are highly centralised and quite rigidly stratified, the *sur-norme* and prescriptive ideas about language (reinforced by the spread of literacy) are exceptionally strong and are not uncommonly used by ruling groups as an instrument of power.

Language codification is a two-sided process: it has a technical side involving the production of unified pronunciation and spelling systems, the writing of grammar-books whose aim is to eliminate variability in the morpho-syntax of the language, and the compilation of dictionaries legitimising the use of certain words but not others, and specifying their meaning and value. It also has a social side involving the identification of those groups in society felt to act as the repository of the most prestigious form of the language, and an observation of their usage. In what follows we will consider briefly the long tradition of grammar- and dictionary-writing in France, before looking in greater depth at changing attitudes to what is considered to be 'the best French'.

THE WORK OF CODIFICATION IN FRANCE

It was F. Brunot who declared that 'le règne de la grammaire . . . a été plus tyrannique et plus long en France qu'en aucun pays' ('the reign of the grammarian has been longer and more tyrannical in France than in any other country') (1966: III, 4). Crystallisation of the norms of the French standard language which reached its culmination in the eighteenth century no doubt began in the Middle Ages as an informal, unconscious process among the literate members of the community (see above, p. 144). However, the numerous practical grammars, word-lists and manuals of conversation produced during that very early period were designed not for French speakers, but for foreigners (notably speakers of English) (see Lambley 1920: 3–57). Among native speakers of French, awareness of the susceptibility of their language to variation and change (in contrast with the perceived permanence and invariability of Latin) was expressed as early as the fourteenth century: a translator of the Psalms from Lorraine laments that:

> pour ceu que nulz ne tient en son parleir ne rigle certenne, mesure ne raison, est laingue romance si corrompue, qu'a poinne li uns entent l'aultre et a poine puet on trouveir a jour d'ieu persone qui saiche escrire, anteir, ne prononcieir en une meismes menieire, mais escript, et prononce li uns en une guise et li aultre en une aultre.

> (Because no one follows unchanging rules, moderation or reason in his speech, the Romance vernacular is so corrupt that scarcely can one person understand anyone else, and scarcely can one find nowadays anyone capable of writing properly or of pronouncing in a consistent way, but each one writes and speaks in one way while someone else does so in another.)
>
> (quoted by Brunot 1966: I, 421)

Complaints such as this became ever more frequent among the literate public, culminating in the celebrated *Champfleury* of G. Tory (1529):

> O Devotz amateurs de bonnes Lettres, Pleust a Dieu que quelque Noble cueur semployast a mettre et ordonner par reigle nostre Langage Francois; Ce seroit moyen que maints Milliers d'hommes se esuerturoient a souvent user de belles et bonnes paroles. Sil ny est mys et ordonné, on trouvera que de cinquante Ans en cinquante Ans La Langue Francoise, pour la plus grande part, sera changee et pervertie. . . . Le Langaige d'aujourd'hui est changé en mille facons du langage qui estoit il y a Cinquante Ans ou environ.

> (O dedicated lovers of fine literature, would to God that some noble heart could employ himself in setting out rules for our French language: it would be a means whereby many thousands of men would strive to become familiar

with good and fine words. If it is not given rules, we will find that every fifty years the French language will have been changed and perverted in very large measure. . . . The language of today has changed in a thousand ways from the language which existed fifty years ago or thereabout.)

(quoted by Pope 1952: 42)

It was then the sixteenth century which saw the first serious attempts to specify correct usage for native speakers of French (see Demaizière 1983). Some of the pressure for codification at that time no doubt came from a desire for a more uniform and hence more efficient instrument of communication (i.e. one which would permit communication over longer distances of space and time). However, this 'disinterested' motivation was supplemented by pressure from two other more 'self-serving' directions. On the one side we find a desire to enhance the external prestige of the language as the badge of a newly form-ing 'nation': many cultured French people in the early sixteenth century wished that their language had the dignity and fixity of Latin and (perhaps more painfully) Italian, and they saw the lack of codification in French as the chief obstacle to external recognition. At the same time, members of the upper classes began seeking to distinguish themselves linguistically from the rest, with the result that ambitious citizens from lower down the hierarchy, who were anxious to gain entry to this group, clam-oured for clear guidance as to what constituted 'the best French'. The first of these preoccupations appears to have pre-dominated in the sixteenth century, while the second seems to have done so thereafter.

Over the subsequent centuries France has seen the accumu-lation of a vast body of prescriptive material dealing with vo-cabulary, grammar, spelling and pronunciation. Let us rapidly glance at each of these areas. Not only is this material more voluminous in French than in most other European languages, it also appears to outsiders to have been more closely co-ordinated, having received the seal of official approval in the first half of the seventeenth century with the setting up of the Académie Française.

In its charter of foundation the Académie was given a brief to 'rendre le langage françois non-seulement élégant, mais capable de traiter tous les arts, et toutes les sciences' ('to make the French language not only elegant, but also capable of handling all the arts and sciences') (see Livet 1858: I, 32). Article 26 of its statutes required it to produce a dictionary, a grammar, a rhetoric and a poetics of French (see Robertson 1910: 13). This institution has clearly influenced the codification of the standard French language and continues to act as a powerful guardian of usage in our own day. However, its overall impact should not be exaggerated. Richelieu's founding of the Académie Française in 1635 may have been motivated to a limited extent by wide social concerns such as enhancing the functional efficiency of the language and standardising usage in order to permit wider communication. However, it is unlikely that Richelieu's motives for setting up the Académie were disinterested. One very obvious purpose for the setting up of the Académie was to enhance the prestige of French on the wider European scene: in a period when the country's cultured elite still felt a certain inferiority *vis-à-vis* Italy, an Académie modelled on the Florentine Accademia della Crusca (set up in 1582) and dedicated to the codification of the literary language was calculated to enhance the status of French at home and abroad. Moreover, as a politician Richelieu was certainly aware of the fact that language codification was a political act and that as such it was too important to be left to the grammarians (see Lapierre 1988: 31). Numerous groups had sprung up in the sixteenth and early seventeenth centuries with the aim of reducing the variability present in the written language (see Yates 1947: esp. 290–7). Richelieu no doubt realised that if codification was to take place, it was the language of power that must set the norm – a political principle established at Villers-Cotterêts a century earlier. He almost certainly realised, too, that praise or blame emanating from a prestigious Académie would be a valuable tool for controlling not only how writers wrote, but also what they wrote, thereby dominating their relationship with the centralist, authoritarian regime he was creating. The membership and activities of the Académie were unofficially but heavily influenced by Richelieu in its earlier years. This can be seen, for example, in its criticisms of Corneille's play *Le Cid* in 1637, regarded by Richelieu as ideologically suspect.

Although the Académie has played an important role in the sociolinguistic history of French – as one of the most powerful guardians of classical usage and inhibitors of change – its prescriptions have never had the force of law and have never been accorded more respect than the contemporary standing of its individual members could command. The *Grammaire de l'Académie* was published only in 1932 and when it emerged it received universally hostile criticism. The Académie's rhetoric and poetics have never seen the light of day.

It is in the *lexical field* that the influence of the Académie has probably been strongest. The first edition of its dictionary was eventually produced in 1694, and it has gone through numerous updatings since that time (1718, 1740, 1762, 1798, 1835, 1878, 1935). However, codification of the French lexicon came about through the efforts of many people in addition to the lexicographers of the Académie Française. The process has been carefully charted by Matoré (1968) and Quemada (1968 and 1972). Glossaries of French words had been compiled in the Middle Ages, but they cannot be said to have contributed to the codification of the language. Their purposes were entirely practical – the interpretation of Latin texts (see Matoré 1968: 49–52). The first lexical inventory resembling a modern French dictionary is R. Estienne's *Dictionnaire François – Latin, autrement dit les Mots françois avec les manieres d'user d'iceux tournés en latin* (1549). The preoccupation with the relationship between French and Latin, evident here, continued throughout the sixteenth century, and it is not until Nicot's *Trésor de la langue françoise* (1606) that we have the first significant monolingual French dictionary. Thereafter, the production of dictionaries became prolific. Here are the principal ones published before the twentieth century:

1680, Richelet, *Dictionnaire françois*, Geneva.
1690, Furetière, *Dictionnaire universel*, Rotterdam.
1694, *Dictionnaire de l'Académie*, Paris.
1704, *Dictionnaire universel françois et latin*, Trévoux.
1765, Diderot and d'Alembert, *Encyclopédie ou Dictionnaire raisonné des sciences, des arts et des métiers*, Neufchastel.
1800 Boiste, *Dictionnaire*, Paris.
1845 Bescherelle, *Dictionnaire national*, Paris.
1872 Littré, *Dictionnaire*, Paris.
1866–76 Larousse, *Grand Dictionnaire universel du XIXe siècle*, Paris.
1890–1900 Hatzfeld, *Dictionnaire général*, Paris.

It is easy to forget that dictionaries, like grammar-books, are not objective mirrors of linguistic reality, but that they are written by people and as such reflect not only the individual value-systems of their authors but also the interests of particular social groups. In their role as legitimisers of certain words at the expense of others and as specifiers of the meaning and value of words, dictionaries have achieved an importance in French culture which is rarely encountered elsewhere. French fascination for dictionaries has certainly not diminished in the twentieth century.

The production of prescriptive *grammar-books* in France over the past four centuries has been no less prolific and we shall look at some of the social reasons for this later. The task of the prescriptive grammarian is to give the seal of approval to certain grammatical forms and to stigmatise others. His initial preferences are usually dictated by social considerations but, as we shall see, grammarians tend to be rather bashful about this, preferring to justify their prescriptions as far as possible on principles possessing greater intellectual credibility. They commonly justify their prescriptions either with reference to some sort of 'logic' or by appeals to etymology and the example of Latin.

Grammatical thinking in sixteenth-century France was concerned very substantially with the relationship (in terms of history and status) between French and languages which at the time possessed greater prestige – Latin, Greek, Hebrew and Italian. Early French grammarians sought to reveal how closely the underlying system of French (stripped of what Saussure would call *parole* variations) 'conformed' to the systems present in one or other or all of these more prestigious languages. According to biblical myth (Genesis 9: 1–9), generally accepted as literal, historical truth as late as the nineteenth century, the original language of Man, spoken in the Garden of Eden, was lost after the episode of the Tower of Babel. Thereafter, the tongues of men were confused and continued on an endless process of degeneration and diversification (see Lusignan 1987: 51–3). In the sixteenth century, with the growth of interest in the vernaculars,

> chacun tente de prouver que sa langue est la plus proche de la langue pré-babélique, comme si cette proximité supposée était la preuve d'une supériorité séculaire.

162

(everyone tries to prove that that his language is the closest to the pre-Babel language, as if this supposed proximity were the proof of an age-old superiority.)

(Calvet 1981: 6)

The first significant French grammar of French was that composed by J. Dubois (often referred to by the latinised version of his name, Sylvius) (1531): *In Linguam gallicam isagoge, una cum eiusdem grammatica Latino-Gallica* ('Introduction to the French language with a Latin–French grammar of the same'). This is, as the title indicates, an etymological grammar: the author wanted to find the underlying system of French in Latin, for he considered French to be but corrupt Latin. In order to uncover its Latin system, the grammarian's task was to strip it of its vulgar accretions. The second French grammar of some importance is that of J. Drosai (1544) entitled: *Grammaticae quadrilinguis partitiones*. This attempts to uncover structural parallels between French and Latin, Greek and Hebrew.

It is not difficult to understand the ascendancy of Latin over the minds of early grammarians. The suppression of optional variation in language, which is the goal of codification, is impossible in anything other than a dead language. Given the enormous prestige of Latin in early modern Europe, given the fact that by the sixteenth century it had become to all intents and purposes a dead language (i.e. a language with no speakers), and given its continued importance as a written language, Latin dominated the thinking of scholars from the sixteenth to the nineteenth century as they grappled with the problem of codifying the vernaculars. Little by little grammarians began to gain in self-confidence and to emancipate French from the tutelage of Latin, and an independent French grammatical tradition emerged (see Chevalier 1968). However, French was seen by many as the natural heir to Latin in the seventeenth and eighteenth centuries, and to give substance to this claim, prescriptive grammarians were usually unable or unwilling to avoid casting the grammar of French in the mould of its illustrious forebear. They retained for many centuries the notion that Latin was the ideal language, that the grammatical categories of Latin could be applied with minimum modification to the analysis of French and that French forms approximating closely to Latin were preferable to those which did not (see Rickard 1981).

The most obvious feature of variability in late medieval written French was *spelling*. The writing system had long since become conventionalised as in the later Middle Ages spelling fell further and further behind changes in pronunciation (e.g. the levelling of diphthongs as in *fait* [fɛ], *fleur* [flœr], and the deletion of final consonants as in *champs* [ʃɑ̃]). Variation was increased by the widespread practice among late medieval scribes of inserting 'etymological' consonants to enhance the Latinate appearance of French words (e.g. *doigt* < *digitum*, *mieulx* < *melius*). Several interesting attempts were made by sixteenth-century scholars to produce unified spelling systems anchored to pronunciation (see Meigret 1550; Peletier du Mans 1550; de la Ramée 1562). These experiments are extremely valuable for historical phonologists, since they embody a good deal of information about sixteenth-century pronunciation. However, they had little impact on contemporary spelling practice, partly because each of the authors produced a different system, but more importantly because printers were unwilling to adopt them. It is safe to maintain, therefore, that it was the *praticiens* (chancery clerks, civil servants and lawyers) in the fourteenth to fifteenth centuries and the printers in the sixteenth century who were chiefly responsible for the fixation of the French spelling system which is still in use today. There have of course been numerous 'reforms' of the system in the intervening centuries (see Catach 1978b: 32–46), and the question continues to generate much heat even in our own day. However, it is worth noting that no heavy premium seems to have been placed upon orthographical correctness before the end of the eighteenth century (see Seguin 1972: 48–50) and that it was the great literacy programmes of the nineteenth century which made spelling the touchstone of educatedness and a uniform spelling system the chief indicator of a uniform language, symbol of a united nation (see below, pp. 213–14).

Whereas uniformity of spelling became relatively easy to achieve with the advent of printing and the spread of literacy, codification of *pronunciation* is exceptionally difficult. It is possible to find examples of the influence of orthography on pronunciation (see Pope 1952: 291–3; Désirat and Hordé 1988: 123–5), *legs* pronounced [lɛg] instead of [lɛ], *cheptel* pronounced [ʃɛptel] instead of [ʃɛtel]. However, codification of French pronunciation took place essentially with reference to the social groups associated with particular modes of speech, and it is to this aspect of codification that we must now turn.

THE DEFINITION OF THE 'BEST FRENCH'

In the rest of this chapter the fundamental question we shall be asking is: how did people decide, at a given period, what was 'the best French'? We shall be tracing the development of the *sur-norme* and its ideological basis in France between the sixteenth and nineteenth centuries. In order to get at 'ideology', which is not often explicitly articulated, we have to read between the lines. We have to interpret the surface symptoms of an underlying intellectual condition. We shall be concerned, therefore, not with the evolution of actual usage, nor with the development of grammatical theory, but with the evolution of dominant social attitudes to language over the period. We shall see how people's attitudes towards 'the best French' went through a series of subtle intellectual shifts between 1500 and 1800: at first the 'best French' was the best because it was the French of the 'best people'; later it was felt to be the best because it was the language of reason and clarity; finally, at the time of the Revolution, since this variety of French was the language of reason, all those wishing to be considered French and reasonable were induced to feel that they had to speak it.

Phase I (1500–1660): 'The "best" French is the best because it is spoken by "the best people" '

Concern for the status of French in relation to other languages may have provided some of the initial impetus to language codification in France, but the most important pressure was social in origin. The essential task involved the detailed selection of the 'correct' forms of French from among numerous competing variants. Which forms were to be considered the best? We saw in the last chapter how in the sixteenth century the superior status of 'the King's French' was finally established at the expense of Latin and of the other Gallo-Romance varieties – the Ordinance of Villers-Cotterêts (1539) set the seal on French as the administrative language of the kingdom. However, by 1539 the precise details of the linguistic norm were far from fixed. In the written language variation had by no means been eliminated, though the development of printing was contributing significantly to its uniformisation. As literacy spread in the sixteenth to eighteenth centuries and as printing made written materials more widely available, writing in French became a powerful agent for the diffusion of the standard. As written forms acquire prestige and are considered to be 'correct', they increasingly exert a pressure on speech. However, we shall see that it is not until the eighteenth century that written forms come to be regarded as the principal yardstick for correct speech. *Spoken* norms are clearly much more difficult to establish than *written* norms and it is these which we will be mainly interested in in what follows.

The spoken standard in French is generally seen as originating in 'le parler de Paris' (see Walter 1988: 82) and we discussed its selection in an earlier chapter (see above, p. 98). This formulation is uncontroversial, but it is also rather unhelpful since the speech of late medieval Paris was far from homogeneous, having shown signs of social stratification from as early as the thirteenth century (see above, p. 144). Let us look first of all at the gulf between the speech of the upper and lower classes in sixteenth-century Paris, then at the variability existing within the usage of the upper social groups, before seeing which variety emerged as the dominant one.

The traditional approach to social differentiation in later medieval French has been to portray the lower social groups in Paris as being the ones who initiated the use of deviant speech-forms. For details of these see above, pp. 145–8. No one can deny the inherently variable nature of the Parisian vernacular, but it would be less prescriptive and perhaps more realistic to put the idea the other way round, portraying the upper class as having initiated its own distinctive speech-norms, no doubt for reasons of group identity and status. As was the case in London (see Leith 1983: 38), the lower class in Paris appears to have spoken a dialect related to those of the surrounding country region. Just as Cockney speech is related to Kentish, the Parisian vernacular appears to have had particularly close links with the dialects situated to the north and west of the city (see Rosset 1911). The rural connections of the Parisian vernacular can clearly be seen in the language of many of the peasants who figure in Molière's plays: the linguistic features which Molière selects to characterise their rural speech consist essentially of items associated with lower-class Parisian speech which had been heavily stigmatised by grammarians since the early part of the sixteenth century (see Lodge 1991). Can the parallel with the development of London English be extended to upper-class Parisian speech, too? It is well known that upper-class London English was derived not from the London vernacular, but from the East Midland dialect (see Leith 1983: 39). Are the origins of upper-class Parisian likewise to be found in the dialect of a different region of France?

Such a hypothesis runs counter to a traditional approach to French cultural history which sees Paris as an exporter, not an importer, of high-status cultural forms, but it should not be excluded without examination. There is a popular belief, current even today, that 'the best French' is spoken in Touraine and it may not be a pure invention of teachers of French to foreigners, as suggested by Gueunier *et al.* (1978). Perhaps it is a reminiscence of a period when the speech of the Loire valley did indeed command high prestige. It is well known, for instance, that before the early part of the sixteenth century the Royal Court had for several decades been peripatetic, and that the kings and aristocracy had shown a marked predilection for their residences in the Loire valley. Writing in 1530 Palsgrave observed that (in matters of correctness) 'I moost followe the Parisyens and the countreys that be conteyned betwene the ryver of Seyne and the ryver of Loyre.' In 1533 Rabelais wrote the following:

> dist Pantagruel, ne sçavez-vous parler Françoys?
> – Si faictz très bien, Seigneur, respondet le compaignon [Panurge], Dieu merci. C'est ma langue naturelle et maternelle, car je suis né et ay esté nourry jeune au jardin de France: c'est Touraine.

> (Pantagruel said: 'Can you not speak French?'
> 'Yes I can, sir, very well,' replied his companion, 'thank God. It is my natural mother tongue, for I was born and brought up in the Garden of France, that is Touraine.')
>
> (Rabelais 1962: 255)

H. Estienne (1578b) declared:

Nous donnons tellement le premier lieu au langage de Paris, que nous confessons que celuy des villes prochaines, qui sont aussi comme du coeur de la France, ne s'en esloigne guere. Et pour ce que Orleans voudroit bien avoir le second lieu, Tours aussi, pareillement Vandosmes, et qu'il est demandé aussi par Bourges, et Chartres d'autres costé y pretend, et quelques autres villes des plus prochaines de Paris; à fin que les unes ne portent point d'envie aux autres, nous laissons ceste question indecise.

(We give the first place so much to the speech of Paris that we confess that the speech of near-by towns, which are also as it were in the heart of France, is scarcely different from it. And because Orléans would like to have the second place, Tours too, Vendôme the same, and because it is also sought after by Bourges, and Chartres also lays claim to it and certain other towns close to Paris; so that none should be envious of the others, we will leave this question unresolved.)

(quoted by Pope 1952: 37)

The famous sixteenth-century quarrel between the *ouystes* and the *non-ouystes* may also be of relevance. Throughout the sixteenth century, controversy raged over the variable pronunciation of the back rounded vowel in words like *nostre, vostre, dos*: speakers favouring the pronunciation /u/ were labelled *ouystes*, while those favouring the pronunciation /o/ were the *non-ouystes*. The /u/ variant was commonly associated with the Loire valley as we can see in the following quotation,

Superiores Galli, ut Aurelii, Turones et Andes . . . gallicas pluresque voces, quas per *o* simplicem effamur, per *ou* eloquuntur: ut in his, *chose, chouse: Iosse, Iousse: gros, grous*.

(Certain people from north Gaul, such as the inhabitants of Orléans, Tours and Angers, pronounce several French words with an *ou* where we pronounce them with a simple *o*, etc.)

(Bovelles 1533, quoted by Thurot 1881: I, 240)

That said, strong evidence enabling us to establish privileged links between upper-class Parisian and the dialect of some other part of France (e.g. Touraine) is not in the end very plentiful. It

168

would be safer to see the spoken norms of the 'best people' as an artificial (and arbitrary) selection of socially marked variables drawn from a multiplicity of sources (Parisian and regional), their essential characteristic being that they were different from forms current among lower social groups. It was no doubt the very arbitrariness of this selection which gave the grammarians the importance they had in seventeenth-century Paris. Upper-class speakers may commonly have preferred forms associated with dialects spoken to the south of Paris (Touraine) precisely because they were the furthest removed from the heavily stigmatised vernacular forms which we saw earlier were associated with dialects located to the north and west of the capital. When the grammarians got to work codifying good usage (the *sur-norme*), one of their major concerns (if not *the* major concern) appears to have been to differentiate the speech of the ruling elite from that of the *peuple*. The strength of upper-class disdain for lower-class speech in the seventeenth and eighteenth centuries implies the existence of a deep antagonism between the two social groups. The spectre of the Paris mob was to haunt the ruling classes throughout the *ancien régime* leading to the decamping of the Court to Versailles in the 1680s and the forced return of the King to Paris a century later at the outbreak of the Revolution.

It would be misleading to suggest, however, that within the ruling elite all was perfect serenity. During the fourteenth to fifteenth centuries, the nature of the monarchy had changed: the kings came increasingly to exercise power through a new bureaucratic class located permanently in Paris and recruited, not in the latinate world of the clergy, but in the vernacular world of the educated bourgeoisie. Moreover, economic power had come to be wielded not only by the great landowners (the Crown, the aristocracy and the Church) but also by the banking and merchant families in the towns, notably in Paris. When the King and his entourage came to establish themselves on a fairly permanent basis in Paris in the second quarter of the sixteenth century (see Braudel 1986: II, 2^e partie 205), the Court had to compete for political (and linguistic) pre-eminence, not only with the body of highly educated officials in the royal administration (the *Chancellerie*), but also with the legal fraternity of the *Palais* (*de Justice*) and in the Paris *Parlement* (a law court, not a democratic legislature), and with the upper echelons of the Paris bourgeoisie

(*la Ville*) (see Brunot 1907). The linguistic debates of the sixteenth to seventeenth centuries reflects the tensions between
these social groups. The terms *Cour, Palais, Ville, Peuple,* etc., are
coded and highly charged: linguistic commentators' evaluations
of the speech of the *Cour,* the *Palais* and the *Ville* are not based
innocently on aesthetic appreciations of the sociolects of the
groups in question: 'L'attitude envers la langue n'est que le
reflet fidèle des préoccupations plus générales de la société'
('Attitudes towards the language are but a faithful reflection of
more general social preoccupations') (Padley 1983: 17).
Commentators' attitudes towards *mots de la Cour* and *mots du
Palais* very often reflect their loyalties in the tension between the
most powerful groups in French society struggling for pre-
eminence. Where was the 'best French' to be found?

There were grammarians in the mid-sixteenth century who
proposed that the bearers of the spoken norm were located in
the *peuple* rather than in the upper social groups (see Glatigny
1989: 19). However, these were exceptions. Most located the
norm-bearers higher up. Tory (1529) seems to accept the *Cour*
and the *Palais* on equal terms: 'le style de parlement et le langage
de cour sont tres bons' ('the style of the *Parlement* and the
language of the Court are both valid'), while others express
preferences one way or the other. Marot (1533), for instance,
regrets that Villon 'n'ait pas été nourri à la cour des rois et des
princes, là où les jugements s'amendent et les langages se
polissent' ('was not brought up at the court of kings and princes
where justice is dispensed and where language becomes refined'). Meigret (1550) looks for the prestige variety at the royal
Court (p. 54v), firmly rejecting the contribution of the people (p.
105r) and the peasantry (p. 121r). Pillot (1550) likewise looks to
the Court, warts and all: 'Hic tanta pollet auctoritate ut praestet
cum ea errare quam cum caeteris bene loqui, et satis sit allegare
ipsa dixit' ('The authority of the court is so powerful that it is
better to commit mistakes with the court then to speak correctly
with other people, and it is sufficient to adduce the principle of
"the language itself said it" '). Ronsard is disarmingly frank
about the dominance of the King's French: 'Nous sommes con-
traints, si nous voulous parvenir a quelqu'honneur de parler son
langage' ('If we want to acquire any honour, we are obliged to
speak his language') (*Art poétique*, 1565), and 'le courtisan est
toujours le plus beau, a cause de la majesté du prince' ('the

courtier is always the more handsome because of the majesty of the prince') (*Franciade*, 1578).

The social conflicts reflected in the Wars of Religion (1562–98) reduced the prestige of the Court, particularly in the eyes of Protestants. Even before the outbreak of violent conflict, R. Estienne had extolled the prestige of the language of the legal fraternity (the *Palais*). While accepting in 1557 that certain of the 'plus savants en nostre langue' are to be found at the royal Court, he nevertheless gives particular weight to the role of

> son parlement de Paris, aussi sa chancellerie et sa cour des comptes; esquels lieux le langage s'escrit et se prononce en la plus grande pureté qu'en tous autres lieux.

> (his *Parlement* of Paris, along with his chancery and his exchequer, in the which places the language is written and spoken with greater purity than in all other places.)
>
> (*Traicté de la grammaire françoise*)

As the religious violence mounted, and particularly after the Massacre of St Bartholomew (1572), the hostility of Protestants to Court speech, influenced as it was by italianising cliques surrounding Catherine de Medici, increased. H. Estienne (1578a) declares that 'autrefois il fallait chercher le meilleur langage entre les courtisans' ('in earlier times one had to seek the best language among courtiers'), but now this is no longer the case. His words are echoed by another Protestant in 1584, Théodore de Bèze (see François 1959: I, 192). H. Estienne does not, however, give uncritical endorsement to the variety used in the *Palais*. Instead, he broadens the base of *bon usage* to the cultivated people of Paris and towns to the immediate south and west such as Bourges, Orléans and Tours (see above, pp. 167–8 and Marzys 1974: 324). Thus, at the end of the century, the *Cour* no longer presented an undisputed reference-point for *bon usage*. Its position was challenged in the eyes of many by the language of the high echelons of the administration and the legal fraternity. Moreover, it contained within itself several conflicting usages, a situation further confused by the arrival on the throne of Henri IV in 1594 with his Gascon entourage and their southern French speech.

It was the seventeenth century which witnessed the most

intense activity directed towards the codification of the linguistic norm. Some traditional accounts of the codification movement attribute the grammarians' endeavours to their aesthetic sensibilities: the exuberance of the sixteenth century left a great deal of 'linguistic untidiness' to be cleared up and 'dead wood' to be pruned (see Rickard 1989: 102). Others portray the French language as an artefact (like a château) which needed to be rendered symmetrical and homogeneous after the wayward fantasies of the linguistic architects of the sixteenth century. Accounts such as these are steeped in prescriptivism, implying as they do that languages can be improved, and they ignore the whole social dimension of the codification process. On the other hand, Wartburg (1962: 171) explains the grammarians' activities with reference to their concern for the long-term needs of the nation: France required a single, uniform language to provide a more efficient means of communication. After the individualistic, even anarchic tendencies of the previous century, the country needed a period of 'rational' social behaviour and national solidarity. The aristocracy's willing acceptance of the grammarians' dictates was a sign of the submission of their individual wills in linguistic as in other matters to the long-term good of the collectivity.

This evocation of a united and disinterested ruling class is somewhat at variance with a substantial body of evidence revealing a seventeenth-century France which continued to be riven with social tension and internal conflict long after the end of the Wars of Religion. Life in fact remained precarious, and competition for basic resources – principally food – was often violent, as the frequent food-riots in Paris and peasant insurrections in the countryside demonstrate quite clearly. Even within the ruling elite conflict was never far from the surface. It took almost seventy years from the arrival of Henri IV in Paris (1594) for the power of the Crown to establish itself fully in the face of pressure from Protestants, the financial/legal bourgeoisie and the centrifugal ambitions of the feudal aristocracy. Analogous social conflict in England led to civil war, the execution of the King in 1649 and the triumph of the London bourgeoisie. Indeed, France itself experienced civil war with the Fronde (1648–52) triggered by a dispute between the Crown (in the person of Mazarin) and the *Parlement* of Paris. Largely through the centralising efforts of Richelieu and Mazarin, the Crown emerged by 1660 as the supreme political force and Louis XIV was able to embark upon fifty-five years of absolute rule, but this ultimate triumph of the Crown was not seen as inevitable in the first half of the century.

It was precisely in this half-century that the process of linguistic codification went through its most feverish and formative phase, and it seems likely that the quest for order in language reflected less an atmosphere of serene rationality and a deep sense of common purpose than one of social insecurity where the boundaries between social groups were ill-defined and a source of conflict. Throughout the seventeenth century the symbolic value of language and the most minute refinements of the linguistic norm were central preoccupations of the upper echelons of a society where 'la beauté du langage est une des principales distinctions' ('beauty of language is one of the chief ways of distinguishing oneself') (Brunot 1966: III, 17). Language had become a crucial marker of social class and the watchword of the codification movement was indeed *la distinction*. Drawing lines around the various 'estates' in society (e.g. Loyseau's *Traité des Ordres*, 1614) and defining the limits of 'acceptable' speech were aspects of one and the same demarcatory mentality. It would be foolish to maintain that the desire to produce a more efficient means of communication for society at large had no place in the thinking of seventeenth-century linguistic codifiers, but it is clear that at the very least there existed at the top of society a conflict between the need for a shared *norme* which would facilitate wider communication across French society and the need felt by the social elite to symbolise its own identity and status through the development of its own *sur-norme*.

F. de Malherbe, who was presented at Court in 1605, became a particularly influential figure in the codification movement with his detailed commentaries on the work of a late sixteenth-century poet named Desportes (1546–1606). His role, however, is not easy to evaluate. He is traditionally portrayed as being the first to engage seriously in the creation of a more efficient linguistic system, with his emphasis on *clarté* and *précision* and with his famous *boutade* to the effect that whatever was written had to be comprehensible to the 'crocheteurs du Port au Foin' ('porters in the Haymarket'). It must be remembered, however, that Malherbe never produced a systematic grammar and that his objectives were actually quite modest: he was concerned exclusively with the distinctive character of Court poetry. There is no evidence to suggest that he had social aims which went beyond the definition of a new literary style, distinct from that of the now unfashionable literary school of the Pléiade.

The style of the Pléiade involved the use of a wide range of vocabulary items (including dialectalisms, italianisms, etc.), convoluted syntax (often influenced by Italian) and multilayered meanings. Any new style, therefore, had to have a restricted vocabulary (shunning dialectalisms, archaisms, loan-words, etc.), a rigorously explicit syntax (*précision*) and unambiguous surface meanings (*clarté*). Since Court fashion now rejected the esoteric, italianate poetry of the late sixteenth century, Malherbe's new style had to be much more accessible – even to the 'crocheteurs du Port au Foin'. What Malherbe did not mean by this remark, however, was that the varieties of French used by the labouring classes should find their way into Court poetry. Quite the reverse. He excluded from fashionable poetry all provincialisms, all *mots bas*, all *mots du palais* and (by definition) all archaisms, words which had fallen out of fashion. His activities not surprisingly earned him the title of 'docteur en négative', but this is the most any prescriptive grammarian can ever expect, his activities being strictly limited to expressing preferences between existing alternatives.

It is doubtful that Malherbe had any wider social aims in his *Commentaires* than the definition of currently acceptable poetic or, at most, Court usage: far from seeking to create a widely available standard language, he was primarily concerned with the production of a literary style which would distinguish the refined minority from the rest. His importance lies, however, in the fact that he set the tone for a whole generation of language codifiers in France, including those of the Académie Française (see above, pp. 159–61).

Engaged for a while on the compilation of the Académie's dictionary was the most famous prescriptive commentator of them all – Vaugelas. Like Malherbe's *Commentaires*, the *Remarques* of Vaugelas (1647) are a miscellaneous collection of comments on features of orthography, pronunciation, lexis and syntax over which there was hesitation in usage. Whereas Malherbe was concerned primarily with the language of Court poetry, Vaugelas widened his brief to cover in addition the spoken language. He produced a sort of linguistic courtesy book whose most avid readership seems to have consisted of ambitious citizens wishing to rise in society and anxious not to have their progress blocked by inability to conform to what were perceived to be the linguistic norms of the dominant elite. Ayres-Bennett (1987: 191–200) has analysed the socioprofessional categories of purchasers of the *Remarques* in Grenoble between 1647 and 1688 and sees among them a predominance of 'financial and judicial office-holders'.

The theoretical base on which the *Remarques* are constructed is somewhat superficial – the theory of *bon usage*. Vaugelas accepts (rather apologetically) that he can detect no fundamental principle (*raison*) at work in the language system which might give coherence to the rather perverse variation present in language use (*usage*): 'l'usage fait beaucoup de choses par raison, beaucoup sans raison et beaucoup contre raison' ('usage does many things according to reason, many without reason and many contrary to reason') (Vaugelas 1970: VI.3). He restricts himself therefore to observing and describing actual usage rather than with speculating about the underlying structures and implicit patternings of language. However, this empirical approach in no sense diminishes Vaugelas's fundamental prescriptivism. In the absence of reliable internal criteria (*raison*) for preferring one linguistic item over another (e.g. should the present participle of *valoir* be *valant* or *vaillant*?), he had recourse to an external social reference-point. He arranged competing linguistic items in a hierarchy corresponding to his view of social stratification. This implicit hierarchy can be represented as in Figure 5.

The development of the standard occasions a rejection of varieties of French which are felt to be outside the norm. The most heavily stigmatised items are those which Vaugelas attributes to the mass of the population in Paris – *le peuple*, or even worse, *la lie du peuple*. No less powerful a deterrent is the association of a particular item with *Province*. Here, however, we can detect suggestions of a hierarchy – some provinces are despised more than others. At the bottom come the regions *au dela Loire* – Poitou and Gascony, followed by Normandy. Slightly more favourable treatment is accorded to Anjou and the region *le long de la rivière de Loire*, no doubt a reminiscence of the tradition we discussed earlier (see above, pp. 167–9).

When Vaugelas attributes a linguistic item to the *Palais* or the *Ville*, he is less categorical in his condemnation of it – he accepts

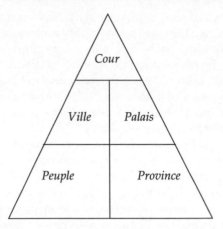

Figure 5   A view of social stratification in seventeenth-century France

that certain members of the bourgeoisie enjoy a status close to that of the *Cour*, i.e. they can be accommodated within the dominant elite. However, ultimately for Vaugelas the ruling group in society was focused on *la Cour*:

> Voicy donc comme on definit le bon Usage . . . c'est la facon de parler de la plus saine partie de la cour, conformement a la facon d'escrire de la plus saine partie des Autheurs du temps. Quand je dis la Cour, j'y comprens les femmes comme les hommes, et plusieurs personnes de la ville ou le Prince reside, qui par la communication qu'elles ont avec les gens de la Cour participent a sa politesse.

> (This is how one defines good usage . . . it is the way of speaking of the most sensible part of the Court, when that accords with the way of writing of the most sensible part of the authors of the day. When I say Court, I include in it women as well as men, and several persons of the town where the Prince resides, who in view of the contacts they have with the Court share in its refinement.)

> (Vaugelas 1970: II.3)

This explicit statement of what constituted the 'best French' would be straightforward were it not for the restriction imposed by the phrase *la plus saine partie*. Clearly court usage was not homogeneous and Vaugelas's problem in these cases was to find plausible grounds for preferring one form rather than another. The justifications he finds are largely *post facto* rationalisations of his personal value-judgements, invoking the precedents set by prestigious authors, euphony, analogy and surface logic (*Raison*), and closely reflecting the current aesthetic and sociocultural ideal of the *honnête homme*. The influence of the aristocratic code of values referred to as *honnêteté* is well illustrated in Vaugelas's handling of the lexicon. The *honnête homme* is a noble, so he naturally avoids using the vulgar language of the populace (*mots bas*). The *honnête homme* does not turn his hand to work, so he naturally avoids using technical vocabulary (*mots techniques*) which may give his society companions the wrong idea. The *honnête homme* is a discreet follower of fashion, so he must avoid using old-fashioned words (*mots vieux*). The *honnête homme* frequents the Court in Paris, so he must avoid any contamination from provincial speech (*mots de province*). The *honnête homme* is exceptionally courteous to ladies, so he scrupulously avoids the use of *mots sales* which may offend their delicate sensibilities. This itemisation of exclusions from acceptable vocabulary reveals the proximity of Vaugelas's activities and those of contemporary authors of courtesy books. Vaugelas's advice is concerned exclusively with the public use of language – the language of literature and the language of society rituals and *mondain* ceremonies. Vaugelas in fact codified a sort of *langue de parade*, the lexical restrictions he imposed being bearable only in public, not in private life.

Purist limitations on the vocabulary acceptable on public occasions inevitably caused difficulties for those wishing to 'shine' linguistically in company. The solution hit upon in the mid-seventeenth century was to compensate for lexical poverty with increasingly bizarre permutations of the small inventory of permissible items. The phenomenon of preciosity was satirised in Molière's *Les Précieuses Ridicules* where armchair = *'commodité de la conversation'* and teeth = *'ameublement de la bouche'*. It is significant that Molière should have taken women as his chief target in his satire, for their role in the codification process was considerable (see Ayres-Bennett 1990). It is well attested that in western societies women are more sensitive to the status connotations of speech than men (see Hudson 1980: 121).

Vaugelas was a perfectly honest linguistic snob, as only a provincial can be (he was brought up in Savoy) – he was serving the identity needs of the ruling elite (and those aspiring to join it) and for him it was quite clear that the 'best French' ultimately was so not because of any intrinsic structural properties such a variety may have possessed, but because the 'best people' spoke like that. Such honesty would not be tolerated by his successors.

Phase II (1660–1789): 'The "best French" is the best because it is the language of reason and clarity'

Louis XIV achieved undisputed dominance of the sociopolitical scene in France (and indeed in Europe) in the second half of the seventeenth century. The identity of the dominant group in French society was by now well established and its members naturally came to believe that French society (and the French language) had reached a state of 'perfection'. From this period and onwards through the eighteenth century the standard language was codified in the minutest detail and its privileged role in society legitimised by the elaboration of what we have referred to earlier as the 'ideology of the standard'. We saw earlier (above pp. 156–7) how this ideology consists of three essential elements:

(1) a belief that only one variety of the language is legitimate and that all non-standard variations are by definition improper;
(2) an ideal model for imitation which prioritises the written language over the vagaries of speech;
(3) a legitimisation of the standard on the basis of its allegedly inherent superiority to other varieties (greater clarity, logic, precision, etc.).

Let us look at the codification of French in the seventeenth to eighteenth centuries with regard to each of these elements in turn.

During the course of the seventeenth and eighteenth centuries *intolerance of all forms of language variation* increased among members of the ruling group in society and perhaps even more ferociously among those who aspired to join it. Society was strongly focused upon a powerful monarch (Louis XIV) who adopted as his emblem that of the 'Sun-King'. With their leader at the peak of his power, the ruling group not surprisingly considered that French society had reached an apogee and that

the French language (*their* language) had reached a corresponding state of 'perfection' (see François 1959: I, 229–402) – a view of
the seventeenth-century French still widely held among guardians of the linguistic norm. The prestige of one variety of
course triggers the disparagement of others, and the period
witnessed an increasing disdain on the part of the upper classes
for language varieties other than their own. As a result, all
provincial and peasant speech-forms could be easily exploited
by writers of comedy as a marker of boorishness and rusticity.
Molière illustrates this in several of his plays (see Dauzat 1946:
37–46; and Leith 1983: 42–3 for a similar development in
English). Gradually the codified language of the ruling group
appropriated for itself the sole right to the the name 'la langue
française'.

For all the concentration of power in the person of the King,
the sociolinguistic situation continued to evolve, particularly
after the death of Louis XIV in 1715. Language variation and
language change continued to confront language codifiers with
the problem: what was the most solid sociolinguistic model to
which the norm could be anchored? During the fifty-five years
of the absolute rule of Louis XIV (1660–1715), the concentration
of power in the person of the King ensured that the Court
remained the arbiter of *bon usage*. Many of Vaugelas's prescriptions were in time superseded, either as a result of language
change, or because they became the object of criticism of other
commentators. However, Vaugelas's empirical conception of
bon usage remained highly influential, numerous commentators
following his example and producing their own commentaries
on variable linguistic items. The most notable of these is perhaps
D. Bouhours with his *Remarques nouvelles sur la langue françoise*
(1675) and his *Suite des remarques nouvelles sur la langue françoise*
(1692). It is known that the playwright Jean Racine regularly
submitted his work to Bouhours for grammatical correction
before it was presented to the public. Court usage likewise
provided the yardstick for Richelet's *Dictionnaire françoise* (1680),
and the long-awaited first edition of the *Dictionnaire de l'Académie
Française* (1694).

However, the strong focus for the linguistic norm provided by
Louis XIV disappeared with his death in 1715. Power ceased to
be concentrated in the royal court at Versailles and came to be
shared more equally with financial and legal circles in Paris. The

highly cultivated bourgeois elite of the city hosted influential literary salons and their use of language (*le bon goût*) began to challenge the supremacy of the sociolinguistic models offered by Versailles. By the second half of the eighteenth century, as in England, it was the upper middle or business class which dictated the norms of the national language, just as they had come to dominate the national economy.

Even during the reign of Louis XIV purist attitudes had not gone unchallenged, especially as regards the lexicon: Furetière's *Dictionnaire universel*, published in 1690 in Rotterdam, out of reach of the Académie's monopoly, granted legitimacy to a far wider range of words than that permitted by the tenets of *bon usage* – it was clear to Furetière, for instance, that to banish technical words from the dictionary was a nonsense, a fact soon acknowledged by the Académie itself when it commissioned Thomas Corneille to produce his *Dictionnaire des arts et des sciences* (1699). This tendency developed strongly in the eighteenth century when a new 'Enlightenment' culture grew up to challenge aristocratic tradition. Technical dictionaries proliferated and the blurring of the distinction between dictionary and encyclopaedia which began with the Dictionary of Trévoux (1704–1771) culminated in the great *Encyclopédie* of Diderot and d'Alembert (1758–72). Eighteenth-century dictionaries clearly reflect contemporary social divisions, with certain dictionaries clinging to the conservative, aristocratic values of the previous century, and others more receptive to new words and ideas and more ready to admit the legitimacy of the aspirations of the lower-status groups in society. The famous *Encyclopédie* of Diderot and d'Alembert produced a significantly more democratic definition of *bon usage* than that produced by Vaugelas:

> *bon usage*: la façon de parler de la plus nombreuse partie de la cour conformement à la façon d'écrire de la plus nombreuse partie des auteurs les plus estimés de temps.

> (*good usage*: the way of speaking of the majority of the court when this accords with the way of writing of the majority of the most highly esteemed authors of the day.)
> (Diderot and d'Alembert 1765: XVI, 517)

However *bon usage* was defined, it continued of course to imply the existence of *mauvais usage*. The stigmatisation of vulgarisms (or *gasconismes* as they were often called) proceeded apace, no doubt leaving most people with a clearer idea of what they were supposed to avoid saying than what the grammarians actually recommended for them. The eighteenth century saw the constitution of a tacitly agreed set of unacceptable linguistic items which were raised almost to the level of shibboleths. Like all stereotypes, the relationship between this set of stigmatised features and actual usage was not fixed.

Indeed, the model used by prescriptive grammarians gradually slipped away from actual spoken usage altogether and *the best form of French was increasingly sought in the written language,* particularly in the writings of the *bons auteurs du Grand Siècle.* The blurring of the social reference for the linguistic norm in the eighteenth century coincided with a weakening of French dominance in international affairs which caused many to look back nostalgically to the days of the *gloire* of Louis XIV. Grammarians increasingly turned away from current usage as the anchor-point for the norm and looked to the writings of the prestigious authors of the previous century. Prominent in this movement was Voltaire:

Il me semble que lorsqu'on a eu dans un siècle un nombre suffisant de bons écrivains devenus classiques, il n'est plus guère permis d'employer d'autres expressions que les leurs, et qu'il faut leur donner le même sens, ou bien dans peu de temps, le siècle présent n'entendrait plus le siècle passé.

(It seems to me that when one has had in a given century a sufficiently large number of good writers whose works have become classics, it is no longer permissible to use any expression other than theirs, and that one must give them the same meaning, otherwise in a very short time, the present century would no longer be able to understand the previous one.)

(quoted by Caput 1975: II, 19)

With the spread of literacy, particularly in the second half of the eighteenth century, written language came to be regarded as the quintessential form of the language, from which other varieties (notably speech) were perverse and regrettable deviations. This primacy accorded to formal, planned, essentially written language is a central feature of standard ideology in French (and indeed European) culture. The 'real French language' is the written language, other varieties (e.g. those used in informal, unplanned, face-to-face interaction) being regarded as un-natural corruptions of it.

We have seen how Vaugelas had justified his prescriptions on empirical grounds, pinning *bon usage* to the usage of a specific social group. The generation of grammarians which succeeded him felt that this expedient contained a dangerous element of contingency – the language of any social group is susceptible to change. What was required now was a means of freezing the language of the current holders of power in perpetuity. The present state of the language had to be permanently fixed and legitimised not by appeals to the vagaries of usage but by the invocation of much more durable authorities. The development of the ideology of the standard requires that society accept the standard variety, not as something imposed by crude political reality, but as flowing naturally from *the intrinsic qualities of elegance, logic and clarity felt to be inherent in that variety.* Many of the efforts of the eighteenth-century grammarians were devoted to discerning the workings of Reason behind the vagaries of French usage.

The gateway to this new avenue was opened by the publi-cation in 1660 of Arnauld and Lancelot's *Grammaire générale et raisonnée* (commonly referred to as the 'Port-Royal Grammar'). This work heralded a renewal of interest among certain gram-marians in the system of language underlying the disparateness of usage. It exerted considerable influence on subsequent gram-matical work, its declared aims being to discover the 'raisons de ce qui est commun à toutes les langues' ('the reasons for that which is common to all languages') and to 'faire par science ce que les autres font seulement par coustume' ('to do through science what others do solely through custom') (quoted by Padley 1983: 89). It is important, however, to distinguish be-tween grammarians interested in theories of language for their own sake and the prescriptive grammarians involved in codify-ing the standard language and in formulating the ideology of the standard.

The seventeenth and eighteenth centuries in France saw im-portant developments in theories of language. During the latter part of the seventeenth century and the first half of the eighteenth, the main thrust of grammatical theory lay in correlating the categories of individual languages with those of universal logic (see Seguin 1972: 65–73). The period saw the publication of numerous grammatical works echoing the principles of Port-Royal, e.g. Restaut's *Principes généraux et raisonnés de la langue française* (1730). Towards the middle of the eighteenth century, linguistic theorists began to question how closely the structures of language could be correlated with the structures of logic. Condillac's *Essai sur l'origine des connaissances humaines* (1746) saw language as governed not by logic, but by 'nature'. Whereas Port-Royal had taken the 'realist', Aristotelian line that thought precedes language (i.e. language gives expression to ideas formulated independently of words), Condillac took the 'nominalist' view that language precedes thought (i.e. language is a conventional structure which predisposes the thought processes of the speech community in particular ways). Each language is a natural phenomenon, encapsulating the 'genius' of the people who speak it and obeying its own internal structural laws rather than the dictates of some universal logic (see Droixhe 1971: 22). Grammatical theorists thereafter lost all interest in universals and became proccupied with the development of particular languages. In his *Traité de la formation méchanique des langues* (1765), de Brosses moves from his inability to attach language to some permanent universal logic to reopen the question of the historical origin of language: he accounted for the irreducibility of languages to unchanging laws of logic with reference to the mutations which have been a feature of languages since their beginning. Only the study of language evolution will then reveal the ultimate truth about language as we trace languages to their source. This paved the way for the great discoveries in historical linguistics made in the nineteenth century.

These later developments in linguistic theory had little impact even on the surface of prescriptive grammar. Prescriptive grammarians continued to promote the belief that the French language ideally replicated the categories of universal logic and reason. Moreover, they remained mesmerised by the apparent regularity and fixity of Latin grammar, seeing the status of the French language as directly related to its conformity to the Latin model (see Rickard 1981). As a result, the eighteenth century saw the gradual development of a formidable prescriptive tradition represented by such works as Mauger's *Nouvelle*

Grammaire françoise (1706) and the influential Lhomond, *Elémens de la grammaire françoise* (1780). These works accumulated detailed and encyclopaedic specifications concerning 'correct' linguistic usage, substantiating their prescriptions with reference to the written models provided by a glittering array of prestigious authors and legitimising them with appeals to the logic, reason and precision inherently present in the structure of the standard variety (see Swiggers 1987).

The ideology of the standard which became crystallised during the eighteenth century served essentially to legitimise the status of the language of the upper classes as the only correct form of expression. Their variety excluded all others and became synonymous with 'the French language' itself. During the eighteenth century this 'French language' was adopted as the language of international diplomacy and became the badge of identity of the aristocracies of Europe, serving an even more demarcatory function in Germany and Russia than it did in France. This variety of French was widely perceived to be superior to all other European languages, the fullest expression of this notion being expressed in Rivarol's lecture *De l'Universalité de la langue française* (1784). Motivated particularly by a desire to demonstrate the superiority of French over English, Rivarol highlighted the clarity and logic of French:

> Ce qui distingue notre langue des langues anciennes et modernes, c'est l'ordre et la construction de la phrase. Cet ordre doit toujours être direct et nécessairement clair. Le Français nomme d'abord le *sujet* du discours, ensuite le *verbe* qui est action, et enfin *l'objet* de cette action: voilà la logique naturelle à tous les hommes . . . la syntaxe française est incorruptible. C'est de là que résulte cette admirable clarté [*sic*], base éternelle de notre langue. Ce qui n'est pas clair n'est pas français: ce qui n'est pas clair est encore anglais, italien, grec ou latin.
>
> (What distinguishes our language from the ancient and the modern languages is the order and structure of the sentence. This order must always be direct and necessarily clear. French names first of all the subject of the discourse, then the verb which is the action, and finally the object of this action: this is the natural logic present in all human beings . . . French syntax is incorruptible. It is from this

that results this admirable clarity which is the eternal basis of our language. What is not clear is not French: what is not clear is still English, Italian, Greek or Latin.)

(Rivarol 1784: 112–13)

Later, Rivarol explains the widespread adoption of French outside France in the eighteenth century on the basis of its internal rationality, coinciding with the rationality which distinguishes human kind in general from beasts: 'Sure, sociale, raisonnable, ce n'est plus la langue française c'est la langue humaine' ('Sure, social and reasonable, it is no longer the language of France, it is the language of humanity') (Rivarol 1784: 119).

The myth of the clarity and logic of the French language has formed a central element in the ideology of the French standard language until our own day. As late as 1962 as eminent a linguist as W. von Wartburg was able to write:

Le 17e siècle, qui a cru pouvoir tout plier aux exigences de la raison, a sans doute donné à la logique l'occasion de transformer dans le sens de la raison la langue française. Aujourd'hui encore il est évident qu'elle répond beaucoup plus que toutes les autres aux exigences de la logique pure.

(The seventeenth century, which believed it could bend everything to the demands of reason, undoubtedly gave logic the opportunity to transform the French language in the direction of reason. Even today it is clear that it conforms much more closely to the demands of pure logic than any other language.)

(Wartburg 1962: 170)

and:

Les qualités de la clarté, de la précision et de l'élégance donnaient au français en Europe une position qu'aucune langue vivante depuis le moyen âge n'avait connue.

(The qualities of clarity, precision and elegance gave the French language a position in Europe which no modern language had known since the Middle Ages.)

(Wartburg 1962: 187)

More recently still, President Mitterrand, opening an exhibition devoted to the French language, declared:

A propos de la langue française, il est difficile d'ajouter, après tant d'autres des éloges tant de fois répétés sur sa rigueur, sa clarté, son élégance, ses nuances, la richesse de ses temps et de ses modes, la délicatesse de ses sonorités, la logique de son ordonnancement.

(On the subject of the French language, after so many others it is hard to add further praising words to those so often repeated concerning its rigour, its clarity, its elegance, its nuances, the richness of its tenses and moods, the delicacy of its sounds, the logic of its word order.)

(quoted by Yaguello 1988: 122–3)

The still current myth of the clarity and logic inherent in the French language reposes on a failure, deliberate or not, to distinguish between *language system* and *language use* (see Milroy and Milroy 1985a: 13). Claims are commonly made by guardians of usage about the superiority of the language *system* of standard French over those of non-standard varieties on the basis of the *use* made of that system by the community's most highly valued writers. Such writers may well produce texts of compelling clarity and logic, but these qualities in their writing spring not from the system itself, but from the use they make of the system. Linguists' analyses of different linguistic systems lead them to the conclusion that, *qua* system, no language variety can be proved to be intrinsically superior to any other. Of course, it is possible to point to differences of complexity between 'developed' and 'undeveloped' languages (see above, pp. 22–3), but such evidence proves nothing about the superiority of one system over another.

Speakers of all languages have deeply held beliefs about the social value of particular varieties, particular words, grammatical structures and speech sounds. Lay people do not share the linguist's doctrine of the artificiality of norms and the arbitrary nature of standard varieties. These speaker perceptions are of extreme interest to sociolinguists, not because of any scientific validity they may have but because of the light they shed on the nature of the speech community concerned. Moreover, particular beliefs about the intrinsic superiority of one variety over others (e.g. the superior logic and clarity of French) are commonly cultivated and exploited by promoters of the standard ideology for rather questionable motives: assertion of the inherent superiority of the standard variety often serves to exclude from power those speakers who do not possess the standard, portraying such speakers as incapable of logic and clarity of thought (i.e. such people are cognitively defective and their social and political aspirations are necessarily flawed).

CONCLUSION

Between the sixteenth and the eighteenth centuries there developed in France a strong set of beliefs about what was and what was not correct in language. These beliefs were a conflation of dos and don'ts from grammarians and practical exemplification from a canon of prestigious authors principally from the seventeenth century (*les grands classiques*). They were reinforced by the development of powerful myths concerning the 'clarity', 'precision', 'logic' and 'universality' of the language, and codified in ever more explicit form during the course of the period. In due course popularising syntheses were produced in the form of such works as Féraud's *Dictionnaire grammatical de la langue française* (1761) and Domergue's *Grammaire générale* (1778), culminating in Girault-Duvivier's *Grammaire des grammaires* (1811). The sociolinguistic importance of these works was immense, for in post-Revolutionary France they came to be used as the basis for the propagation of the standard variety in the dialect-speaking provinces.

The ideology of the standard involves a good deal of self-deception (wilful or otherwise), construing features of language use as characteristics of the language system, and principally for reasons of social demarcation it had become well established by the end of the eighteenth century. At that point this ideology was to receive even greater reinforcement through being harnessed to the centralist and nationalist forces which emerged with the French Revolution. It is paradoxical that the prestige variety devised in the seventeenth century as a means of social differentiation should have been taken up by the French Revolution and propagated by post-Revolutionary governments as a means of increasing social solidarity between Frenchmen and of marking them off from their hostile neighbours. Since French was the language of Reason, it became mandatory for everyone wishing to be considered 'French' and 'reasonable' to speak it. But here we move from the process of 'Codification' to that of 'Acceptance'.

7

ACCEPTANCE

Following Haugen's (1966) analysis of the process of standardisation we come, after 'selection', 'elaboration of function' and
'codification', to the process of 'acceptance': the selected dialect
has ultimately to be adopted by the relevant population as the
principal language of the community, in the case of certain
societies as the 'national language'. Whereas 'elaboration of
function' and 'codification' are processes bearing upon the
linguistic corpus of that dialect, 'selection' and 'acceptance' are
sociological processes, affecting its role and status in society.
The distinction made here between 'selection' and 'acceptance'
is useful as an expository device, but it is at bottom rather
artificial. We saw in Chapter 4 how the variety current in the
King's Court was 'selected' (unconsciously) in the late twelfth
century as the one to be developed into the standard language.
Now, given that the very process of 'selection' of a prestige
dialect implies an 'acceptance' of its special status by at least
some speakers of other dialects, there is a sense in which its
'acceptance' (i.e. its functional, social and spatial diffusion) got
under way in France as early as the twelfth century.

However, many centuries were to elapse before this dialect
became the omnifunctional language of the majority of the
French population, particularly in the Occitan-speaking south.
We saw in Chapter 5 how it took till the middle of the sixteenth
century for the King's French to take over the principal H
functions in society, at the expense of Latin (in the north), and
of Latin and Occitan (in the south). Even then, however, the
proportion of the population actually participating in those H
functions (education, the law, government, banking, literature,
etc.) remained tiny: low levels of literacy and the social struc-

tures of a relatively primitive agricultural economy excluded from these the mass of ordinary people in the fields. As far as the L functions were concerned (i.e. everyday conversation), the process of acceptance took longer still, and the *patois*, character-ised by infinite variation, were to reign supreme among a pre-dominantly rural population until very recent times.

Before taking this subject further it might be useful to reflect on what was eventually 'accepted' by speakers of different language varieties, as the standard was diffused across the area which is now French-speaking. What was or is 'the standard language'? Are we to view it as a variety like any other, with 'its dimensions of variation, including that of informality–formality, since for many people it must function as the medium of every-day conversation' (Leith 1983: 37), or is it best seen as something more abstract? Standardisation may well be achievable in a written language, but it is doubtful that a spoken language (our chief concern in this chapter) can ever be fully standardised. Where do we find the spoken standard in its pure form? It is not possible to find a body of speakers whose usage may be reliably taken to represent fully and unwaveringly the spoken standard. The cultivated Parisian bourgeoisie is often said to constitute such a group (see Picoche and Marchello-Nizia 1989: 26), but in so far as language is often used as a criterion for determining membership of that group in the first place, and in view of the fact that the speech of the Parisian middle classes is not homo-geneous, this reference-point is of dubious value. In the light of this, it is probably better to see the standard language less as a particular variety than as 'a set of abstract norms to which actual usage may conform to a greater or lesser extent' (Milroy and Milroy 1985a: 23).

What then are the norms in question? They obviously com-prise to an important degree the highly codified norms we discussed in the last chapter, though these must be taken to include specifications about permitted levels of variability along the axis formality–informality, enabling the standard language to be used in everyday conversation. Such norms (as we have seen) are based on and are followed most closely in upper-class usage, that is the usage of a minority of the population, and for reasons which we shall look at shortly, they are extremely powerful. However, it would be inaccurate to maintain that these are the only speech-norms to have emanated from Paris during the past three or four centuries. We need to bear in mind that most contacts between Paris and the provinces have always taken place at a lower social level, between ordinary people moving to and from the capital in the course of their everyday lives. It seems reasonable to maintain, therefore, that the speech-norms which have been diffused across France in the course of the last two or three centuries comprise not simply the norms of *le bon usage*, but also (to an extent) those of the lower-class Parisian vernacular.

In the first part of this chapter we shall sketch in the stages whereby the various norms of Parisian French were diffused through society – at the expense of those of the *patois* and the regional languages. In the second, we shall discuss the main factors which brought this about, looking in particular at the notion of dominant languages.

CHRONOLOGY OF DIFFUSION OF THE STANDARD LANGUAGE

General conditions of diffusion

The diffusion of Parisian French throughout the Gallo-Romance area was a multidimensional process: (a) most obviously, it involved *spatial* diffusion, with the norms of the capital taking longer to reach inaccessible areas near the periphery than places having more sustained contact with the 'core'; (b) it involved *functional* diffusion as Parisian norms penetrated different domains of use: in many cases formal occasions first, informal usage later; urban affairs (local government, the law, finance, long-distance trade) before rural matters (agricultural techniques, the local market, village get-togethers and so on); (c) it involved *social* diffusion as Parisian norms were adopted by government functionaries, the provincial aristocracy, literati, then by the inhabitants of towns, and eventually by the mass of ordinary people in the fields (at rates varying with sex and age).

The diffusion of the standard took place in the *langue d'oïl* area in a different way from that of the *langue d'oc*, Brittany, etc., the dialects in the former being engaged in a process of gradual 'convergence' with the norms of the capital, and those in the latter undergoing a process of 'language shift' or, as some have called it, 'language death' (see above, p. 15). Examples of linguistic *convergence* are to be found in the relationship between the standard language and the *langue d'oïl* dialects, for here similarities in linguistic structure are such that, as Parisian norms became more powerful, *patois* speakers gradually moved in varying degrees towards the standard, producing a continuum of transitional varieties from French-like *patois* to *patois*-like French (see Warnant 1973 and Walter 1984a). Examples of the process of language *shift* are to be found when speakers of languages not closely related to French (e.g. Breton, Basque, Flemish) shift to the dominant language: interference between the subordinate and the dominant language undoubtedly occurs during the shift and in contact situations, but the differences of linguistic structure are such that mixed, transitional varieties appear to be less common.

The distinction made here between language shift and convergence is not at all clear-cut, however, for when we come to shifts into French from the Occitan dialects, we are dealing with varieties which, although quite closely related to French, nevertheless manifest very substantial differences of linguistic structure. Mixed Franco-Provençal varieties have long been common: Chambon (1990: 384), writing about the linguistic situation in Auvergne at the beginning of the seventeenth century, declares:

> il pouvait exister à cette date, y compris chez les locuteurs cultivés, des variétés intermédiaires hybrides, résorbées par la suite, que nous imaginons mal à partir de la situation du 20ᵉ siècle et qui témoignaient probablement d'une interpénétration et d'une superposition extrêmement poussées de deux codes aux niveaux phonologique, lexical et même morphologique.

> (there may well have existed at this time, even among cultivated speakers, hybrid, intermediary varieties which have subsequently been eliminated and which we have difficulty in imagining given the twentieth-century situation, and which in all probability manifested an extremely advanced state of interpenetration and superimposition of two codes, on the phonological, lexical and even morphological levels.)

Southern varieties of French speech still differ markedly from those of the north as a result of residual Occitan influence (see

Schlieben-Lange 1977). Language shifting and linguistic convergence are then perhaps best seen as a continuum rather than as discrete sociolinguistic processes (see Carton 1981).

The most basic condition for language shift is societal bilingualism (i.e. where two or more languages are widely used throughout a society). However, it needs to be pointed out that the existence of societal bilingualism does not mean that language shift will inevitably take place: such a state may survive for centuries before one of the languages is lost (see Weinreich 1968: 106–10), as can clearly be seen in the case of Occitan and French in the southern part of France. It has been noted that almost all cases of language shift come about through intergenerational switching (see above p. 15). In other words, bilingual speakers tend not to give up the use of one language and substitute another during the course of their own lifetime. Typically, one generation is bilingual but only passes on one of its two languages to the next. However, one can visualise a whole range of types of individual bilingualism strung out along a continuum between monolingualism in L 1 and monolingualism in L 2. In the context of Gallo-Romance this could be schematised as follows:

L 1	monolingual	(1)	*patois* only
		(2)	*patois* + standard (receptive only)
	bilingual	(3)	*patois* + standard
		(4)	*patois* (receptive only) + standard
L 2	monolingual	(5)	standard only

For a variety of reasons related to what has just been said, it is impossible to determine precisely the numbers of speakers of French and other dialects and languages in France, even at the present time, to say nothing of the situation in times past. This means that any statistics quoted in what follows have relative rather than absolute value and are offered only by way of illustration.

Diffusion of the standard: seventeenth to eighteenth centuries

Systematic information about language use across early modern France is simply not available until the time of the French Revolution: in earlier periods we have to rely on fragmentary sources such as the comments made on provincial speech by travellers (usually upper-class) from Paris. Evidence such as this is entirely anecdotal, and as we attempt to gauge its significance, we need to make allowance for the fact that, in reporting their provincial tours to their Parisian peers, such travellers were no doubt strongly tempted to exaggerate the outlandishness of life away from the capital. However, their reports are unanimous concerning the predominance of *patois* speech in the French countryside. The linguistic state of the Gallo-Romance area was clearly dominated right up to the nineteenth century (and possibly beyond) by the presence of a wide variety of regional vernaculars. These traditional manners of speech were firmly entrenched in a population which was overwhelmingly rural, living principally in small self-sufficient communities with close internal ties but loose external ones.

In the seventeenth and eighteenth centuries *patois* speech was omnipresent. Speakers whose usage approximated closely to the standard remained a small minority, so practical guides on how to rid one's speech of regionalisms were produced in great numbers:

> Pourquoi tombe-t-on dans les gasconismes? . . . Tout gasconisme vient du patois du pays. . . . Les enfants parlent le patois avant de parler français . . . Dominé par l'habitude on ne sait que le traduire lorsqu'on parle français. Quand quelqu'un ouvre les yeux des Gascons et leur fait remarquer les fautes qu'ils font, ils les reconnaissent avec surprise: ils sont étonnés d'avoir parlé ridiculement toute leur vie. Ils sont les premiers à reconnaître la source du mal, le patois.
>
> (Why do people fall into gasconisms? . . . All gasconisms originate in the local *patois*. . . . Children speak *patois* before speaking French. . . . In the thrall of habit people can only translate when they speak French. When one opens the eyes of Gascons and points out the mistakes they make, they recognise them with some surprise: they are amazed that they have spoken in a ridiculous way all their life. They are the first to acknowledge the source of the problem, their *patois*.)
>
> (Desgrouais 1776: iv, quoted by de Certeau *et al.* 1975: 51)

The *Encyclopédie* (XII, 174) defines *patois* as: 'langage corrompu tel qu'il se parle presque dans toutes nos provinces. . . . On ne parle la langue que dans la capitale' ('a corrupt manner of speaking used in more or less all our provinces. . . . The [French] language is spoken only in the capital').

The speech of the Franco-Provençal and Occitan areas was found by Parisian travellers to be quite incomprehensible. In an often-quoted letter written in 1661 Jean Racine declares:

> J'avois commencé dès Lyon à ne plus guère entendre le langage du pays, et à n'être plus intelligible moi-même. Le malheur s'accrut à Valence, et Dieu voulut qu'ayant demandé à une servante un pot de chambre elle mit un réchaud sous mon lit. . . . Mais c'est encore bien pis dans ce pays (Uzès). Je vous jure que j'ai autant besoin d'interprète qu'un Moscovite en auroit besoin dans Paris.

> (Once I had reached Lyon I could no longer understand the local language and could no longer make myself understood. This misfortune got worse at Valence, for God willed it that I asked a maid for a chamber-pot and she pushed a heater under my bed. . . . Things are even worse in this locality (Uzès). I can assure you that I have as much need of an interpreter as a Muscovite would have in Paris.)
>
> (quoted by Walter 1988: 105)

La Fontaine fares better in the area north of Limoges, but makes a similar observation about the unintelligibility of the *langue d'oc*:

> Comme Bellac n'est éloigné de Limoges que d'une petite journée, nous eûmes tout le loisir de nous égarer, de quoi nous nous acquittâmes fort bien et en gens qui ne connaissaient ni la langue, ni le pays.

> (Since Bellac is less than a day's ride from Limoges, we had every opportunity to get lost, and in this we acquitted ourselves exceedingly well, for we had no acquaintance either with the language or with the locality.)
>
> (quoted by Walter 1988: 105)

Madame de Scudéry tells of the almost complete inability of Marseille society ladies to converse in French in 1644 (see Brun 1923: 466–7). Several similar reports are quoted in Brunot (1966: V, 544–9), Braudel (1986: I, 73–8) and Brun (1923: 465–72). Even allowing for a degree of exaggeration for the benefit of Parisian audiences supremely disdainful of the backward ways of the provinces, the unanimity of the reports is compelling.

The vitality of dialectal speech in the *langue d'oïl* area attracted less comment, presumably because problems of comprehension were less dramatic. However, when a town councillor in Amiens harangued Louis XIV in Picard dialect, the inappropriateness if not the unintelligibility of his speech was considered to be very noteworthy (see Dauzat 1930: 545). Northern dialectal speech seems to have been regarded by upper-class people less as a separate linguistic system than as a comic deviation from high-status norms, produced by people who did not know any better. Burlesque works incorporating a large number of *patois* forms enjoyed great popularity in the mid-seventeenth century and continued to be published well into the eighteenth century (for example *Virgille virrai en bourguignon*, Dijon, 1711; see Brunot 1966: VII, 19–21).

Perhaps the best-documented of the northern vernaculars at this period is that of the Ile-de-France and Paris itself (see Wüest 1985). Its importance in the history of French is considerable for it is quite clear that certain of its features have been diffused across the country in tandem with upper-class speech-forms. Satirical texts such as the *Agréables Conférences de deux paysans de Saint Ouen et de Montmorency sur les affaires du temps* (1649–51) (Deloffre 1961) provide precious information about the speech of this area. Very similar features are to be found in the mouths of peasants appearing in the more 'up-market' theatre of the time, e.g. in *Le Pédant joué* by Cyrano de Bergerac and in several of Molière's plays (see above, pp. 166–7 and Dauzat 1946: 37–46). The tradition continues throughout the eighteenth century with the *Sarcelades* of Nicolas Jouin (1730) (see Nisard 1872: 363), and the so-called *genre poissard*, best represented by the writings of Jean-Joseph Vadé (1719–57) (see Moore 1935). The language of these texts is to a considerable degree conventionalised (see Brunot 1966: VI, 1213–15, X, 259–70), but it would unwise to assume that the relationship between stereotype and actual usage was nil. It seems highly likely, in fact, that there existed a distinctive vernacular in Paris and the surrounding region, analogous to Cockney speech in London. What distinguishes the subsequent sociolinguistic histories of the two capitals is the virtual disappearance of *poissard* during the course of the nineteenth century, and the survival of Cockney to the present day.

Against the background of a predominantly *patois*-speaking population, which social groups were the first to adopt Parisian speech-norms? The most obvious direction for the social diffusion of the standard language was top–down, that is imitation by groups of provincial speakers of the cultivated speech of the aristocracy and the urban elite. By the seventeenth century there had grown up in most of the provinces of the kingdom a small nucleus of people in the upper echelons of society (the gentry and the well-to-do bourgeoisie in particular) on whom it had become incumbent to adopt the standards cultivated by 'the best people' in the capital. As the prestige of the royal Court increased during the long reign of Louis XIV (1643–1715), and as the status connotations of speech became greater, the ability to speak a 'pure' form of French, i.e. one which conformed closely to the norms of *bon usage*, was an essential key to upward social mobility and one of the principal badges of social distinction. Demand for prescriptive manuals like Vaugelas's *Remarques* was considerable. Provincial academies were set up in a large number of towns in imitation of the Académie Française with the ostensible purpose of 'atteindre à la pureté et à l'élégance de la langue, de la cultiver, de l'augmenter, de l'enrichir, de l'embellir' ('bringing about the purity and elegance of the language, of cultivating, expanding, enriching and enhancing it') (Brunot 1966: V, 84).

In the 1730s observers appear to have become aware that a change had come about in the linguistic usage of the provincial elites. The following comment made in 1733 about the sociolinguistic situation in Montferrand (Puy-de-Dôme) is revealing. It will be recalled that French had been adopted as the language of written record in that town's administration as early as 1390 (see above, p. 125). Nevertheless, according to the author of the following text, two and a half centuries later (*c*. 1660) even the upper classes in the town used French in speech only rarely. Writing about the local Auvergnat poet J. Pasturel (1625–76), the editor explains in his preface:

De son tems, dans les meilleures maisons de la Ville et de la Campagne, la langue ordinaire étoit le Patois: dans les repas de plaisir même, on n'en parloit guère d'autre. Le François en ce tems-là étoit une langue de parade, dont on n'usoit que dans les grandes occasions et dans les cérémo-

196

nies. Cet usage se conserve encore dans quelques Provinces du Royaume, ou les Dames, surtout ne parlent communément que le Patois de leur pays. Il n'est donc pas surprenant, qu'un homme de beaucoup d'esprit, & accoutumé d'ailleurs à parler habituellement la Langue de son pays, en ait saisi tous les tours, toutes les finesses & toutes les expressions propres à rendre ses pensées sur toutes sortes de sujets.

(In his day the everyday language in all the best houses of the town and the county was *patois*: even in meals with invited guests, this was virtually the only language used. French at that time was a language of formal show which people used only on important occasions and in ceremonies. This usage still persists in certain provinces of the Kingdom, where ladies in particular generally speak only in their local *patois*. It is not surprising, therefore, that a highly intelligent man, accustomed to habitual use of his local language, should have grasped all its nuances and subtleties and all the expressions required to communicate his thoughts on all manner of subjects.)

(Pasturel 1733: avis de l'imprimeur)

The author clearly implies that by 1733 the use of spoken French among the upper classes in Auvergne had expanded significantly: the number of bilinguals had increased, firstly among upper-class males and somewhat later among females. It was to take several generations more, however, for these bilinguals to be able to dispense with Auvergnat *patois* completely.

So far we have been assuming that the chief direction for the diffusion of Parisian speech-norms was top–down. This assumption is not necessarily a safe one: it is reasonable to think that many members of the lower social groups were themselves in contact with Parisian speech, given that most contacts between Paris and the provinces involved ordinary people going about their ordinary business (see Brunot 1966: VII, 188–231). Seasonal movements of men in search of work had long been considerable (see Braudel 1986: I, 82), and Paris had a sizeable population of provincials many of whom would have retained links with their rural homes and families. It may not be realistic to speak of a national market in goods before the late eighteenth century, but the massive importance of Paris as a commercial and administrative centre led to much long-distance travelling to and from the great city from as early as the thirteenth century. Economic expansion and the transport revolution which began in the mid-eighteenth century significantly increased the geographical mobility of the people of France, and seem to have coincided with a marked expansion in the use of French in provincial towns in the south. Low-level contacts between Paris and the provinces undoubtedly involved the diffusion of the norms of the uncultivated Parisian vernacular rather than the norms of *bon usage*. Evidence to support this is understandably sparse, but the long-standing presence of low-status Parisianisms and *argot* terms in the surviving modern dialects and regional varieties suggests that this is the case (see Gardette 1983: 776 and Sainéan 1920: 46–9).

The most explicit evidence we have concerning the dialectal situation in France at the end of the eighteenth century comes from the remarkable survey carried out between 1790 and 1794 by Abbé Grégoire, resulting in his report: *Sur la nécessité et les moyens d'anéantir les patois et d'universaliser l'usage de la langue française* (1794) (see de Certeau *et al.* 1975). As the title shows, the scientific aspect of Grégoire's survey was more than a little overshadowed by the political objectives of the author and of his fellow Jacobins – the political and ideological homogenisation of France. The survey was conducted by means of a questionnaire completed by forty-nine informants located in various parts of France. The distribution of informants across the country was not uniform, reduced coverage being given to the *langue d'oïl* area where the linguistic distance between dialect and standard was relatively small. The correspondents selected by Grégoire tended to be concentrated in the south and in peripheral areas (Brittany, Flanders and the east) where linguistic problems were known to be greatest. The informants were in the large majority educated men (clergy, lawyers, doctors) and one can suppose that they shared at least some of Grégoire's advanced political ideas. The questions put to them cover a disconcerting mixture of religious, political and cultural topics, as well as linguistic issues – clearly Grégoire was above all seeking political ammunition to promote his belief that 'l'unité de l'idiome est une partie intégrante de la Révolution' ('linguistic unity is an integral part of the Revolution').

Summing up the findings of his survey, Grégoire declares:

On peut assurer sans exagération qu'au moins six millions de Français, surtout dans les campagnes, ignorent la langue nationale; qu'un nombre égal est à peu près incapable de soutenir une conversation suivie; qu'en dernier résultat, le nombre de ceux qui la parlent n'excède pas trois millions, et probablement le nombre de ceux qui l'écrivent correctement est encore moindre.

(We can affirm without exaggeration that six million French people, above all in the countryside, are in complete ignorance of the national language; that a similar number is more or less incapable of holding a continuous conversation; that as a final result, the number of people who speak French does not exceed three million, and no doubt the number of those who write it correctly is even smaller.)

(quoted in de Certeau *et al*. 1975: 302)

Grégoire's statistics were no doubt calculated to have the maximum political effect, leaving scientific considerations some way behind, but they are not without interest even so. Given a total population of 26 million at the time, Grégoire estimates the number of speakers with little or no control of the standard language ('la langue nationale') at 46 per cent, and those with complete control at a mere 11.5 per cent. Presumably the 46 per cent of non-French speakers were located principally in the Occitan south and in the peripheral provinces (Brittany, Flanders, Alsace in particular), while the 11.5 per cent who spoke French were the inhabitants of the principal towns of the north, notably Paris, and those of the rural Ile-de-France. We are left with a residue of some 40 per cent of the population which Grégoire does not specify but which are to be located, one assumes, somewhere between the two poles with regard to knowledge of French. No doubt Grégoire implicitly placed in this category rural speakers of the *langue d'oïl* dialects outside the Ile-de-France.

More interesting than these global figures are perhaps the correspondents' replies themselves (see Gazier 1880 and de Certeau *et al*. 1975): they contain a wealth of first-hand information on the sociolinguistic situation in the localities covered. They highlight the profound gulf separating the *langue d'oïl* area (where the standard language could at least be understood) and the Occitan-speaking south. While showing the dominance of the *patois* in rural areas and among the lower classes in the towns, they fairly consistently point to the spread of the Parisian norms in urban communities, not only among the well-to-do, but also among artisans. They also draw attention to the extreme diversity of the *patois* and to a sizeable degree of linguistic interference from Parisian speech upon the structures used by many *patois* speakers – though this can partly be accounted for by prescriptive attitudes on the part of correspondents who tended to regard the *patois* as debased corruptions of Parisian speech rather than as autonomous linguistic systems.

Diffusion of the standard: nineteenth to twentieth centuries

As France, along with other west European countries, moved along the path of development from a small-market, rural economy towards a large-market urban one, the bureaucratic superstructure became progressively more sophisticated and documentation about all aspects of social life more plentiful and systematic. Linguistic behaviour was not spared from bureaucratic intrusion. The nineteenth century provides an increasing amount of information about the state of the regional vernaculars, beginning with E. Coquebert-Montbret's survey of 1808, eliciting dialectal versions of the Parable of the Prodigal Son (see Coquebert-Montbret 1831 and Simoni-Aurembou 1989), and culminating in the monumental *Atlas linguistique de la France* (Gilliéron and Edmont 1903–10). It emerges that the diffusion of the standard language, for all the centralist rhetoric of the Revolutionary period, continued to be painfully slow until the last quarter of the century.

The tenacity of the *patois*, particularly in the south and east, is illustrated in Map 15 based on A. Hugo's survey published in 1835. The value of the information given here is, it must be said, severely limited. It is by no means clear what is meant by 'wholly French-speaking'. Are the *patois* of the *langue d'oïl* area (so widely used at this time according to Bonnaud 1981: 470, 482) to be identified with French? If so, why are the *patois* of the east of France (e.g. Lorraine) treated differently from those of the west (e.g. Norman)? The use of *patois* in Normandy and Picardy is still attested even today. It may be that long contacts between Paris, Picardy and Normandy had accustomed Paris-

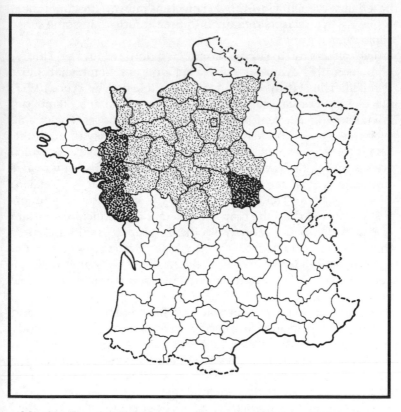

Map 15   French-speaking departments in 1835 (from Weber 1977)

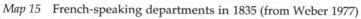   Wholly French-speaking

   Largely French-speaking but with some
cantons holding to their own dialects

based observers to view these dialects as subvarieties of French, while eastern dialects remained in their minds as in some sense separate.

The results of a survey conducted in 1863 by V. Duruy, Napoleon III's Minister of Education, are somewhat more detailed. The statistics produced are published by Weber 1977: 498–501, and reveal that out of a population of almost 30 million, 7.5 million (25 per cent) were monolingual in *patois*. The overall picture is charted on Map 16. This map is not easy to interpret. The uncertainty about what is French and what is *patois* which we saw in the 1835 survey reappears here: the term *patois* relates primarily to Occitan and the peripheral languages (Catalan, Basque, Breton, Flemish, Alsatian, Corsican), but the information provided on the map implies that it also includes certain *langue d'oïl* varieties. Duruy seems to adopt a traditional view that Norman and Picard are 'basically French', whereas the eastern *patois* are not. What is clear, however, is that dialectal speech was still firmly entrenched in the south and in peripheral areas in the north.

An acceleration in the diffusion of the standard language and a drop in the incidence of *patois* monolingualism apparently occurred in the last third of the century. Whereas the proportion of *patois* monolinguals in the 1863 survey had been 25 per cent, a survey of men conscripted into the army in 1867 showed that 69.1 per cent habitually spoke French, 20.4 per cent spoke French 'très imparfaitement', and 10.1 per cent spoke no French at all, the remaining 4 per cent being unaccounted for (see Furet and Ozouf 1977: I, 325). The drop in the number of *patois* monolinguals between the two surveys is very substantial, but these figures provide only a loose guide to what was happening in reality – younger males (the group conscripted into the army) cannot be regarded as typical of the rural population in general, for they appear to have led the way in the shift to the standard language. What is to be regretted in the nineteenth-century statistical surveys of dialectal speech is their absence in the crucial last quarter of the century and their failure to inquire into the extent of bilingualism and code-switching across the country (see Sauzet 1988: I, 212–14). This is known to have become increasingly widespread at this time among Occitan-speakers (see Bonnaud 1981: 39).

After the 1867 survey, no comparable linguistic inquiry was

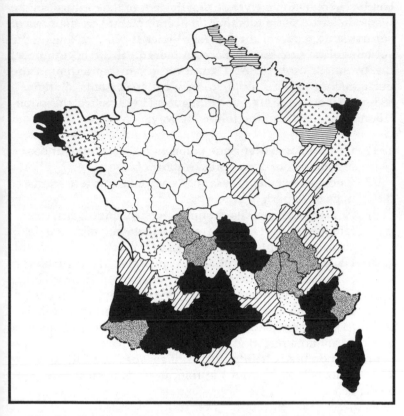

Map 16 *Patois*-speaking departments in 1863 (from Weber 1977)

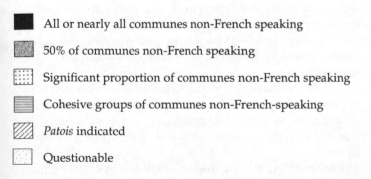

All or nearly all communes non-French speaking

50% of communes non-French speaking

Significant proportion of communes non-French speaking

Cohesive groups of communes non-French-speaking

Patois indicated

Questionable

conducted at national level during the rest of the century, so the historian has to piece together an overall picture on the basis of various scattered local surveys (see Vigier 1979). Working on the sociolinguistic situation in Basse-Auvergne at the beginning of the twentieth century, A. Dauzat observed that although the great majority of his population were 'patoisants d'origine', most speakers were by now bilingual. He classified the population linguistically in the following way:

1) Ceux qui ne parlent que patois et ne comprennent pas le français ont à peu près disparu.
2) Quelques vieilles paysannes comprennent le français mais ne le parlent pas.
3) A la campagne les hommes de quarante ans, les femmes de plus de trente, parlent généralement le patois, accidentellement et mal le français.
4) Les plus jeunes, sont, à la campagne, de véritables bilingues.
5) Certains parlent couramment le français, accidentellement le patois: habitants des villes, à l'exception des faubourgs, et, à la campagne, châtelains, petits bourgeois, notaires, médecins.
6) De nombreux habitants des villes telles que Clermont, Riom, Thiers, parlent le français sans comprendre le patois.

1) Those who speak only *patois* and do not understand French have more or less disappeared.
2) Some old peasant women understand French without being able to speak it.
3) In the countryside men of 40 and women over 30 normally speak *patois*, and only occasionally French, and then badly.
4) In the countryside the youngest are truly bilingual.
5) Some speak French fluently and occasionally *patois*: inhabitants of towns (excluding the suburbs) and in the country the gentry, petty bourgeois, lawyers and doctors.
6) Many inhabitants of towns like Clermont, Riom, Thiers speak French without understanding *patois*.)

(quoted from Chaurand 1985: 350–1)

We could infer from this report that the standard language had come to play a significant role in village life only in the previous twenty-five years, older speakers having hardly acquired the standard language at all, middle-aged speakers having only a poor control of it, and only younger speakers possessing it securely. The state of bilingualism and diglossia described here was highly unstable, and it is not unreasonable to assume that it was replicated across the country with the standard reaching different stages of advancement in different regions.

Predictably, as the twentieth century has advanced the number of bilinguals has diminished massively, and the regional languages and dialects have undergone the process of language shift widely attested in other countries (see Gal 1979; Williamson and van Eerde 1980). The working out of the process in Occitan is graphically described in Maurand 1981. The decline of the *patois* and regional languages of France in the twentieth century has not been uniform and regular (see Tabouret-Keller 1981). Certain languages (e.g. Alsatian, Breton and Corsican) have survived more strongly than others (e.g. Flemish, Basque and Catalan). The decline of Occitan has taken place at very different rates over the vast area of France where varieties of that language were previously spoken. Hadjadj (1983), for instance, points to significant differences in rates of decline in two villages located very close to each other in the vicinity of Thiers (Puy-de-Dôme). Her findings are derived from a survey conducted in 1975. The horizontal axis in the graphs in Figures 6a and 6b indicates the dates of birth of the various age-groups of informants. The vertical axis indicates the percentage of the informants who (a) understand the local *patois*, and (b) use it during their everyday life. Interestingly, the decline in these dialects and languages seems to have accelerated particularly during the two great wars of the twentieth century.

Global estimates of numbers of speakers of *patois* and regional languages in contemporary France have been attempted. Wardhaugh (1987: 104–17) hazarded the following figures for the number of speakers who currently use the traditional minority languages in addition to French in the course of their daily lives:

Occitan	–	2,000,000
Breton	–	400,000
Alsatian	–	'bilingualism is a fact of life'
Flemish	–	'fewer than 100,000'
Corsican	–	'the vast majority of the 200,000 inhabitants'
Catalan	–	'a very small number'
Basque	–	'disappearing'

Pottier (1968) shied away from head-counts and offered an impressionistic categorisation of various degrees of bilingualism attested across rural France (see Map 17). It is clear from this map that the surviving *patois* and regional languages are all located in geographically peripheral areas, and that they exist only in a diglossic situation with regard to the standard language. It is equally clear that in most cases their existence is now very precarious.

CAUSATION

Having outlined the stages whereby over the past two centuries Parisian speech-norms all but displaced not only the *langue d'oïl* dialects closely related to it but also major regional languages (particularly Occitan) previously spoken by up to half of the population, we must now tackle the question of causation. Such a major sociolinguistic change implies the operation of numerous forces all pulling in the same direction. The question of languages in competition (see Wardhaugh 1987) and of dominant languages (see Grillo 1989) has recently received a good deal of attention. In this section we shall look first at the operation of overt political factors in the diffusion of the Parisian standard (language planning policies), then at more deep-rooted and probably more powerful factors related to general economic and demographic change.

The past three centuries have seen the emergence in France of what is (geographically speaking) the largest and the most centralised state in western Europe. The *ancien régime* saw the steady accumulation of political power by the King and the apparatus of the state focused on Paris. Post-Revolutionary governments continued the process of political centralisation thrusting the tentacles of bureaucratic power ever deeper into the nooks and crannies of national life. A powerful national

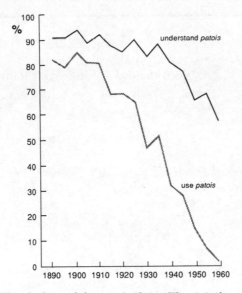

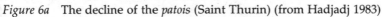

Figure 6a The decline of the *patois* (Saint Thurin) (from Hadjadj 1983)

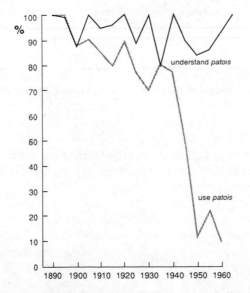

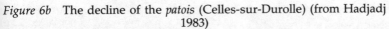

Figure 6b The decline of the *patois* (Celles-sur-Durolle) (from Hadjadj 1983)

207

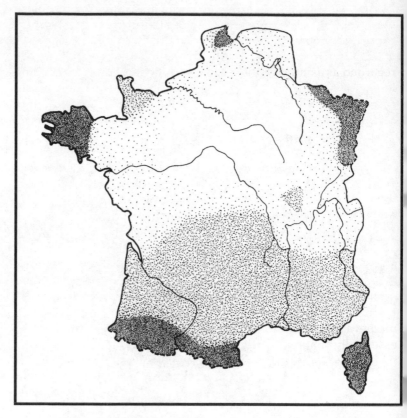

Map 17 Rural bilingualism in 1968 (from Pottier 1968)

 Sporadic

Usual

Intense

identity was created dwarfing all regional identities and squeezing out by the same token the regional modes of speech which expressed them.

In a modern world where the nation-state is still widely regarded as a natural, unalterable sociopolitical unit, 'nation and language have become inextricably intertwined. Every self-respecting nation has to have a language. Not just a medium of communication, a "vernacular" or a "dialect", but a fully developed language. Anything less marks it as underdeveloped' (Haugen 1966: 103). However, the definition of a nation raises complex problems for historians and social scientists who, unlike the layperson, consider that it corresponds to no universal and unchanging reality. The notion of nation seems to have undergone particularly significant modifications in European thinking over the course of the eighteenth century. Grillo (1989: 22–3) distinguishes between 'nation as community' and 'nation as association', the former signifying 'relationships derived from likeness, from commonalities of blood and locality, kinship and affinity', the latter being 'based on exchange and rational will', typified by towns, industry and larger units such as states. In medieval and early modern Europe the word 'nation' signified essentially 'nation as community', and was not automatically bound up with the state. During the eighteenth century, however, the notion of 'nation as association' appears to have become dominant, and in consequence there developed demands to make the 'nation' and the state synonymous and to cement the bonds of association within the 'nation' by means of a common language and a shared ethnicity.

During the seventeenth and eighteenth centuries the kings of France conducted a successful policy of political expansion (see Map 13, p. 121) and of political centralisation. Power was concentrated in the person of the King and wielded through a small and cohesive dominant elite. Their language was inevitably the dominant language, the only language which mattered in society, and as such offered a magnetic attraction to all those who wished to gain position and influence within the state. However, just as the state remained a feudal rather than a bureaucratic one, so its attitude to language prescribed the use of the King's French in matters of state, but left the mass of the population to use their traditional languages in all other domains. The France of the *ancien régime* remained until the end a sprawling multicultural, multilingual community, a federation of provinces which owed allegiance to the Crown, but jealously guarded their local laws and customs. The political system remained firmly rooted in the medieval categories of feudalism and the Christian religion. The role of the Crown (in theory at least) was the preservation of the peace and the administration of justice. The provincial fiefdoms were subject to the King's authority but retained innumerable local customs and privileges inherited from the feudal past which the King, by virtue of his own feudal tenure of office, was powerless to overturn. He was concerned with the fidelity of the provinces, not with their homogeneity. The France of the *ancien régime* has been defined as an 'agro-literate' society where 'the state is interested in extracting taxes, maintaining the peace, and not much else, and has no interest in promoting lateral communication between its subject communities' (Grillo 1989: 28).

We have seen in an earlier chapter, that the state in the *ancien régime* was engaged to some extent in language planning – status planning with the Ordinance of Villers-Cotterêts (1539) which prescribed the King's French as the sole judicial language of the kingdom, and corpus planning with the setting up of the Académie Française (1635) with official instructions to engage in linguistic codification. However, these developments do little to demonstrate the *ancien régime*'s commitment to a conscious policy of linguistic uniformisation through the assimilation of the *patois*-speaking provinces. The fact that the use of French in courts of law created in the provinces a nucleus of French speakers who could 'spread the word' does not mean that this particular effect was intended or encouraged. Likewise, the fact that linguistic codification in the seventeenth century produced a clear linguistic model for others to imitate does not mean it was intended for anyone other than members of the dominant elite or for individuals who felt themselves to be within striking distance of it.

The *ancien regime*, like any state, was anxious to maintain a degree of ideological cohesion between its component parts, but it saw this cohesion lying primarily in the Catholic religion and in the sovereignty of the King, rather than in ethnic and linguistic commonality. Michel de l'Hospital expressed the position clearly in the sixteenth century: 'La division des langues ne fait pas la séparation des royaumes, mais celle de la religion et des lois' ('Separation of kingdoms comes about not through division of languages but through that of religion and laws') (quoted by Peyre 1933: 10). The motto of the French monarchy was 'Une foi, une loi, un roi' ('One faith, one law, one king').

No efforts were spared to bring about religious uniformity within the domains ruled over by the King of France, as we can see from Richelieu's campaigns against the Protestants in the 1630s, the Revocation of the Edict of Nantes (1685) (which ended a century-old policy of religious toleration for Protestants) and the bloody persecution of the Camisards (1702–5) (Protestant communities living in the Cévennes). On the other hand, the *ancien régime* seems to have seen the link between language and nationhood only in the most indistinct terms.

It is true that as new provinces were annexed in the seventeenth and eighteenth centuries (Béarn 1607, Alsace 1648, Flanders 1659, Roussillon 1659, Franche-Comté 1668, Lorraine 1738, Corsica 1768) the King's French was imposed as the official language, but that was merely an extension of the long-established principles of Villers-Cotterêts. It appears that moves were made in the cases of annexed provinces with links to outside linguistic groups (Flanders, Alsace, Roussillon) to assimilate them linguistically through the appointment of teachers of the French language. However, these moves were half-hearted and aimed (significantly) only at the gentry. The absence of any real will to operate a policy of linguistic assimilation is most clearly illustrated in Alsace where the strength of the Germanic dialect was such that French was imposed only in the uppermost levels of the administration. Louis XIV apparently justified his annexation of Franche-Comté on the grounds that it was French-speaking, but this smacks of *post hoc* legitimisation rather than of a serious exposition of his expansionist motives.

Outside the apparatus of the administration of law and finance, the state could in theory have applied a policy of linguistic assimilation through the schools, and schools in the *ancien régime* undoubtedly played a part in the dissemination of the standard language (see Brunot 1966: VII, 1332–82). With the object of strengthening religious orthodoxy throughout the kingdom in the wake of the Revocation of the Edict of Nantes (1685), the King ordered the establishment of a (fee-paying) elementary school in every parish in 1698. The educational priorities were firstly to inculcate the mysteries of the Faith and secondly to teach basic reading, writing and arithmetic. French was taught in these schools, but essentially only as a means to Latin. Ambitious citizens naturally enough saw the social and economic advantages that command of the King's French would bring, and as a result many municipalities were induced in the eighteenth century to offer some sort of elementary schooling. However, the state's commitment to the process was only luke-warm, and indeed certain royal intendants were overtly hostile to the education of all but the upper social groups, as can be learnt from the following statement made by an intendant named d'Etigny in 1759:

Je ne crois pas qu'il soit nécessaire de faire de grands raisonnements pour prouver l'inutilité des régens dans les villages. Il y a de certaines instructions qu'il ne convient pas de donner aux paysans; rien n'était si commun lorsque je suis arrivé dans cette généralité que de voir des enfants de petits laboureurs, vignerons, même de journaliers, abandonner leurs villages pour chercher à sortir de leur état, soit en apprenant à écrire pour pouvoir entrer chez les procureurs et dans des bureaux, soit en se donnant au latin pour devenir avocats ou prêtres, ce qui peuplait le pays de fainéants et de mauvais sujets qui, en diminuant le nombre des cultivateurs, augmentaient celui des gens inutiles et sans ressources pour la société. . . . Dans l'exacte vérité, l'on se plaint, dans presque tout mon département, qu'on ne trouve pas d'ouvriers pour travailler les fonds. Ce seul article demanderait qu'on empechât les paysans d'ap-prendre à lire . . . aussy est-ce une des principales raisons qui m'a fait prendre le party de supprimer les régens, surtout dans les endroits qui ne sont habités que par des laboureurs, vignerons ou journaliers.

(I do not believe one has to employ sophisticated reasoning to demonstrate the uselessness of primary school teachers in villages. There are certain types of teaching that one should not dispense to peasants; nothing was more com-mon when I first came to this generality than to see the children of small ploughmen, winegrowers, even daily-paid farm-workers, leaving their villages in an attempt to change their station in life, whether it be by learning to read in order to work for procurators or in lawyers' offices,

or whether it be by devoting themselves to Latin in order
to become barristers or priests: all this peopled the country
with layabouts and petty criminals who, by reducing the
number of cultivators, increased the number of useless
people who produced no benefit for society. . . . The fact
of the matter is that people complain almost everywhere in
my department that they cannot find workers to work the
land. This fact alone would require us to prevent peasants
from learning to read . . . consequently, that is one of the
main reasons which made me decide to suppress primary
school teachers, especially in places inhabited only by
ploughmen, winegrowers and daily-paid farm-workers.)

(quoted in Brun 1923: 438)

Even if we argue that d'Etigny is untypically extreme in his
views on popular education, it seems clear that, generally
speaking, the state in the eighteenth century did not seek to use
the schools in pursuance of a policy of linguistic assimilation.
Indeed, we can find no evidence to show that the *ancien régime*
wished to pursue a serious policy of linguistic assimilation at all.
It was at best indifferent to the language used by the mass of its
subjects, at worst very ready to exploit the advantages it gained
from the linguistic exclusion of the peasantry from economic
and political power.

At the end of the eighteenth century, the French Revolution
brought about a dramatic change in the nature of the power of
the state. The old tradition of political centralisation was maintained, but the reality of political power was transformed: the
state now began to concern itself with every area of the life of
the citizen as the feudal state became a bureaucratic state. In the
new ideology the notion of 'nation' was fundamentally changed
and language came to assume an entirely new role in society.
Whereas previously the 'nation' had been the social group of
variable dimensions wherein one had been born, now it designated a larger social group bound together by Reason, the
'General Will' and the 'Social Contract'. This 'nation as association' required that all its members speak the same language.
Language became the essential symbol of the nation. Whereas
the motto of the *ancien régime* had been 'Une foi, une loi, un roi',
that of the new post-Revolutionary state was 'République une,
langue une: la langue doit être une comme la République'. The

213

'national language' began to be used to stimulate 'a loyalty beyond the primary groups' and to discourage 'any conflicting loyalty to other nations. The ideal is: internal cohesion – external distinction' (Haugen 1966: 104). This concept of nationhood has been widely adopted across the world, but in no European country did it take deeper root than France, with far-reaching sociolinguistic consequences.

The Revolutionary leaders were clearly motivated in their linguistic policy by a need to increase the internal cohesion of the nation through the diffusion of a standard language. This desire to improve communicative efficiency is paralleled in their replacement of the disparate old systems of coinage and weights and measures by a uniform decimal system of francs, grams, litres, etc. After a brief flirtation with linguistic pluralism under the Girondins (who proposed official status on a regional basis for certain dialects and minority languages), the Jacobin policy of linguistic assimilation was adopted – regional varieties were proscribed in the face of the traditional Parisian norm: non-Francophone communities within the borders of France had to be assimilated linguistically:

> Le fédéralisme et la superstition parlent bas-breton; l'émigration et la haine de la République parlent allemand; la contre révolution parle italien et le fanatisme parle basque. Brisons ces instruments de dommage et d'erreur. . . . La monarchie avait des raisons de ressembler à la tour de Babel; dans la démocratie, laisser les citoyens ignorants de la langue nationale, incapables de contrôler le pouvoir, c'est trahir la patrie, c'est méconnaître les bienfaits de l'imprimerie, chaque imprimeur étant un instituteur de langue et de législation. . . . Chez un peuple libre la langue doit être une et la même pour tous.

> (Federalism and superstition speak Breton; emigration and hatred of the Republic speak German; counter-revolution speaks Italian and fanaticism speaks Basque. . . . We must smash these instruments of harm and error. . . . The monarchy had its own reasons for being like a Tower of Babel; in a democracy, leaving citizens in ignorance of the national language and incapable of placing a check on the people in power is to betray the fatherland, it is to misunderstand the benefits of the printing-press, each printer

being an elementary teacher of language and the law. . . .
Among a free people language must be one and the same
for everyone.)

(B. Barère, quoted by Caput 1975: II, 106)

The belief in the identity of nation and language automatically led to attempts to embrace within the borders of France (by force if necessary) Francophone communities attached to foreign states (notably in Belgium (1792) and Switzerland (1798)). Language now served not only as an instrument of 'internal cohesion', but also as a means of achieving 'external distinction', that is dividing off the essential French nation from surrounding nations. In the xenophobic climate of 1792 this led to prolonged wars between France and its neighbours.

The new political and administrative order brought about by the Revolution and subsequently by the Emperor Napoleon immeasurably increased the real power of the centralised state: the new administrative system focused on Paris entailed the intrusion of Parisian power into every corner of society. These developments almost certainly had a more decisive impact on the diffusion of the standard language into the provinces than did the state's overt moves into the domain of language planning. The material steps it was able to take to bring about the acceptance of Parisian speech-norms throughout the community were very limited. The effectiveness of language planning depends crucially upon good information and adequate communication. The Revolutionary leaders saw this clearly – it was they after all who commissioned Grégoire's survey of the linguistic state of the country and they took immediate steps to promote the standard language through state education. The Décret du 8 pluviose 1794 ordered

> L'établissement dans un délai de dix jours, d'un instituteur de langue française dans chaque commune de campagne des départements où les habitants ont l'habitude de s'exprimer en bas-breton, italien, basque et allemand.

> (The establishment within ten days of a French-speaking teacher in every rural commune in those departments where the inhabitants normally express themselves in Breton, Italian, Basque and German.)

(See Seguin 1972: 227)

Catalan was later added to the list. State education, however,

215

was painfully slow to develop – the 'école primaire gratuite et obligatoire' had to wait for almost a century after the French Revolution before it became a reality.

Perhaps the Revolution's greatest contribution to the diffusion of the standard in France lies in fact in its rhetoric, in its formulation of the new ideology of the standard. It is paradoxical that since the Revolution of 1789 the French state has sought in the name of democracy and egalitarianism to impose a standard variety which had been crystallised under the *ancien régime* as a hallmark of class distinction. This contradiction has done nothing to weaken the ideology of the standard in France. It is probably the reverse which is true: on to a stock of beliefs about the elegance, precision, logicality, universality, etc., of the standard variety inherited from the *ancien régime*, were grafted new political connotations associating this variety with national identity and libertarian values. Since French was the language of Reason, it became mandatory for people who wanted to be considered reasonable and truly French to speak French 'correctly'.

The nineteenth century witnessed an ever-increasing tendency towards the centralisation of political power in France. Progress was relatively slow in the first part of the century, with a restored monarchy nostalgic for the political ideology of the *ancien régime*. The Second Empire (1852–70) and more particularly the Third Republic (1871–1940) carried the notion of the centralised state to an extreme degree, seeking the absorption of all regional identities into the single national identity of a monolithic state. To this end, the last quarter of the nineteenth century witnessed the implementation of a vigorous policy of language-planning.

French government policy since the end of the eighteenth century towards the *patois* and the minority languages used within French borders has often been held up as a classic example of linguistic assimilation (see Bourhis 1982): French is the only language with official status, the regional vernaculars (Occitan, Breton, Basque, etc.) having only in the past half-century or so moved from 'proscribed' to 'tolerated' status, the sole exception being Alsatian which, because of its peculiar history, retains a status approaching that of a 'promoted' language. The state in an increasingly centralised and bureaucratic society was able to influence linguistic behaviour through its own administrative machinery and through the armed forces – ever since the general mobilisation of the French population in 1792 a period of military service has been obligatory for all French males and has undoubtedly contributed significantly to the linguistic homogenisation of France, though the linguistic norms disseminated in the army were predominantly the low-status norms of the Paris vernacular rather than the high-status norms of *bon usage*. That said, the chief instrument for state policies of language planning has always been education.

Civil and foreign wars prevented the Revolutionary Convention from effectively implementing a policy of elementary state education. Napoleon created schools for his new social elite – the *lycées* and the *Grandes Ecoles* – but handed back the task of educating the masses to the Church. The Restoration's attempts (1815–30) to revive the social structures of the *ancien régime* inevitably failed, but moves by the July Monarchy (1830–48) and the Second Empire (1852–70) (in the persons of Guizot and Duruy respectively) to institute universal primary education were half-hearted and met with only partial success. Guizot's law of 1832 established state primary schools in every *commune*, but they were to be neither free nor compulsory. One is forced to the conclusion that before the last quarter of the nineteenth century, while the French state may have willed the linguistic assimilation of the provinces, it was not prepared to dig deep into its pockets to bring it about.

The shock of defeat in the war with Germany (1870–1) induced a popularisation of the ideology linking language and national identity. The Jacobin rhetoric of the previous century was revived by the Third Republic and given practical application after decades of only sluggish activity. All the human resources of the nation had to be mobilised, the slumbering particularisms of the diverse provinces had to be swept away, and a united nation speaking with one voice (and in one language) had to be created (see Quéré 1987). Between 1881 and 1886 J. Ferry instituted his celebrated 'enseignement gratuit, obligatoire et laïc' ('free, compulsory and secular schooling') – primary schools (*écoles communales*) were to spearhead the education of the masses and to bring 'the national language' into every home in the land. All tuition was conducted in French, the written French language had pride of place in the curriculum, the use of *patois* or the regional languages even in the playground being severely punished:

> A favourite punishment, inherited from the Jesuits (who had ironically used it to enforce Latin on their French-speaking charges), was the token of shame to be displayed by the child caught using his native tongue. The token varied. It could be a cardboard ticket (Dorres, Pyrénées-Orientales), a wooden plank (Err and Palau, Pyrénées-Orientales), a bar or stick (Angoustine, Pyrénées-Orientales), a peg (Cantal), a paper ribbon or metal object (Flanders), or a brick to be held out at arm's length (Corrèze). A child saddled with such a 'symbol' kept it until he caught another child not speaking French, denounced him, and passed it on. The pupil left with the token at the end of the day received a punishment. In the country schools of Brittany the symbol of shame was a sabot.
>
> (Weber 1977: 313)

Such ferocious treatment of the rural languages inevitably sparked off resistance, particularly in the south. It was not unknown for the local priest to spring to the defence of the *patois* beloved of so many members of his flock and to use language as yet another weapon in his struggle with the secular *instituteur* sent from Paris as a direct challenge to his authority in the community. At a higher social level the second half of the nineteenth century saw the development of the Félibrige movement led by the Provençal poet Frédéric Mistral – its aim was to revive the literature of the *langue d'oc* and to give the language a literary standard. The conservative and Catholic political attitudes of the movement aroused the deepest suspicions in Paris, but more seriously, the movement failed to attract popular support even in the south. In fact, it was popular and left-wing agitation in the Languedoc which proved a much greater challenge to the unitary state in the first decade of the twentieth century, culminating in the Winegrowers' Revolt of 1907 – resentment at the humiliating treatment meted out by Paris to regional feelings and to the Occitan language in particular apparently played a significant role (see Weber 1977: 276).

During the twentieth century the regional languages (including Occitan), located as they are in the peripheral areas of

France, have frequently been associated with social and economic problems. In these areas French often came to be regarded as a symbol of oppression from the centre, whereas the local language served as an identity-shield (see Bazalgues 1973). Defence of the regional language has tended to be associated with demands for local autonomy ranging from federation to complete independence, and in the cases of Breton and Corsican this has led to violent action. In the years up to the Second World War, political action related to the regional languages tended to be right-wing in orientation, leading in certain cases to acts of collaboration with Nazi forces during the Occupation. Since then, regionalism has been associated more conspicuously with left-wing politics (see Ager 1990: 29–30).

In recent decades, coinciding no doubt with a realisation that the *patois* and regional languages no longer pose a serious threat to the linguistic and political unity of the state, attitudes towards them have become more favourable. The Loi Deixonne of 1951 allowed the teaching of Breton, Basque, Occitan and Catalan in state schools, thereby giving them 'promoted status'. It did nothing for Flemish and Corsican, however, which had to await the decentralisation legislation introduced by the Socialists in 1982. In the meantime, numerous semi-official bodies emerged devoted to the protection of the regional languages, notably Occitan (see Bazalgues 1973). Various moves have been made to standardise them (see Alibert 1935 and Armengaud and Lafont 1979: 883–98 for Occitan; Fabre 1964 for Catalan), but they appear to have had little impact in a society which now associates these languages with nostalgia for a rural past.

In the consciousness of many French people (including linguistic historians) it is the state, through the intermediary of the school system, which was the principal agency responsible for the diffusion of French throughout France and for the suppression of the *patois* and regional languages. There can be no doubt that the educational programme initiated by Jules Ferry was a major vehicle for carrying the ideology of the Parisian standard across the community. As we have seen, by the end of the nineteenth century (one generation after the introduction of the *écoles communales*) the number of monolingual *patois* speakers had become almost negligible. Two generations later (after the end of the Second World War) the number of bilingual *patois* speakers had likewise entered a serious decline. Defenders of regional cultures commonly refer to Parisian linguistic and cultural 'imperialism', and adhere firmly to the belief that legislative and educational measures could contribute significantly to the resuscitation of their dying languages. The reality, however, is more complex, for the activities of the state have to be seen as a single facet of a much deeper socioeconomic development: the shift from a traditional, peasant society rooted in the land, to an advanced industrial society with a mobile, urbanised population. Historians argue endlessly on the question of the priority to be given to politics or economics in social developments: was it the development of a centralised state which created a 'national market', or was it the growth of a 'national market' which called forth the centralised state? Did trade follow the flag, or was it the other way round? Clearly both were facets of the same phenomenon, but let us now turn our attention from political to economic factors in sociolinguistic change in France.

The *patois* and regional languages of France were the linguistic expression of a traditional peasant economy. They had developed to serve the needs of a society organised in this way (see Chapter 3, pp. 83–4) and when this society was superseded, they disappeared with it. The decline of the French peasantry in the second half of the nineteenth century has been admirably described by Weber (1977) and much of what follows is derived from him.

The traditional peasant economy was rooted in the land, moulded itself to the possibilities offered by the land, and was heavily dependent upon the vagaries of climate and natural phenomena. It often provided the means to little more than subsistence. The peasant population lived in small, fairly static, introspective communities. The level of technology was generally low: age-old farming methods persisted late in France, for although the French Revolution freed the peasantry from the exactions of feudal *seigneurs*, it did not bring an agrarian revolution with modern techniques of husbandry and marketing. Village communities remained static: goods tended to be transported within a radius of about 15 km to the nearest market, but little further. The necessities of life were either grown or made by the peasant's family itself – or, if all else failed, bartered. In many parts of the country money was little used, for the peasant's land often produced no surplus to sell.

This autarkic framework had been the peasant's lot since time immemorial, and when change came it was uneven, proceeding at different rates in different parts of the country – a line could be drawn between Saint Malo and Geneva, north and east of which social and economic development went ahead significantly more rapidly than in the south and west. Change was also a good deal slower in France than in Britain and in certain other parts of Europe. In many regions of France traditional peasant society, which had disappeared from much of Britain in the eighteenth century, persisted until well into the twentieth century.

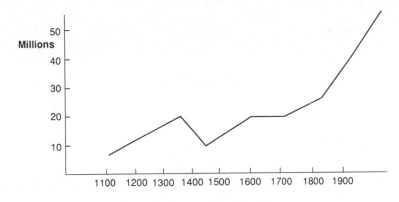

Figure 7   Population growth in France

The population of France had remained relatively stable for several centuries up to about 1750, but at about that time demographic growth began to take place again. Little by little the economy of France, like the economies of most western European countries, moved away from traditional peasant structures towards the constitution of urban, industrialised societies. A spiral of three interlocking developments was set in motion which contributed significantly to the diffusion of a single linguistic norm: urbanisation and industrialisation, technological progress and the spread of literacy, and the constitution of a national market in goods.

The past 150 years have witnessed in France as elsewhere in western Europe a shift of population from country to town, and this has entailed a language shift from the highly localised *patois*

221

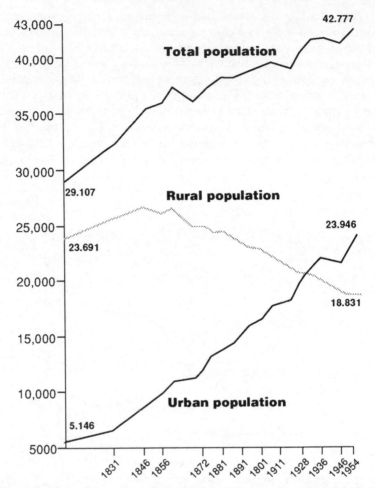

Figure 8   The urban and rural population in France (from Braudel 1986)

to urban speech which approximated much more closely to Parisian norms. Until about 1850 the rural population of France continued to make up about 85 per cent of the whole. Since that date this proportion has steadily declined, though at a slower rate than in other countries like Britain and Germany. It was in fact only in 1931 that the French urban population began to outnumber the rural one.

Regional centres of population like Lyon and Marseille developed significantly in the nineteenth century, but the chief centre of urbanisation was Paris which increased its population five-fold between 1801 and 1891. The strength of Parisian speech-norms can only have been increased as a result.

Urbanisation was linked of course to industrialisation. A first wave of industrialisation got under way in France in the 1850s, focused primarily on Paris, but with important developments in areas located on or near the coal-fields like Lille-Roubaix and Saint-Etienne. However, this first wave was relatively small and it required a second in the years which followed the Second World War to bring the French economy to the levels previously attained by Britain and Germany. It is this relatively late indus-trialisation which perhaps explains the fact that the long-established working-class communities possessing their own distinctive speech-norms which are to be found in British cities are relatively rare in France.

Technological progress in the nineteenth century transformed not only life in the towns, but it had ever-increasing effects on life in the countryside. Little by little, improvements in agricul-tural methods (particularly in fertilisation of the soil and in techniques of ploughing and processing agricultural products) raised peasant life above the level of subsistence. Peasants be-gan to dominate their environment instead of being for ever at its mercy. A persistent feature of life in medieval and *ancien régime* society had been famine and consequential food-riots. The nineteenth century had its share of these, but they had more or less come to an end by the last quarter of the century (see Weber 1977: 18). The peasant was moving from the world of isolated subsistence towards integration with a wider society. Improvements in agricultural efficiency also meant that the agri-cultural workforce was gradually reduced, and that age-old rural technologies little by little slipped into oblivion. Every stage of the drift of population from country to town meant a weakening of peasant culture and language. Gonon (1973) has shown how the replacement of traditional country crafts like basket-making and carpentry in the Forez region by new methods led to the disappearance of whole swathes of rural vocabulary. Techniques and knowledge traditionally handed down orally from one generation to the next were gradually superseded by technologically more advanced methods trans-mitted essentially through writing. The old oral culture gave way to a culture dominated by the written word.

The spread of literacy in France has been charted in some detail by Furet and Ozouf (1977: I, 352):

> L'universalisation de l'alphabétisation naît de l'économie du marché, qui développe la division du travail et répand la communication par l'écrit, du haut vers le bas du corps social.

> (The universalisation of literacy was born of the market economy which develops the division of labour and disseminates written communication downwards through the body of society.)

Literacy rates in France showed a considerable increase from the middle of the eighteenth century, particularly among the middle classes and particularly in the developed part of France located north and east of the Saint Malo-Geneva line. They progressed steadily in the nineteenth century to a figure of around 95 per cent in 1906. Schooling clearly had a role to play in the spread of literacy, but it was not necessarily only the schooling imposed from above which produced the results: demand for education developed from below as people recognised their needs within the new economic order. Furet and Ozouf have shown that as early as 1850 73 per cent of 6–13-year-olds attended school and that by 1876 58 per cent of that age-group attended free schools. They conclude therefore that the Ferry reforms of the 1880s served principally to 'boucher les trous de la scolarisation' ('plugging the gaps in the school system') (Furet and Ozouf 1977: I, 175). Growth in literacy like the diffusion of French followed deep-rooted social and economic developments rather than political fiats.

The spread of literacy in the nineteenth century was undoubtedly a major vehicle for the diffusion of authoritarian language attitudes. French people in the country at large gradually adopted the belief that the most valid form of language was to be found in writing. The language of speech, in so far as it diverged from the norms of the written language and from the structures of formal, planned discourse, became progressively disparaged. In this way millions of French people developed the idea that they had only an inadequate grasp of their own language. Given that the *patois* generally had no written form, they were denied the status of language altogether. Illiteracy became synonymous with barbarism. Inability to handle all the details of the written language was gradually seen as a symptom not simply of ignorance, but of moral depravity, even of religious laxity. Accuracy of spelling acquired particularly great symbolic value, serving to identify not only those who had had greater exposure to education, but more importantly people with superior intelligence. The widespread belief in the central importance of orthographic uniformity colours all discussion of spelling reform even in our own day.

Urbanisation and industrialisation called into being a national market in goods which far surpassed the scale of previous ones. The tight local networks of previous generations were gradually opened up into the broader and looser networks of a mercantile economy. Developments in transport and communications from the mid-eighteenth century onwards stimulated and were stimulated by the growth of a national market. In France the way was led by the intendants of the *ancien régime* who equipped the country with a fine network of trunk roads between 1750 and 1780 (see Maps 18 and 19).

A second major impulse came in the 1840s with the development of railways. Migrations of people – for military and civilian purposes – had always taken place, but now the movement of people and goods was gradually transformed. Little by little, small village communities were drawn into the larger world. This larger world was focused on Paris, for all the road and rail networks radiated from the capital. The sheer size of France, however, made such progress slow. The great trunk roads and the railways could only serve the major regional centres. The network remained loose until the last two decades of the nineteenth century: a major and unsung contribution to the tightening of the mesh in rural areas was the Plan Freycinet which from 1879 financed the construction of thousands of kilometres of minor roads enabling the remoter rural communities to be connected to the national network. Even then, the gulf between town and country remained great until the widespread use of motor cars, telephone, radio and television in the 1950s.

Progressively, the tight but fragmented social networks of traditional peasant society gave way to the looser and much larger social network represented by the 'nation'. The looser networks facilitated greatly the diffusion of the standard language. As Paris came to assume an increasingly dominant role

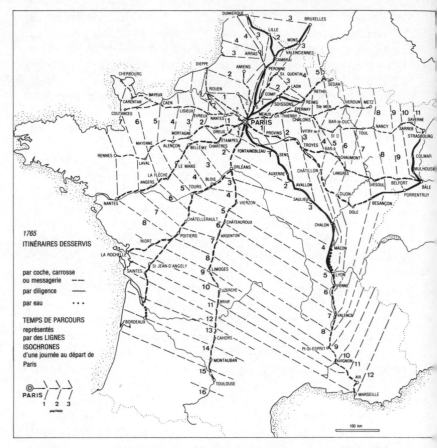

Map 18 Travelling time from Paris in 1765 (from Arbellot 1973)

in the economy of France, likewise its language came to play an increasingly important role in outlying provinces which had previously existed in an economic semi-independence.

CONCLUSION

In this chapter we have traced the process of 'acceptance' whereby Parisian speech-norms were gradually extended to a greatly enlarged speech community, and the French language became in many people's minds a powerful symbol of national identity. At the end of the twentieth century there remain in France relatively few speakers of the once widespread rural

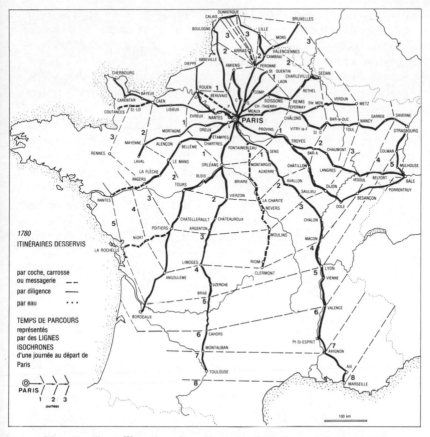

Map 19 Travelling time from Paris in 1780 (from Arbellot 1973)

patois and regional languages, and we have attempted to answer the question why. Have we been witnesses to cases of 'language death' (from natural causes) or of 'language murder' (see Aitchison 1981: 208–21)? The defenders of regional languages commonly argue that the decline of languages like Occitan and Breton has been brought about principally by deliberate action on the part of the state. Indeed, this *volontariste* approach to history – the belief that the nation's destiny is ultimately controlled by the decisions of legislators and teachers – is widely shared by people on both sides of the language debate in France. We saw how from the late eighteenth century onwards language and shared ethnicity were enlisted by centralist

227

politicians to cement bonds of association within society and to differentiate the French nation from surrounding nations. However, in this chapter we have also seen that, while much of government policy in the century and a half following the French Revolution was directed towards 'killing off' the *patois*, the state was acting by no means alone. It was in fact simply adding its power to deeper economic and social forces promoting the dominance of Paris and the destruction of the small autarkic communities of which the *patois* were the natural expression.

Over the course of many centuries France has become what is probably the most highly focused society in Europe, with Paris eclipsing regional economic and cultural centres to a greater extent than any other European capital. Within France (and to an extent without it too, if we consider social attitudes in French-speaking Belgium and Switzerland) Paris has come to be regarded as the epitome of power, prosperity and progress, setting the tone and imposing its models in all areas of social life. The provinces in consequence became associated unerringly with backwardness. Attitudes to the different language varieties current in France evolved in tandem with general social attitudes: intolerance of regional varieties became progressively more widespread, local and regional speech-norms being gradually displaced by norms emanating from Paris. By the end of the nineteenth century the ideology of the standard had assumed a particularly rigid form in France. With the spread of the belief in the identity of language and nationhood in the nineteenth century, the promotion of linguistic uniformity according to Parisian norms became a prime duty of citizenship. Those who deviated from these norms diminished proportionately their claim to Frenchness.

Paradoxically, the dominance of Paris in French sociolinguistic history has been such that the speech-norms that it has exported to the rest of France are not only those of the educated upper class, but include those of the lower social groups as well. Speech-norms in a conurbation as large as nineteenth-century Paris were many and varied, those of the dominant group being inevitably different from those of the lower class (see Sainéan 1920). It is an oversimplification to see the Parisian society of the day as being divided into two, for there have clearly always existed intermediate groups between the upper reaches of the bourgeoisie and the *peuple*. However, social polarisation un-doubtedly occurred: fear of the Paris mob haunted the dominant class before the Revolution (see above, p. 169) and continued to do so for much of the nineteenth century. The need to control the teeming populace by breaking up the working-class com-munities of Paris was probably the chief motive behind Haussman's construction of the *grands boulevards* in the 1860s. Class conflict in the capital erupted into civil war in the bloody suppression of the Paris Commune in 1871. These social ten-sions were inevitably reflected in the language, and it is clear that the forces promoting the ideology of the standard operated with as much ferocity against speakers of the 'debased' French of the capital as against *patois* speakers in the provinces. Their success is to be measured by contrasting the survival of Cockney speech in London and the near obliteration of a distinctive lower-class vernacular in Paris. This vernacular has not vanished without trace, however, for we shall see in the next chapter how it has played an important role in the development of informal speech-norms across contemporary France. If the diffusion of Parisian French into the provinces had been solely top–down and principally the result of official education poli-cies, we would have expected speakers of French in the pro-vinces to use few forms derived from the Parisian vernacular (e.g. lexical items commonly labelled as *argotique* (see Sainéan 1907)). This is patently not the case and we have in fact seen how low-level contacts between Paris and the provinces (through migrations of workers seeking employment, through conscription and military service) undoubtedly had a major, though largely undocumented, role to play in the linguistic 'unification' of the country.

8

MAINTENANCE OF THE
STANDARD

In previous chapters we have charted the development of standardisation in French with reference to the four processes distinguished by Haugen – selection, elaboration of function, codification and acceptance. Having seen these processes at work in the history of French, the uniformisation of the language should now, theoretically, be more or less complete. In our final chapter we will see that this of course is not the case: linguistic usage in French, as in all living languages, is far from homogeneous. The ideal goal of standardisation may well be the halting of change and the suppression of variation through the diffusion of a single norm. However, short of the language becoming a dead language (i.e. a language with no speakers) this goal is unlikely ever to be achieved. Any language with a reasonably large number of speakers will develop dialects reflecting the barriers separating groups of people from one another. In pre-industrial societies these barriers were predominantly geographical. In advanced, technological societies with a high degree of geographical mobility, barriers of class and ethnic group have gained relatively in importance. Furthermore, although fixity and uniformity can be brought about to an extent in writing (though even here in a complete way only in spelling), speech in face-to-face interaction is highly resistant to them. Here the achievement of uniformity would actually be dysfunctional since it would destroy the elasticity of language which is essential for effective communication (see Weinreich *et al.* 1968: 101). We shall see in this final chapter that standardisation in French is not something which occurred during a particular historical period as a one-off event, rather it is a continuous process involving permanent tension between factors promoting and factors inhibiting linguistic uniformity.

There is a tendency among observers of variation in the contemporary French language to take a static, taxonomic approach which seeks to isolate, describe and label particular varieties of French. For example, on the stylistic axis of variation observers have differentiated the varieties shown in Figure 9.

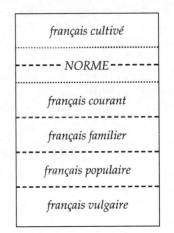

Figure 9 A model of stylistic variation (Müller 1985: 226)

On the spatial axis we find the classification shown in Figure 10.

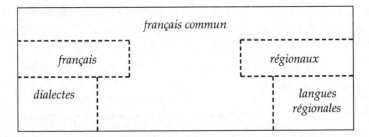

Figure 10 A model of regional variation (Müller 1985: 159)

Although it is invariably stressed that these varieties are not hermetically sealed (hence the use of dotted lines in Figures 9 and 10), the idea persists that there exist alongside the standard language reasonably homogeneous sub-varieties each possessing a fairly coherent and stable structure. This approach owes a good deal to Saussurean structuralism, but it is also reminiscent of earlier Romantic ideas, widely held at one time by dialectologists, namely the belief in the existence of 'pure dialect' – forms of local speech hidden in the depths of the countryside, surviving in their natural state unsullied by contacts with other dialects or with the standard language and broadly homogeneous within themselves.

The approach we shall take is a very different one. We shall assume that language varieties, particularly spoken ones, are inherently variable – as a rule and not as an exception – and that there are no pure varieties of contemporary French, merely quantitative differences in the distribution of key language variables. This means that labels like *français populaire, français familier, français régional* can be profoundly misleading, for they imply the existence of discrete sociolinguistic varieties rather than an observer's arbitrary division of variable linguistic continua. In what follows we shall then be less concerned with the structures and delimitations of particular varieties of French than with the competing forces pulling speakers in opposing directions. We shall separate *social* forces from *stylistic* forces rather in the way Halliday (1964) distinguished between 'variation according to user' and 'variation according to use' (see above, p. 13).

On the *social* axis of variation the norms of the standard language are at all times threatened by the existence of rival norms among speakers of the language. There

> is a constant tension between a tendency on the one hand to ever-increasing *divergence* . . . and a tendency on the other for the primary function of language to be facilitated by the diffusion of a norm or standard among ever larger groups of people.
>
> (Harris 1978: 2)

Linguistic norms develop among all types of social grouping. They are closely bound up with questions of identity and their

232

constraining effect varies with the degree of focusing in the group concerned (see Le Page and Tabouret-Keller 1985: esp. 187). In a particular society one might be able to identify local norms (operating, say, at the level of a single village), supralocal norms (operating at a broader regional level) and supraregional norms (operating, say, at 'national' level). The revolution in transport and communications which has taken place over the past century has ensured that regional factors now have a reduced role to play in language variation, but this does not mean that subgroups within French society have been eliminated. Romaine and Reid (1976) distinguish between *social* norms (operating within society at large) and *community* norms (operating within various subgroups which make up that society). Institutional and other pressures may pull speakers in the direction of the former, but bonds of small-group solidarity exert powerful pressures in the opposite direction. Conformity with the former may well bring 'overt prestige', while conformity with the latter will bring another sort of prestige, related to membership of the subgroup and referred to as 'covert prestige'.

On the *stylistic* axis of variation, language varies according to different purposes and situations of use, and there is a constant tension between form and function: as we have seen, the ideal goal of codification is 'minimal variation in form' and that of elaboration 'maximal variation in function'. Codification and the suppression of variation in form operate successfully only in the written language and in formal, planned discourse; uniformity has much less place in the unplanned spoken discourse of face-to-face interaction which makes up the vast majority of language activities. Where the tension between form and function is maintained in equilibrium, all well and good. But it is possible for codification to become so rigid as to prevent the use of the codified form for other than formal purposes, giving rise to a functional separation of H and L forms and ultimately to a situation of diglossia.

In this chapter we shall attempt to uncover the principal lines of force in the tension between homogeneity and heterogeneity in contemporary French. We could summarise them as in Figure 11.

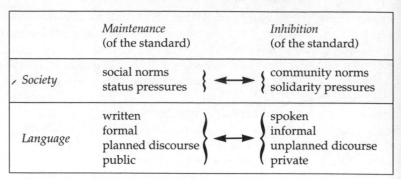

	Maintenance (of the standard)	*Inhibition* (of the standard)
Society	social norms status pressures } ⟷ {	community norms solidarity pressures
Language	written formal planned discourse public } ⟷ {	spoken informal unplanned dicourse private

Figure 11 Factors maintaining and inhibiting the standard

SOCIAL PRESSURES

Pressures promoting the maintenance of the standard

The social role of standard languages varies considerably from one speech community to another. In many communities (e.g. in the German-speaking world) the norms represented by the standard language are relaxed to the extent that the use of non-standard varieties, in the appropriate contexts, is viewed quite positively. In other communities – and France and Britain are prime examples – the use of non-standard varieties is viewed a good deal more negatively. Although linguistic prescriptivism operates in each of these countries in a somewhat different way – in France it tends to be explicit and overt, in Britain more implicit and covert – nevertheless, the 'social norms' represented by the standard language exert strong pressures on speakers and deviation from the standard is tolerated less readily. This intolerance of language variation has its roots deep in the histories of these countries (as we have seen) and can be correlated to a degree with their highly centralised and rather rigidly stratified social structures.

The strength of the 'ideology of the standard' (see above, pp. 156–7) in France at the end of the twentieth century is evident from the use of the very name *la langue française*: it is reserved in most French people's minds (including many linguists), for educated Parisian usage, particularly that found in written or in formal contexts. Non-standard social varieties are still commonly dismissed as not being French at all: 'Ce ne serait pas une boutade de dire que le français populaire n'est pas vraiment le français' ('It would not be merely frivolous to say that popular French is not really French at all') (quoted by Blanche-Benveniste and Jeanjean 1987: 13). About a non-standard word one frequently hears remarks such as: 'Ce n'est pas du français ça, c'est de l'argot.' Similar exclusion of non-standard stylistic variants (informal, unplanned discourse for example) will be discussed later. What we wish to sketch in here are the principal factors at work in contemporary French society to give the standard ideology its continuing power.

It could well be that the most powerful underlying force promoting the standard language in France is the centralised structure of French society and the continuing dominance of Paris in French political, economic and cultural life. We have seen how until quite recently the French economy was primarily agricultural and the French population thinly distributed over a vast geographical area. The exception to this was (and is) Paris with its long-established urban population and industrial/commercial economy. Paris continues to act as the central focal point of French society, as a glance at a French railway map will show. It is still the unchallenged commercial, administrative and political centre of France, despite recent steps taken in the direction of decentralisation. One-fifth of the French population lives in the Paris region and a high proportion of these people are recent migrants from other parts of France. Increased communication between Paris and the rest of France through the media and highly developed transport systems gives the French of Paris an immense power of penetration throughout the country. The highly focused nature of French society gives great strength to Parisian norms, not only in language, but in all aspects of social behaviour. Paris leads the field in all areas of fashion (including language) and (gladly or not) is universally seen in France as the ultimate source of all material reward (in terms of money and status).

The most powerful institutional vehicle for the promotion and maintenance of the standard is probably the centralised education system, staffed by teachers who, from the level of *instituteurs* to the Society of *agrégés*, tend to retain highly prescriptive linguistic attitudes and a firm belief in the immutability of the standard. Debates about the teaching of French in France and the position of grammar and spelling are conducted with a passion unknown in other European countries (see Chervel 1977). It is no doubt through the school system with its emphasis on the primacy of the written language, on the priority of planned over unplanned discourse, on the unacceptability of non-standard linguistic forms, that the ideology of the standard is promoted most vigorously and effectively.

Institutional concern for the state of 'the language' is not restricted to the confines of school, however. The great writers of the past and *la belle langue* have a particularly strong focusing role in French society: a major element in the shared culture of the population of France is literary. The French language is commonly seen to exist in its quintessential form in the words of the writers whom French people have come to value so highly – Corneille, Pascal, Racine, Voltaire, Rousseau, Stendhal, Flaubert, Gide, Mauriac and so on. It is widely felt that the French language was indeed 'created' by such writers as these. This rich literary heritage confers high prestige on the norms of the standard language, and these have to be mastered by anyone wishing to be identified with 'cultivated people'. The question of the maintenance of the literary standard stimulates regular discussion in the press and holds an obviously interested readership (see Quemada 1972). The same public concern is reflected in the prolific production of new dictionaries of French which monitor and legitimise lexical developments, and the regular re-edition of Grevisse's celebrated *Le Bon Usage* (12th edition 1986).

As if these general centralising pressures were not enough, they are reinforced by vigorous official action to promote and maintain the standard language. What distinguishes the defence of the standard in France from the process of language maintenance in other European countries is the explicit and overt involvement of the state and official bodies in the business of language planning. The 'defence of the French language' in the twentieth century has been the subject of numerous studies (see in particular Bengtsson 1968 and Gordon 1978), so it is not our intention to do more than sketch in the outlines here. Since the 1930s (perhaps as a result of the replacement of French by English as the principal language of international diplomacy, particularly after the Second World War) numerous official bodies have been set up in France alongside the Académie Française to defend not only the position of French as a world language, but also to maintain traditional norms within France in the face of the depredations of the 'enemy within' (slang and sloppy use of language) and the 'enemy without' (principally English loan-words). These bodies have such names as *Office de la langue française* (founded in 1937), the *Office du vocabulaire français* (founded in 1957), the *Haut comité pour la défense et l'expansion de la langue française* (founded in 1965) and the *Haut Conseil supérieur de la langue française* (founded in 1989). Their activities complement a series of governmental legislative measures relating to the French language, beginning with the *Arrêté ministériel du 26 février 1901* outlining certain grammatical and orthographic *tolérances* (see Grevisse 1986: 1696–1708), followed by the various 'linguistic laws' of the 1970s and 1980s directed principally against anglicisms.

French linguistic *dirigisme* is much derided by English-speaking observers. However, disdainful reactions of this sort may be misplaced, for they overlook the extreme potency of the French language as a symbol of French national identity. The old Jacobin tenet that 'la langue doit être une comme la République' is still widely accepted. French politicians are clearly well aware of the symbolic power of the language, and it is not inconceivable that the legislation they initiate with respect to the language is their way of harnessing that power to serve their own political purposes. It is of course impossible to measure the effectiveness of official steps to maintain the standard. They bear essentially on very restricted parts of the language (i.e. spelling and specified lexical items) and are concerned only with public and written uses of the language, leaving largely unscathed the majority of language uses which take place in face-to-face spoken interaction. However, they reflect a deeply held belief in France that the standard language represents in a profound sense the values of French democracy and nationhood, and the fact of official involvement in language matters adds weight to the other forces pulling speakers of French in the direction of the standard language.

Of course, the guardians of usage cannot achieve their aim of halting linguistic change and bringing about linguistic uniformity. To that extent their endeavours are permanently doomed to failure. However, failure in absolute terms does not mean lack of effect. The cumulative effect of a powerful literary tradition, the centralised education system and explicit regulatory action by official bodies has been to maintain the norms of the standard language at the front of public consciousness, making Brunot's statement of eighty years ago still true today: 'le règne de la grammaire . . . a été, en France, plus tyrannique et plus long qu'en aucun pays' ('the reign of the grammarian has been longer and more tyrannical in France than in any other country') (Brunot 1966: III, 4). Since access to power and status in French society depends to a considerable extent on complying with the high-prestige linguistic standard, French speakers are under very strong pressure to move their speech in the direction of the national linguistic norm.

Pressures inhibiting the progress of the standard

In view of the social gains which accrue from adopting a form of speech close to the standard, and in the light of the strong institutional pressure to relinquish vernacular forms, what is surprising is the vitality of language variation in contemporary France and the continued existence of rival linguistic norms alongside those of the standard. Why do low-prestige varieties persist? (See Ryan 1979.) In French, as in other European languages, the 'pull' of standard norms varies with the sex, the age, region of origin, social class and ethnic origin of the speaker. Let us look briefly at the workings of these speaker variables, bearing in mind that although we shall discuss each one separately, in reality they operate conjointly. Language varieties influenced by the first two of these factors (gender and age) are the result of social *difference* – i.e. different social attitudes and different behaviour are expected from men and women, and, increasingly nowadays, from young and old. Language varieties springing from the latter two (geographical/ethnic group and social class) result from social *distance*. (See Trudgill 1983: 88.)

It has long been recognised that men and women speak differently, but in French the differences are generally subconscious and not very obvious. Differences in language behaviour between the sexes have been observed in interactive discourse – women being apparently more 'co-operative' than their male counterparts (see Aebischer 1985) – and in lexical usage – women avoiding the use of slang and swear-words more consistently than men (see Lodge 1989). What have been noted above all are differences of language attitude between men and women. It appears to be the case in France as in other western societies that women seek to push their speech in the direction of high-prestige norms more readily than males. We find anecdotal evidence for this in the sixteenth and seventeenth centuries when women are reported to have been more caught up in hypercorrection than men, and to have provided the main public of prescriptive grammarians (see Ayres-Bennett 1990). It could be inferred that women's attitudes to language are more conservative than men's, but this term would be inappropriate since the low-status forms preferred by certain groups of males are very often highly traditional (see Ashby 1981: 685–6). The social class variable needs to be taken into account at the same time, but in the latter stages of language shift from the *patois* to standard, it has been noted that women were often a generation ahead of men (see Gauchat 1903).

How are these differences of attitude to be accounted for? Explanations offered to date invoke biological factors (women's *retenue naturelle* – see Müller 1985: 176), their child-rearing role (see Hadjadj 1989: 238), the power structure in society (women's alleged *docilité sociale* – see Bourdieu 1977a: 32), their greater preoccupation with appearance and self-presentation resulting from their exclusion from positions of real power and status in society. Some of these explanations carry greater weight than others (Müller's suggestion being particularly difficult to sustain), but all carry the implication that it is women's behaviour in this matter which requires explanation and not men's. An equally legitimate question would be to ask why men have greater recourse to vernacular forms than women, particularly in the lower socioeconomic groups. Here the different sorts of social relationships contracted by men and women may be an important factor: traditionally men have interacted more closely with professional colleagues outside the home, while women have tended to be either isolated within the family group or divided uneasily between home and workplace. In these circumstances we can see how men may develop a stronger sense of group identity with their workmates, and how this may in turn call for linguistic markers of male solidarity. As usual in such situations, the broad social norms which convey *overt* prestige are rejected in favour of 'community norms' bringing *covert* prestige – among his workmates a man is considered more manly the less his speech conforms to the social norms of the

239

standard language. Once the vernacular is associated with man-liness, femininity can be registered linguistically only by greater rejection of vernacular norms in favour of those of the high-prestige standard (see Bourdieu 1977a: 32). As Trudgill (1983: 94) puts it: 'Sex varieties, then, are the result of different social attitudes towards the behaviour of men and women, and of the attitudes men and women themselves consequently have to language as a social symbol.'

Differences between the speech of people of different age-groups have been widely attested in French as in other lan-guages. In his celebrated study of the pronunciation of French officers in a prisoner-of-war camp in Germany during the Second World War, Martinet (1945: 76) demonstrated for in-stance that the tendency to distinguish two *a*-sounds (/ɑ/ and /a/) in *pâte* and *patte* diminished as he descended the age-scale: older speakers 99 per cent; middle-aged 96 per cent; younger speakers 92 per cent. In a later study (Martinet 1969: 168–90), it was suggested that linguistic differences of this type between the generations can be taken to indicate the linguistic changes which are currently in progress. This approach was simul-taneously adopted by W. Labov (1970) who saw in the 'vernacu-lar' of adolescents (i.e. the relaxed spoken style in which the least conscious attention is being paid to speech) the general direction of change in American English. He established a useful distinction between changes in 'real time' (changes observed between the speech of comparable groups of speakers separated by significant periods of time), and changes in 'apparent time' (differences observed between the speech of different gener-ations but existing at the same time).

Labov's interest in the 'vernacular' led him to pay particular attention to the speech of adolescents, since he felt that here access to the 'vernacular' was most direct (see Labov 1970: 181). It is clear that in French, as in the American English studied by Labov, it is speakers in the 15–25 age-group who are most resistant to high-status social norms. The non-standard nature of much French adolescent speech has been noted in phonology (see Léon 1973) and in syntax (Ashby 1981: 683), but it is in lexis that it is most conspicuous (Walter 1984b). The mechanisms of lexical innovation involve semantic shift (e.g. *méchant* = 'great' rather than 'malevolent'), change of word-class (e.g. *sexe* =

'sexy' rather than 'sex'), derivation (e.g. the use of new suffixes like *-os* and *-ing*), abbreviation (e.g. *appart = appartement*), anglicism (e.g. *cool*). However, many other 'innovations' used by the young involve the upward diffusion of much older items traditionally used by low-status groups (e.g. Parisian slang like *mec* = bloke, *tire* = car, and *verlan* creations like *meuf = femme*).

Clearly, the linguistic differences between the generations which we have just pointed to may well be indicative of linguistic 'change in progress'. However, 'there is no theoretical reason why [generation differences] should not be simply recurrent features characteristic of particular age-groups, to be adopted or abandoned by the individual speaker as he passes through the generation sequence' (Bynon 1977: 206). This 'age-grading' is obviously the case with baby-talk, but it may well be happening in the speech of adolescents, too. There is plenty of evidence to suggest that the young are under strong pressure to conform to a group identity which distinguishes them from children and from adults. The shared experiences of young people throughout France (educational establishments, military service, etc.) and the specific targeting of this group by commercial purveyors of 'youth culture' (teenage music, dress, leisure activities) have combined to create a separate 'youth identity', symbolised inevitably by age-specific linguistic usage. Such age-specific usage generally demands a rejection of high-status norms (to which they are so heavily exposed in educational establishments) and increased use of the vernacular (see Lodge 1989).

Regional variation and social variation in France are closely intertwined. Trudgill's model, constructed with reference to English, could be usefully applied to French (see Figure 12 after Trudgill 1983: 42). Dialectal diversity tends to increase proportionately to the degree of communicative isolation between groups. Barriers separating groups of people may be geographical ones (e.g. physical obstacles like mountains, forests and marshes or barriers of sheer distance), but they may also be ones of social class (e.g. a rigidly stratified social structure which impedes social mobility). The greater the communicative isolation of groups, the longer it will take for a central norm to be diffused across them. However, we cannot explain *all* social differences in language in terms of pre-existing barriers to communication: speakers' *attitudes* to particular language varieties

241

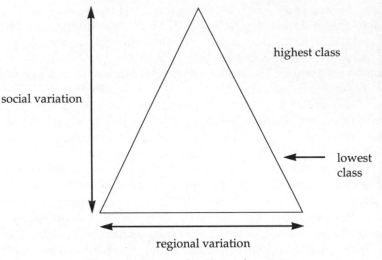

Figure 12   Regional and social variation

can also vitally affect the preservation/removal of dialect differences. The maintenance of local norms in the face of pressure from an outside standard can reflect the identity needs of the groups concerned and the degree of 'focusing' within them. The maintenance of 'community norms' in relation to regional groups (e.g. speakers of Gallo, the Romance dialect of eastern Brittany), ethnic groups (e.g. the Muslim community) and certain low-status working-class groups (e.g. northern French mining communities) is often related to the use of language as an identity shield.

We looked in the last chapter at the extent to which the *patois* and regional languages such as Breton, Alsatian, Basque, Occitan, etc., are still spoken in France. These will not therefore concern us here. What we shall be interested in will be the spatial variation observable within 'French itself'. Since the virtual extinction of the old rural *patois*, French dialectologists have increasingly turned their attention to the description of particular *français régionaux* (see Brun 1946; Müller 1985: 157–70). Success in this enterprise has often proved elusive. Offord (1990: 148–9) expresses the problem clearly:

> It is extremely difficult to draw up a definitive map of regional French . . . since it is essentially an unstable and

unpredictable variety of French. . . . Because regional French exists mainly by virtue of local words, rather than local accents and syntactical usages – although, as we have seen, these do figure to a small degree – it is not appropriate or practical to study it as a separate, self-contained linguistic system.

Offord is obviously right when he claims that no *français régional* exists 'as a separate, self-contained linguistic system'. This is the central difficulty raised by studying *all* vernaculars, not solely regional varieties of French, for they appear to be inherently variable, as a rule rather than as an exception. In most regions of France, speakers use varieties which fall at particular points along a continuum from the standard language to varieties close to the now almost extinct *patois* (see Carton 1973, 1981). The point on the continuum at which any one of them falls will vary with factors like age, sex, occupation and, of course, the context of situation. Dialect-switching, like style-shifting, has then to be described quantitatively in terms of the relative frequencies of key variables, rather than in terms of abrupt switching between tightly structured linguistic systems. Regional differences are most obviously perceptible in pronunciation ('accents'), but other levels of language (syntax and lexis) are also affected (see Brun 1931 and Séguy 1950). Here are some examples.

The most obvious pronunciation differences within France are those differentiating the north of the country from the south, corresponding to a certain degree to the historical zone of influence of the Occitan *substratum* (see Walter 1982: 205). Salient points of difference are the incidence of schwa (e.g. 'Je me le demande' is typically pronounced /ʒɔmlɔdmɑ̃d/ in the north and /ʒəmələdəmandɔ/ in the south), and the extent of nasalisation of vowels (e.g. 'pain' is typically pronounced /pɛ̃/ in the north and /pɛⁿ/ in the south). Other significant regional variants include the distribution of the mid-vowels /e/, /ɛ/, /o/ and /ɔ/ (e.g. /Roz/ in the standard is pronounced /Rɔzə/ in the south). Regional variations in syntax are less easy to find since most grammatical items are less frequent than phonological ones. However, observers point to regional variation in the tense system (e.g. the widespread use of the *passé surcomposé* – *j'ai eu chanté* – in the south-east of France, and retention of the *passé simple* – *je chantai* – in the west). (See Walter 1988: 170–2.) Because of the sheer number of lexical items in any linguistic system, regional variation in lexis is common – most speakers of French have acquired lexical items whose use is restricted to a region smaller than the whole of France. These are in most cases survivals of earlier *patois* forms (e.g. *éclairer* = *allumer* in Saint Etienne, *guetter* = *garder* in the Orléanais, *coufle* = *rassasié* in Auvergne).

The features which characterise the speech of the different regions of France originate, for the most part, in interference from the earlier *patois* and regional languages. Alsatian French, for instance, contains features (e.g. the voicing of voiceless plosives – *police* > *bolice*) carried over from the Germanic Alsatian dialect which is still spoken by a large proportion of the population. Likewise, many features of southern French speech can be seen as continuations of pre-existing Occitan features (e.g. the distribution of mid-vowels, nasalisation and the incidence of schwa). However, this correlation between features present in the various *français régionaux* and in the pre-existing *patois* is not a simple and direct one. For instance, the geographical distribution of the key schwa-retention variable (e.g. *une petite fille*) does not overlap with the traditional Oc–Oïl boundary: schwa retention is most frequent in Languedoc and in the south-west, but becomes sparser as one moves northwards, disappearing north of a line running along the southern borders of Limousin and Auvergne, areas traditionally regarded as having been Occitan-speaking in centuries past.

What factors pull speakers from the standard towards a more strongly regional speech? The first factor is no doubt geographical – regional speech-norms are stronger in certain areas than in others and their strength is in turn related to the degree of integration of the regional community into national life focused on Paris. Walter (1982: 206) observes that outside the Ile-de-France, Parisian norms of pronunciation are strongest in areas immediately to the west (Maine-Orléanais) and to the east (Champagne) of the capital. Regional norms, on the other hand, are particularly strong in northern Picardy, in Alsace and in the erstwhile Occitan-speaking areas. Remoteness from Paris (e.g. the south-west) and historical factors like the period of political and economic integration (e.g. Alsace and Savoy which were integrated relatively late) have a central role to play here. Related to this is the question of urban or rural residence.

While the great provincial cities of France possess their distinctive 'accents' – Lille, Lyon, Marseille, Bordeaux, etc. – regional speech tends to be more strongly marked in the country than in the towns, where the population is less mobile and where the old rural *patois* exert a correspondingly greater residual influence. Speaker-variables like age, sex and social class membership clearly have a determining influence on the 'pull' of regional norms on individual speakers. Regional norms are weaker with younger speakers than with older ones and with female speakers than with male speakers. They are stronger in the lower socioeconomic groups than in the higher. In addition to such speaker-variables as these, the 'pull' of regional norms is related to a significant degree to the context of situation. Carton (1981: 24) demonstrates a correlation between the incidence of regionally marked forms and particular pragmatic functions. Regional speech-forms are felt to be most appropriate in informal contexts where the intention is to express feelings of solidarity and friendliness. Local 'community norms' have an important function here, particularly among males belonging to the lower socioeconomic groups. Striking examples of this are to be found in northern industrial towns (e.g. Lille and Roubaix) where large urban proletariats adopted as their vernacular the local pre-industrial *patois* (known since the time of the First World War as *chtimi*) (see Lefebvre 1988: 270–3 and Gueunier *et al*. 1978: 122–3). Mounin (1975: 68–70) describes an analogous situation in the village of Vieux Rouen located on the borders of Normandy and Picardy.

Until the end of the nineteenth century (and perhaps later), social stratification in France was reflected sociolinguistically above all in the opposition between the Paris-oriented usage of the upper classes and the *patois* spoken by an overwhelmingly rural population. The major exception to this pattern was, as we have seen, Paris itself, which from an early date manifested a considerable gulf between the norms of upper-class usage (*le bon usage*) and those of the vernacular spoken by the majority of Parisians (*la langue du peuple*). We have seen how during the past century the sociolinguistic situation has changed radically: the *patois* have been all but displaced by varieties more closely related to Parisian French, and major conurbations have developed in the provinces (e.g. Lille, Lyon, Marseille), attracting immigrants not only from other parts of France, but also from outside (especially Spain, Portugal and north Africa). As a consequence, the opposition between standard language and rural dialect has been displaced throughout France by class-based differences *within varieties of French*, and, among the immigrant communities, by class-based bilingualism.

Discussions of class-based differences within French have traditionally centred on the notion of *le français populaire*. This term is widely used to designate the speech of the lower socioeconomic groups in Paris (see Guiraud 1965: 7). *Le français populaire* is seen as differing from the *patois*, which (apart from those of the Ile-de-France) are usually regarded as quite separate linguistic systems, and also from the various *français régionaux* (though observers point to regional forms of *le français populaire*). Most importantly, however, *le français populaire* is defined in contradistinction to *le français cultivé*. The latter is seen as the prerogative of the educated middle classes, though these may in their unguarded moments slither towards popular speech in a variety labelled *le français familier*. As well as being seen traditionally as a variety quite discrete from the other varieties we have just mentioned, *le français populaire* is believed to possess a substantial degree of homogeneity: 'Le français populaire . . . a conservé la simplicité, l'homogénéité, la vigueur et la naïveté d'une économie naturelle' ('Popular French . . . has retained the simplicity, homogeneity, vigour and naïvety of a natural [language] economy') (Guiraud 1965: 12).

The approach to social-class variation outlined here raises problems: the clear-cut boundaries posited between the various language varieties listed and the suggestions of homogeneity within them run counter to the generally observed characteristic of vernaculars, which is their inherent variability. Class-based differences have to be measured in quantitative rather than in absolute terms. Like all western societies, French society is stratified on social-class lines, but the barriers between the classes are not uncrossable and there is now a considerable measure of social mobility. It is well attested that speakers representing the dominant sociocultural group use in their spontaneous style features which they attribute to members of less prestigious sociocultural groups. It has to be conceded, moreover, that traditional depictions of lower-class speech rely frequently on upper-class stereotypes portraying the Paris working class not only as simple and uncultivated but also as a united group posing an organised threat to the wealth and status enjoyed by the upper social groups. Stereotypical attitudes like this have an important effect on individuals' linguistic behaviour, but should not influence the approach of an observing linguist. Let us glance at simple examples of class-based variation in phonetics/phonology, syntax and lexis in French.

Reichstein (1960) compared the pronunciation of key phonological variables like the oppositions /a/~/ɑ/, /e/~/ɛ/ and /ɛ̃/~/œ̃/. She discovered uncontroversially that in general the pronunciation of children from the upper social groups (here those attending private schools) approximated more closely to the high-prestige norm than did that of children from the lower groups (those attending state schools).

There exist a large number of non-standard grammatical forms which are heavily stigmatised and attributed to the less-educated social groups – for example, interrogatives of the type 'Où que tu vas?' (instead of 'Où est-ce que tu vas?'), use of the relative *que* in 'C'est le film que je t'ai parlé' (instead of 'C'est le film dont je t'ai parlé'), generalised use of the conjunction *que* in 'Que ça serait de l'eucalyptus, que ça m'étonnerait pas' (instead of 'Si cela était un eucalyptus, cela ne m'étonnerait pas') (see Gadet 1989: 161–8). However, the social distribution of these forms has not been fully analysed. The social-class correlates of negative forms has, however, received detailed attention. Ashby (1981: 682) studied the frequency with which speakers in Touraine deleted the first element of the negation *ne . . . pas*. He was able to point to quite pronounced class-based differences:

Social class	Deletion rate
Highest	55%
Mid	53%
Lowest	84%

Here the classic situation emerges where the social group with the most 'correct' speech is not the highest but the intermediate one (see below).

Lodge (1989) studied speakers' perceptions of their use of a set of fifty non-standard lexical items in French in Clermont-Ferrand. A questionnaire was completed by seventy informants made up of equal numbers of males and females, divided equally between seven age-bands going from 10 to 70, and spread representatively across the socioeconomic groupings.

Informants were asked first to estimate the frequency with which they used each of the non-standard words on the list (e.g. *bouquin* = 'book', *fric* = 'money', *bagnole* = 'car'). It seems safe to assume that they based their estimate principally upon their perceived usage with family, friends and workmates. Secondly, they were asked to evaluate the readiness with which they felt they might use these words with strangers (of the same age and sex as themselves). The average scores which speakers in four occupational classes awarded themselves in response to question 1 is set out in the following table:

Top management	72.1
Lower management	65.3
Employees	88.0
Manual workers	74.3

Examination of the figures produced by Ashby and by Lodge indicates that while the upper social groups tend to conform more closely to high-prestige norms than do the lower ones, the progression from high to low is not regular: it is the group located just below the top group which produces (or thinks it produces) the 'most correct' French. This hypercorrectness on the part of lower middle-class speakers was first observed and measured in Labov's classic study of New York speech (1970: 191–4) and has subsequently been noted widely in French linguistic behaviour (see Bourdieu 1977a: 26). It is explained with reference to this group's alleged 'linguistic insecurity'.

A further feature which can be said to differentiate the speech of the upper and lower social-class groups concerns their different abilities to shift styles according to context. In the Clermont-Ferrand survey the average scores of the four social groups in response to both questions are as follows:

	q. 1 (with intimates)	q. 2 (with strangers)
Top management	72.1	57.2
Lower management	65.3	43.7
Employees	88.0	85.1
Manual workers	74.3	69.8

What is interesting here is the difference between the two sets of scores: whereas the two upper groups see themselves shifting style (upwards) very markedly in the presence of strangers, the two lower groups shift style (upwards) to a much smaller extent. This echoes the findings of Bernstein (1971) to the effect that middle-class speakers have control of both 'restricted' and 'elaborated' codes, by dint principally of their greater exposure to formal education, whereas working-class speakers have substantially reduced control of the 'elaborated code'.

To sum up, then, what seems to differentiate middle-class speakers from lower-class speakers is the greater approximation of middle-class speakers to the high-status linguistic norms. It would be wrong, however, to assume that low-status forms are invariably the prerogative of lower-class groups. Middle-class speakers are quite capable of using many of these, sometimes ironically, sometimes out of a desire not to appear stilted (a reaction sometimes referred to in French as *encanaillement*), though the forms involved are principally lexical, rarely syntactic – middle-class speakers tend to avoid highly stigmatised syntactic forms like 'qui que c'est ti qui vient?' ('Qui est-ce qui vient?') very strenuously. On the other side, it would be equally wrong to assume automatically that lower-class speakers cling to low-status forms out of ignorance of the 'correct' way to speak. It is clear that they very often use low-status forms as a symbol of group cohesion and identity. Conscious that they do not 'belong' to the middle-class groups who 'speak well', they often come under strong solidarity pressures to conform to their own 'community norms'. We have seen how conformity with 'community norms' confers its own special sort of prestige within the group ('covert prestige') – see above, p. 233, and Bourdieu 1977a: 31–3.

The strength of 'community norms' seems to be related to the structure of the social groups concerned: tight-knit groups located at the top and at the bottom of society appear to have the most constraining community norms, the majority of the population comprising geographically and socially mobile speakers falling somewhere between these two poles. Examples of powerful community norms operating at the top of society are to be found in the *Précieux* movement in seventeenth-century Paris (see above, p. 177) and in the public schools of nineteenth- and twentieth-century Britain (see Honey 1989: 177). Examples of such norms operating at the bottom of society are to be found in France in certain closed working-class communities, like the mining village of Vieux Rouen studied by Mounin (1975: 68–70).

Ce groupe exerçait en matière de langage une attitude normative et répressive spontanée contre tout ce qui pouvait diminuer la distance linguistique séparant sa propre variété des variétés voisines.

(In linguistic matters this group exercised a spontaneous, normative and repressive attitude to everything which might reduce the linguistic distance between its own speech variety and neighbouring ones.)

(Garmadi 1981: 72)

Second-generation members of north African immigrant communities in France (referred to as 'les Beurs') appear to have developed their own community norms in a similar way, though paradoxically this involves heightened use of French vernacular forms rather than north African ones.

Other manifestations of community norms in France are perhaps to be found in the numerous *argots* coined by various self-contained subgroups within society, not all of which are low status, but which use language as a badge of identity nonetheless (e.g. the *argots* of *lycéens* and of students in the *Grandes Ecoles*). The special norms of *argot* bear of course only on lexical usage, not on phonology and syntax. The most well-known of all the French *argots* is that of the criminal fraternity in pre-nineteenth-century Paris (see above, pp. 145–6). The *jargon de l'argot*, along with its alternative lexical codes of *verlan* (= 'à l'envers') and *loucherbem* (= 'le boucher'), has received a good deal of scholarly attention (see Guiraud 1976). In *verlan* syllables are inverted in two-syllable words (e.g. *l'envers* = *verlan*) and phonemes in single-syllable words (e.g. *femme* = *meuf*). In *loucherbem* the first consonant of the word is replaced by *l* and a suffix is added (e.g. *boucher* = *loucherbem* and *jargon* = *largonji*). The marginality of the groups which developed these codes and their association with criminality inevitably led to the conviction among the wider public that they were designed expressly to disguise the speakers' law-breaking activities. Perhaps this was too malevolent an interpretation – the *argot* of the Parisian underclass could well have developed simply as an identity shield, as commonly happens in communities which feel themselves to be under some sort of threat. At all events, the tight social networks holding in this group did not survive the nineteenth century. The modernisation of Parisian social and economic life, large-scale works of town-planning, the development of effective policing, bureaucracy, and spatial and social mobility brought about a loosening of these social networks and the spread of *mots argotiques* into the broader system of lower-class Parisian speech.

The ideal goal of language standardisation is the halting of change and the suppression of variation through the imposition of a single norm: in the first part of this chapter we have looked at the tension between the powerful social forces pulling users in the direction of the traditional norm and countervailing pressures exerted by alternative norms related to the various age/sex and geographical/social class identities to which speakers aspire. In the second part of this chapter we shall look at tension within the norms of contemporary French operating on a different axis of variation: variation according to context.

CONTEXTUAL PRESSURES

No language is limited to a single code or style applicable in all situations, for if it were it would be incapable of 'indicating respect, insolence, mock seriousness, role distance, etc., by switching from one variety to another' (Hymes 1967: 9). Agreement has not yet been reached between linguists about which labels are the most suitable for the variable elements which make up these codes and styles, but in what follows we shall use the terms which seem to have gained the widest currency, namely those proposed by Halliday (1964): 'field', 'mode' and 'style'. We shall define these terms as we come to them. The totality of linguistic varieties available for the many different contexts of use is known as the community's 'verbal repertoire'. Competence in a language involves more than mastery of a single style and more than 'grammatical competence'. Hymes highlighted in particular the notion of *appropriateness*. Knowledge of what sort of language is appropriate for what sort of social context forms a vital part of what Hymes terms our 'communicative competence': 'The goal of a broad theory of competence can be said to be to show the ways in which the systemically possible, the feasible and the appropriate are linked to produce actually occurring linguistic behavior' (Hymes 1971: 286).

The thrust of standard ideology is to restrict the number of varieties admitted to the verbal repertoire: certain varieties (written, formal and planned uses) are granted greater legitimacy than others (spoken, informal and unplanned uses), creating tensions between the communicative requirements of the particular situation and the pressures exerted by the high-prestige (usually written) norm. The power of this ideology is such that it leaves many French people firmly convinced that they speak their own language badly. In this section we shall explore some of the areas of tension between the dictates of standard ideology and the needs of normal communication.

Field

This category embraces basically different sets of vocabulary items. Put simply, different subject-areas (different 'fields') require their own areas of vocabulary. A discussion about cooking will require different words from a discussion about clinical pathology. A society will develop extremely complex and elaborate vocabularies in the fields which are culturally important for it. Each professional subgroup within society will evolve its own technical vocabulary to meet its own specialist needs. In Chapter 5 we saw how the 'elaboration of function' in French as it passed from being an oral vernacular to being a 'developed' language was the expansion of its lexicon (largely through borrowing from Latin) to enable it to function in a wider range of fields.

Guardians of usage, however, do not maintain a neutral attitude towards the various lexical fields in the language's repertoire. Social attitudes to particular vocabularies reflect the values of the dominant cultural tradition. The cultural model of the *honnête homme* (see above, p. 177) still retains considerable power in France, conferring higher status upon words pertaining to high culture (aesthetics, science, 'high tech', etc.), but disparagement upon words belonging to lower-status fields (e.g. rural activities and the various *argots de métier* discussed by Dauzat 1929).

Mode

This heading embraces variation resulting from the differences between speech and writing. A central feature of the 'elaboration of function' discussed in Chapter 5 was the development of a writing system as an adjunct to speech. The differences between speech and writing in French, and the ways in which these have become blurred in some contexts due to the development of new technologies like telephone and radio/television broadcasting, have been frequently enumerated (see Offord 1990: 101–19), so it is not our intention to examine them in detail here. The central point we wish to make concerns social attitudes prevalent in France towards the relative statuses of the two modes.

We have seen in earlier chapters how the development of standardisation and the spread of literacy promoted the belief that writing is a more valid form of language than speech. The fact that something approaching uniformity is achievable in writing led codifiers to the belief that the written code is the ultimate reference-point in standardisation: the 'real' French language is the written French language and speech is merely a corrupt version of it. Languages without a written form are deemed not to be languages at all, but *idiomes*, *patois*, *parlers*. Beliefs such as these are still deeply engrained in contemporary France. A recent survey of attitudes to varieties of spoken French (see Gueunier *et al*. 1983: 779) has revealed that

dans 35% des entretiens apparaît l'idée que la prononciation, 'le parler' sont moins importants que l'écrit. Ah! si nous avions travaillé sur les fautes d'orthographe ou la grammaire. . . . Oublieuse de son apprentissage de la langue maternelle, la majorité des enquêtés pense que l'écrit détermine l'oral.

(In 35 per cent of the interviews the idea emerges that pronunciation and speech are less important than writing. If only we had worked on our spelling mistakes and our grammar. . . . Oblivious to the way they learnt their mother tongue, the majority of the people interviewed think that speech is determined by writing.)

Mastery of the written code is widely felt to be synonymous with a high level of linguistic competence. The high social premium set on accuracy in spelling is reflected in the massive popularity of the TV personality Bernard Pivot's annual national spelling competitions. At a less mundane level, the reverence in which the community's great literary authors are held (in some quarters at least) is a further testimony to the high value placed upon the written word in French culture. Speakers of French then come under correspondingly high pressure to align their speech with the model of writing.

Such pressure on speakers to produce writing-like speech creates inevitable tension with the requirements of normal interactive discourse. Whereas interactive speech involves a negotiation of meaning between the participants and a profound level of interplay between language and the immediate situation of utterance, writing is heavily decontextualised communication, with writer and recipient separated from each other in space and time and making up for the lack of situational support for the message by total reliance on exclusively linguistic signals. Spoken utterances are often incomplete and ungrammatical, and frequently effective communication demands that they be so: 'a person who chooses occasions and sentences suitably, but is the master only of fully grammatical sentences, is at best a bit odd. Some occasions call for being appropriately ungrammatical' (Hymes 1971: 277).

A related difference between speech and writing concerns *planned* and *unplanned discourse*. Of course, not all speech is unplanned – public speeches are usually planned in great detail and much speech in the media is in fact spoken writing – but most speech happens, nevertheless, in spontaneous, interactive discourse. For fairly obvious reasons, society places greater value on planned than upon unplanned discourse, upon information-bearing utterances than upon utterances fulfilling other functions like maintaining solidarity and friendliness, reassuring, amusing, etc. The greatest part of the effort involved in teaching French in France in the school system is devoted to enhancing the pupils' skills in written, planned, information-bearing discourse, often with the implication that these skills ought ideally to be transferred as far as possible to the pupils' speech. While such transfers are feasible to a certain extent, much of everyday speech remains stubbornly beyond the reach of planning: in order for it to be effective, it has to be spontaneous. In other words, standardising pressures pushing speakers to produce writing-like speech can run counter to the 'elasticity of language which is essential for effective communication' (see Weinreich *et al.* 1968: 101).

Style

The broad and ambiguous reference of the term 'style' in every-day use has tended to discourage linguists from using it as a technical term. We shall use it here in its Hallidayan sense referring to language variation linked to 'the relations among the participants' in a language activity, particularly the level of formality they adopt. Many factors can influence the level of formality in the language used. A first factor concerns the nature of the situation: for instance, is it public or private? Public speech situations normally call for a more formal, careful style than intimate ones. A second factor concerns the nature of the addressee. Here a complex nexus of variables comes into play: the relative ages and sexes of the participants, the length of time they have known each other, the difference in status between the participants, the warmth and closeness of their relationship with one another, etc. It is very apparent that speakers 'accom-modate' their style to suit their addressee and the way they 'design' their language for their 'audience' has recently begun to attract growing attention from sociolinguists (see Bell 1984). A third factor influencing the level of formality is derived from the function of the discourse in question. Brown (1982: 77) draws a broad distinction between two main functions of spoken lan-guage: listener-oriented utterances and message-oriented utter-ances. The former are primarily concerned with establishing and consolidating the relationship between the speakers. The latter seek primarily to communicate a message which will bring about a specific change in the listener's state of knowledge. There are of course few pure types, most utterances in fact containing elements of both. However, it is clear that listener-oriented utterances are likely to call for less formal, less careful style than message-oriented utterances.

The complex and variable nature of the phenomenon of 'style' makes the problem of style-labelling a particularly intractable one. In French, traditional terminology is confused: *vulgaire – populaire – familier – courant – cultivé*. The problem with these labels is that they are not based on a consistent set of defining criteria – some label a style with reference to a particular social group (*populaire, cultivé*), some with reference to social accepta-bility (*vulgaire, familier*) and one with possibly a reference to rates of frequency (*courant*). In what follows we shall make a simple distinction between H (High) and L (Low) styles: H items are those segments of the community's linguistic *répertoire* which are highly valued and which are reserved for formal or public situations; L items are those which are less highly valued and which are used in situations perceived as more informal and intimate. In so doing, we are not unaware of the fact that stylistic variation in French forms not a simple duality, but a continuum not unlike the gradations observed in English by Joos (1962): intimate – casual – consultative – formal – frozen. Stylistic variation affects phonology, syntax and lexis. Let us look at a few examples.

In *pronunciation* we can observe the following:

Reduction of consonant clusters:

H	L	
/ɛksplike/	/ɛsplike/	'expliquer'
/səlɥi/	/sɥi/	'celui'

Neutralisation of certain vocalic oppositions:

/Rɛzɔne/	/Rezɔne/	'raisonner'
/pɑt/	/pat/	'pâte'

(see Valdman 1976: 55–70)

In addition one could cite numerous variables in French connected speech such as liaison and elision which differ significantly in H and L style (see Green and Hintze 1988).

The *syntactic differences* between H and L styles in French are particularly strongly marked. Whole tense-systems present in H have been eliminated from L: the past historic (e.g. *je chantai*), the past anterior (e.g. *j'eus chanté*), the imperfect subjunctive (e.g *que j'eusse chanté*). As we saw earlier, the two-part negation (e.g. *ne . . . pas*) has become exceedingly rare in informal style, in favour of a one-part system (e.g. *pas*). Verb-subject inversion so common in H style is scrupulously avoided in L style, even in interrogatives (e.g. *Où est-ce que vous allez?* (H) *Où c'est que vous allez?* (L)).

It is probably in the *lexicon* that style-shifting in French is indicated most obviously. The French lexicon has seen the development of what has been referred to as a 'vocabulaire parallèle' (see Sauvageot 1964: 244), that is to say a large number of paired items, one in H and one in L for commonly referred to objects:

H	L
voiture	bagnole
argent	fric
médecin	toubib

Such pairs include verbs and adjectives as well as nouns:

manger	bouffer
se promener	se balader
travailler	bosser
amusant	marrant

This development has led over the past decade or so to the proliferation of dictionaries contrasting L and H forms:

1977, F. Caradec, *Dictionnaire de français argotique et populaire*
1980, G. Sandry and M. Carrière, *Dictionnaire de l'argot moderne*
1980, J. Cellard and A. Rey, *Dictionnaire du français non-conventionnel*
1986, P. Merle, *Dictionnaire du français branché*
1986, A. La Rue and C. Casciani, *Dictionnaire d'argot*
1987, E. Nouguier, *Dictionnaire d'argot*
1991, J.-P. Colin and J.-P. Mével, *Dictionnaire de l'argot.*

CONCLUSION: FRENCH DIGLOSSIA?

In his article 'Dialect, language, nation', which has been so influential in the inception of the ideas developed in this book, Haugen (1966: 108) states:

> Elaboration of function may lead to complexity of form, and contrariwise, unity of form may lead to rigidity of function. This area of interaction between form and function is the domain of *style*. A codification may be so rigid as to prevent the use of a language for other than formal purposes. Sanskrit had to yield to Prakrit, and Latin to the Romance languages, when the gap between written and spoken language became so large that only a very few people were willing to make the effort of learning them. Instead of being appropriate for 'all purposes for which the

language is used', the standard tends to become only one of several styles within a speech community. This can lead to what Ferguson (1959) has described as 'diglossia'; sharp cleavage between 'high' and 'low' style. Or it may be a continuum, with only a mild degree of what I have called 'schizoglossia', as in the case of English (Haugen 1962).

Could it be that, in the tension between standard and non-standard, modern French is heading towards a situation describable as 'diglossic'?

We began the latter part of this chapter by observing with Hymes that a feature of normal speakers' communicative competence is their ability to shift between different parts of the verbal repertoire according to the different contexts in which they find themselves. We have seen how French speakers have to make sometimes very sizeable shifts of style as they move from one context to another. In certain speech communities different domains of use entail a switch from an L variety of the language in informal contexts to an H variety which is very divergent from it and highly codified, reserved for formal situations. This is the situation of diglossia which we discussed in earlier chapters in connection with the relationship between Latin and the Romance vernaculars in medieval France and between Parisian French and the regional languages of France in more recent times. Since Ferguson's original definition of diglossia (see Ferguson 1959), Fishman (1967) extended use of the term to cover separate languages distributed functionally within the community. He quoted as an example of such a situation the relationship between Guarani (L) and Spanish (H) in Paraguay. More recently Fasold (1984: 52–4) has proposed a further extension of the term to cover stylistic differences within 'the same language'. The grounds for this extension have been called into question (see Trudgill 1983: 114), but it is nevertheless worth asking whether the switching between H and L varieties which occurs within French is not now approaching the situations Fasold chooses to call diglossic. The answer to this question depends on how we handle two sets of factors, the one social, the other stylistic.

A key question in the definition of diglossia concerns the distribution of H and L forms across the community. Are the varieties in question current throughout the community with a purely functional distinction between them, or is their distribution to a significant degree class-based? Does any group in society ignore the functional distinction, and, for instance, use the H variety as a medium of everyday conversation? We saw earlier that the speech of the upper social groups tends to approximate more closely to the high-prestige norm than does that of the lower groups, though in France as elsewhere it is the lower middle class which shows the greatest concern for correctness. We saw, too, that there are in France significant class-based differences in the degree of control of the community's verbal repertoire, the upper groups having greater skill in handling the H code in addition to the L. That said, while greater mastery of H may give them a freer choice between H and L varieties, it does not preclude them from using the L variety when the occasion demands it, i.e. in everyday conversation. Indeed, it would be most unusual to find members of the upper social groups using H as their everyday language, even though they may themselves attribute features in their own spontaneous style to members of less prestigious sociocultural groups. Conversely, it is extremely difficult to maintain that there exists in French class-based vernaculars which are the prerogative of particular socioeconomic groups. Possession of H forms is undoubtedly correlated with 'educatedness', but it is not possible to attribute H and L varieties of French very clearly to particular social groups.

A second key question in the definition of diglossia is the following: do H and L varieties of French represent 'distinct varieties', or do they merge in a stylistic continuum? It is difficult to demonstrate the existence of a sharp cleavage between H and L forms of French. It is most reasonable to claim that the phonetic and syntactic differences between H and L are to be measured quantitatively on a sliding scale rather than qualitatively with an abrupt break. Likewise in lexis, we are probably dealing in French with lexical items located on a sliding scale of acceptability, e.g. *demoiselle*, *jeune fille*, *nénette*, *gonzesse*, rather than with a simple system of binary pairs. That said, there is little doubt that native speakers of French are themselves very aware of the gap now separating the codified form of the language and the highly variable L forms. The topic is raised very frequently in the press, with purists endlessly deploring their compatriots' reluctance to 'talk properly', and with 'progressives' endlessly ridiculing the stilted nature of the traditional standard. Comic and satirical writers constantly play upon the gap between H and L and upon the grotesque linguistic incongruities which can be discovered or engineered. The co-occurrence of H and L features is normally strenuously avoided, e.g. 'Sans doute a-t-il bousillé sa bagnole.' However, comic writers like Queneau, San Antonio and journalists such as Claude Sarraute (in her regular column in *Le Monde* entitled 'Sur le vif') make such incongruities the basis of their humour. The most accurate formulation would perhaps be to say that although the space between H and L varieties in French is occupied by a continuum, nevertheless it appears that at a certain point along its length this stylistic continuum is being stretched almost to breaking-point.

It would then be an exaggeration to say that the present-day sociolinguistic situation in French is diglossic. However, it is clear that the rigid codification imposed upon the written language and the powerful institutional pressures promoting standard ideology, which we described earlier in this chapter, have brought about a greater rigidity in the standard form of French than is to be found in many languages in the modern world. Success in slowing the evolution of the written and formal varieties of the language can only result in a widening gap between them and the evolving spoken and informal varieties, increasing the possibility of diglossia in the long run. The ongoing debate about the *crise du français* focuses (among other things) on the widening gulf between 'bad French' and the norms of the traditional standard. Such agonising is often looked upon rather patronisingly by English speakers, but this is to misunderstand the fundamental importance of the standard language as a symbol of identity and national unity in France.

REFERENCES

Aebischer, V., 1985. *Les Femmes et le langage*. Paris: PUF.
Adenet le Roi, 1963, *Berte aus grans piés*, ed. A. Henry. Brussels: Université Libre.
Ager, D., 1990. *Sociolinguistics and Contemporary French*. Cambridge: Cambridge University Press.
Aitchison, J., 1981. *Language-change: Progress or Decay*. London: Fontana.
Alibert, L., 1935. *Grammatica occitana*. Toulouse: Société d'Etudes Occitanes.
Antoine, G. and Martin, R. (eds), 1985. *Histoire de la langue française, 1880–1914*. Paris: CNRS.
Arbellot, G., 1973. 'Les routes en France au XVIIIe siècle'. *Annales ESC*, 28: 765–91.
Armengaud, A. and Lafont, R., 1979. *Histoire d'Occitanie*. Paris: Hachette.
Arnauld, A. and Lancelot, C., 1660. *Grammaire générale et raisonnée*. Paris: Le Petit.
Ascoli, G. T., 1878 (first appeared 1873). 'Schizzi franco-provenzali'. *Archivio Glottologico Italiano*, 3: 61–130.
Ashby, W. J., 1981. 'The loss of the negative particle *ne* in French: a syntactic change in progress'. *Language*, 57: 674–87.
Ayres-Bennett, W., 1987. *Vaugelas and the Development of the French Language*. London: MHRA.
Ayres-Bennett, W., 1990. 'Women and grammar'. *Seventeenth Century French Studies*, 12: 5–25.
Aymon de Varennes, 1933. *Florimont*, ed. A. Hilka. Göttingen: Gesellschaft für romanische Literatur.
Bacon, R., 1859. *Compendium studii philosophiae*, ed. J. S. Brewer. London: Rolls Series.
Bacon, R., 1897. *The 'Opus Majus' of Roger Bacon*, ed. J. H. Bridges. Oxford: Oxford University Press.
Balibar, R., 1985. *Institution du français*. Paris: PUF.
Banniard, M., 1980. 'Géographie linguistique et linguistique historique. Essai d'analyse analogique en occitan-roman et en latin tardif'. *Via

Domitia, 24: 9–34.

Batany, J., 1982. 'L'amère maternité de la langue française'. *Langue Française*, 54: 29–39.

Bazalgues, G., 1973. 'Les organisations occitanes'. *Les Temps Modernes*, 324–6: 140–62.

Beaune, C., 1985. *Naissance de la nation France*. Paris: Gallimard.

Beaune, C., 1987. 'La notion de nation en France au moyen âge'. *Communications*, 45: 101–16.

Bec, P., 1967. *La Langue occitane*. Paris: PUF (Que Sais-Je?).

Bédard, E. and Maurais, J., 1983. *La Norme linguistique*. Quebec: Le Robert.

Bell, A., 1984. 'Language style as audience design'. *Language in Society*, 13 (2): 313–48.

du Bellay, J., 1549. *Defense et illustration de la langue françoise*. Paris: Arnoul l'Angelier.

Benedict, P., 1989. *Cities and Social Change in Early Modern France*. London: Unwin Hyman.

Bengtsson, S., 1968. *La Défense organisée de la langue française*. Uppsala: Almquist & Wiksells.

Bergounioux, G., 1989. 'Le francien (1815–1914): la linguistique au service de la patrie'. *Mots/Les langages du politique*, 19: 23–40.

Bernstein, B., 1971. *Class, Codes and Control, vol. 1: Theoretical Studies towards a Sociology of Language*. London: Routledge & Kegan Paul.

Berschin, H., Felixberger, J. and Goebl, H., 1978. *Französische Sprachgedichte*. Munich: Max Huber.

de Bèze, T., 1584. *De francicae linguae recta pronuntiatione*. Geneva: Vignon.

Blanche-Benveniste, C. and Jeanjean, C., 1987. *Le Français parlé*. Paris: Didier.

Bonfante, G. and Bonfante, L., 1983. *The Etruscan Language. An Introduction*. Manchester: Manchester University Press.

Bonnaud, P., 1981. *Terres et langages. Peuples et régions* (2 vols). Clermont-Ferrand: Auvernho Tara d'Oc.

Bonnet, M., 1890. *Le Latin de Grégoire de Tours*. Paris: Hachette.

Bouhours, D., 1675. *Remarques nouvelles sur la langue françoise*. Paris: Mabre-Cramoisy.

Bouhours, D., 1692. *Suite des remarques nouvelles sur la langue françoise*. Paris: G. et L. Josse.

Bourdieu, P., 1977a. 'L'économie des échanges linguistiques'. *Langue française*, 34: 17–34.

Bourdieu, P., 1977b. *La Distinction*. Paris: Minuit.

Bourhis, R. Y., 1982. 'Language policies and language attitudes: le monde de la francophonie'. In: E. B. Ryan and H. Giles, *Attitudes towards Language Variation*. London: Arundel.

de Bovelles, C., 1533. *Sur les Langues vulgaires et la variété de la langue française*, ed. and trans. D. Dumont-Demaizière, 1972. Paris: Klincksieck.

Braudel, F., 1986. *L'Identité de la France, t. 1: Les hommes et les choses; t. 2: (2 parties) Espace et histoire*. Paris: Arthaud-Flammarion.

REFERENCES

de Brosses, C., 1765. *Traité de la formation méchanique des langues*. Paris: Saillant.

Brown, G., 1982. 'The spoken language'. In: R. Carter (ed.), *Linguistics and the Teacher*. London: Routledge.

Brun, A., 1923. *Recherches historiques sur l'introduction du français dans les provinces du Midi*. Paris: Champion.

Brun, A., 1931. *Le Français de Marseille*. Marseille: Bibliothèque de l'Institut Historique de Provence.

Brun, A., 1935. 'La pénétration du français dans les provinces du Midi du XVe au XIXe siècle'. *Français Moderne*, 3: 149–61.

Brun, A., 1936. 'Linguistique et peuplement'. *Revue de Linguistique Romane*, 12: 165–251.

Brun, A., 1946. *Parlers régionaux: France dialectale et unité française*. Paris: Didier.

Brun, A., 1951. 'En langage maternel françois'. *Français Moderne*, 19: 81–6.

Brun-Trigaud, G., 1990. *Le Croissant: le concept et le mot*. Lyon: Université Jean Moulin.

Brunel, C., 1922. 'Les premiers exemples de l'emploi du provençal dans les chartes'. *Romania*, 48: 335–64.

Brunel, C., 1926, 1952. *Les Plus Anciennes Chartes en langue provençale* (2 vols). Paris: Picard.

Brunot, F., 1907. 'La langue du Palais et la formation du "bel usage" '. In: *Mélanges Chabaneau*, 1973. Erlangen: Slatkine.

Brunot, F., 1966. *Histoire de la langue française* (13 vols). Paris: Colin.

Busquet, R., Bourilly, V.-L. and Agulhon, M., 1976. *Histoire de la Provence*. Paris: PUF (Que Sais-Je?).

Bynon, T., 1977. *Historical Linguistics*. Cambridge: Cambridge University Press.

Calvet, L., 1981. *Les Langues véhiculaires*. Paris: PUF (Que Sais-Je?).

Caput, J.-P., 1972, 1975. *La Langue française. Histoire d'une institution*, t. 1: *842–1715*; t. 2: *1715–1934*. Paris: Larousse.

Caradec, F., 1977. *Dictionnaire du français argotique et populaire*. Paris: Larousse.

Carpentier, E. and Glénisson, J., 1962. 'La démographie française au XIVe siècle'. *Annales ESC*, 17: 109–29.

Carton, F., 1973. 'Usage des variétés de français dans la région de Lille'. *Ethnologie Française*, 3: 235–44.

Carton, F., 1981. 'Les parlers ruraux de la région Nord-Picardie'. *International Journal of the Sociology of Language*, 29: 15–28.

Catach, N., 1978a. *L'Orthographe française à l'époque de la Renaissance*. Geneva: Droz.

Catach, N., 1978b. *L'Orthographe*. Paris: PUF (Que Sais-Je?).

Cellard, J. and Rey, A., 1980. *Dictionnaire du français non-conventionnel*. Paris: Hachette.

de Certeau, M., Julia, D., and Revel, J., 1975. *Une Politique de la langue*. Paris: Gallimard.

Chambers, J. K. and Trudgill, P., 1980. *Dialectology*. Cambridge: Cambridge University Press.

Chambon, J.-P., 1990. 'L'occitan d'Auvergne au XVIIe siècle'. *Revue de Linguistique Romane*, 54: 377–445.

Chaurand, J., 1972. *Histoire de la langue française*. Paris: PUF (Que Sais-Je?).

Chaurand, J., 1983. 'Pour l'histoire du mot "francien" '. In: C. Deparis, F. Dumas and G. Taverdet (eds), *Mélanges de dialectologie d'oïl à la mémoire de Robert Loriot*. Dijon.

Chaurand, J., 1985. 'Les français régionaux'. In: G. Antoine and R. Martin (eds), *Histoire de la langue française 1880–1914*. Paris: CNRS.

Chaytor, J., 1945. *From Script to Print*. Cambridge: Cambridge University Press.

Chervel, A., 1977. . . . *Et Il Fallut Apprendre à Ecrire à Tous les Petits Français*. Paris: Payot.

Chevalier, J.-C., 1968. *Histoire de la syntaxe*. Geneva: Droz.

Cicero, 1965. *Pro Archia*, ed. N. H. Watts. London: Heinemann (The Loeb Classical Library).

Citron, S., 1987. *Le Mythe national*. Paris: Editions ouvrières.

Clanchy, M. T., 1979. *From Memory to Written Record: England, 1066–1307*. Cambridge: Cambridge University Press.

Cohen, M., 1953. *L'Ecriture*. Paris: Editions sociales.

Cohen, M., 1987. *Histoire d'une langue: le français*. Paris: Messidor/Editions sociales.

Colin, J.-P. and Mével, J.-P., 1991. *Dictionnaire de l'argot*. Paris: Larousse.

de Condillac, E., 1746. *Essai sur l'origine des connaissances humaines*. Amsterdam: Mortier.

Conon de Béthune, 1921. Chansons, ed. A. Wallensköld. Paris: Classiques français du moyen âge, 34.

Coquebert-Montbret, E., 1831. *Mélanges sur les langues, dialectes et patois*. Paris: Bureau de l'Almanach du Commerce.

Corneille, T., 1699. *Dictionnaire des arts et des sciences*. Paris: Coignard.

Cyrano de Bergerac, 1977. *Le Pédant joué*, ed. J. Prévot. In: *Oeuvres complètes*. Paris: Belin.

Danesi, M., 1991. 'Latin vs Romance in the Middle Ages'. In: R. Wright (ed.), *Latin and the Romance Languages in the Early Middle Ages*. London: Routledge.

Dauzat, A., 1929/1956. *Les Argots*. Paris: Delagrave.

Dauzat, A., 1930. *Histoire de la langue française*. Paris: Payot.

Dauzat, A., 1946. *Les Patois*. Paris: Delagrave.

Dauzat, A., 1947. *Dictionnaire étymologique*. Paris: Larousse.

Decrosse, A., 1987. 'Un mythe historique: la langue maternelle'. In: G. Vermes and J. Boutet (eds), *France, pays multilingue, t. 1*. Paris: Logiques Sociales. L'Harmattan.

Dees, A., 1980. *Atlas des formes et constructions des chartes françaises du 13e siècle*. (Zeitschrift für Romanische Philologie, Beiheft 178). Tübingen: Niemeyer.

Dees, A., 1985. 'Dialectes et scriptae à l'époque de l'ancien français'. *Revue de Linguistique Romane*, 49: 87–117.

Dees, A., 1987. *Atlas des formes linguistiques des textes littéraires de l'ancien français*. (Zeitschrift für Romanische Philologie, Beiheft 212). Tübingen: Niemeyer.

Delattre, P., 1970. 'Substratum theory'. *Romance Philology*, 23: 480–91.

Delbouille, M., 1962. 'La notion de "bon usage" en ancien français'. *Cahiers de l'Association Internationale des Etudes Françaises*, 14: 10–24.

Delbouille, M., 1970. 'Comment naquit la langue française?' In: *Mélanges offerts à M. Georges Straka, t. 1*. Lyon-Strasbourg: Société de linguistique romane.

Deloffre, F. (ed.), 1961. *Agréables Conférences de deux paysans de St Ouen et de Montmorency*. Paris: Les Belles Lettres.

Demaizière, C., 1983. *La Grammaire française au XVIᵉ siècle*. Paris: Didier.

Descimon, R., 1989. 'Paris on the eve of Saint Bartholomew: taxation, privilege, and social geography'. In: P. Benedict (ed.), *Cities and Social Change in Early Modern France*. London: Routledge.

Desgrouais, M., 1766. *Les Gasconismes corrigés*. Toulouse: Robert.

Désirat, C. and Hordé, T., 1988. *La Langue française au 20ᵉ siècle*. Paris: Bordas.

Deutsch, K. W., 1968. 'The trend of European nationalism – the language aspect'. In: J. A. Fishman (ed.), *Readings in the Sociology of Language*. The Hague/Paris: Mouton.

Diderot, D. and d'Alembert, J., 1765. *Encyclopédie ou Dictionnaire raisonné des sciences, des arts et des métiers*. Paris: Briasson.

Doblhofer, E., 1959. *Le Déchiffrement des écritures*. Paris: Arthaud.

Dollinger, P., 1956. 'Le chiffre de population de Paris au XIVᵉ siècle'. *Revue historique*, 216: 35–44.

Domergue, U., 1778. *Grammaire générale*. Paris: Houel.

Dorian, N., 1973. 'Grammatical change in a dying dialect'. *Language*, 49: 413–38.

Dottin, G., 1920. *La Langue gauloise*. Paris: Klincksieck.

Drinkwater, J. F., 1983. *Roman Gaul*. London: Croom Helm.

Droixhe, D., 1971. 'L'orientation structurale de la linguistique au XVIIIᵉ siècle'. *Français Moderne*, 39: 18–32.

Drosai, J., 1544. *Grammaticae quadrilinguis partitiones*. Paris: Perier.

Dubois, C. G., 1970. *Mythe et langage au XVIᵉ siècle*. Bordeaux: Ducros.

Dubois, C. G., 1972. *Le Développement littéraire d'un mythe nationaliste*. Paris: Université de Paris.

Dubois, J., 1531. *In Linguam gallicam isagoge, una cum eiusdem grammatica Latino-Gallica*. Paris: R. Estienne.

Duby, G., 1980. *Histoire de la France urbaine* (5 vols). Paris: Seuil.

Dudley, D., 1975. *Roman Society*. Harmondsworth: Penguin.

Duval, P.-M., 1952. *La Vie quotidienne en Gaule pendant la paix romaine*. Paris: Hachette.

Duval, P.-M., 1972. 'De la préhistoire à la Gaule romaine'. In: A. François (ed.), *La France et les Français*. Paris: Pléiade.

Eisenstein, E. L., 1979. *The Printing Press as an Agent of Change* (2 vols). Cambridge: Cambridge University Press.

Elcock, W. D., 1960. *The Romance Languages*. London: Faber & Faber.

Ernst, G., 1985. *Gesprochenes Französisch zu Beginn des 17. Jahrhunderts*. (Zeitschrift für Romanische Philologie, Beiheft 204). Tübingen:

Niemeyer.

Estienne, H., 1565. *Traicté de la conformité du langage françois avec le grec.* Geneva: H. Estienne.

Estienne, H., 1578a. *Deux Dialogues du nouveau langage françois italianizé.* Geneva: H. Estienne.

Estienne, H., 1578b. *La Précellence du langage françois.* Paris: Mamert Patisson.

Estienne, H., 1582. *Hypomneses de gallica lingua.* Geneva: H. Estienne.

Estienne, R., 1557. *Traicté de la grammaire françoise.* Paris: R. Estienne.

Fabre, P., 1964. *Grammaire catalane.* Paris: Les Belles Lettres.

Falc'hun, F., 1963. *Histoire de la langue bretonne d'après la géographie linguistique, t. 1 texte.* Paris: PUF.

Falc'hun, F., 1977. *Les Origines de la langue bretonne.* Rennes: CRDP.

Falc'hun, F., 1981. *Perspectives nouvelles sur l'histoire de la langue bretonne.* Paris: Union Générale d'Editions.

Faral, E., 1924. *Les Arts poétiques du XIIe et du XIIIe siècle.* Paris: Champion.

Fasold, R., 1984. *The Sociolinguistics of Society.* Oxford: Blackwell.

Fauchet, C., 1581. *Recueil de l'origine de la langue et poésie françoise, ryme et romans* (2 vols). Paris: R. Estienne.

Féraud, J.-F., 1761. *Dictionnaire grammatical de la langue françoise.* Paris: Vincent.

Ferguson, C. A., 1959. 'Diglossia'. *Word*, 15: 325–40. Reprinted in P. P. Giglioli (ed.), *Language and Social Context*, 1972. Harmondsworth: Penguin. (This pagination is used here.)

Ferguson, C. A., 1968. 'Language development'. In: J. A. Fishman, C. A. Ferguson and J. Das Gupta (eds), *Language Problems of Developing Nations.* New York: Wiley.

Fierro-Domenech, A., 1986. *Le Pré carré.* Paris: Robert Laffont.

Fiorelli, P., 1950. 'Pour l'interprétation de l'ordonnance de Villers-Cottcrêts'. *Français Moderne*, 18: 277–88.

Fishman, J., 1967. 'Bilingualism with and without diglossia, diglossia with and without bilingualism'. *Journal of Social Issues*, 32: 29–38.

Fishman, J., 1972. *Language in Sociocultural Change.* Stanford: Stanford University Press.

Fishman, J. A., 1972. *Language and Nationalism: Two Integrative Essays.* Rowley, Mass.: Newbury House.

Fishman, J. A., 1985. *Sociolinguistics in France.* Berlin/New York: Mouton.

Fleuriot, L., 1982. *Les Origines de la Bretagne.* Paris: Payot.

Foulet, L. and Foulon, C., 1944–5. 'Les scènes de taverne et les comptes du tavernier dans le *Jeu de S. Nicolas* de Jean Bodel'. *Romania*, 68: 422–43.

Fournier, P.-F., 1955. 'La persistance du gaulois au VIe siècle'. In: *Recueil de travaux offerts à M. Clovis Brunel, t. 1.* Paris: Société de l'Ecole des Chartes.

Francis, W. N., 1983. *Dialectology: an Introduction.* London: Longman.

François, A., 1936. 'D'une préfiguration de la langue classique au XVIe siècle'. In: *Mélanges offerts à M. Abel Lefranc.* Paris: Droz.

REFERENCES

François, A., 1959. *Histoire de la langue française cultivée des origines à nos jours* (2 vols). Geneva: A. Jullien.

Furet, F. and Ozouf, J., 1977. *Lire et écrire: l'alphabétisation des Français de Calvin à Jules Ferry* (2 vols). Paris: Éditions de Minuit.

Furetière, A., 1690. *Dictionnaire universel*. Rotterdam: A. et R. Leers.

Gadet, F., 1989. *Le Français ordinaire*. Paris: Colin.

Gal, S., 1979. *Language Shift*. New York: Academic Press.

Gamillscheg, E., 1938. 'Germanische Siedlung in Belgien und Nordfrankreich', *Abhandlungen der preussischen Akademie der Wissenschaften*, XII.

Gardette, P., 1983. *Etudes de géographie linguistique*. Paris: Klincksieck.

Gardette, P., 1983a. 'Une grande méconnue: la langue lyonnaise'. In: *Etudes de géographie linguistique*. Paris: Klincksieck.

Gardette, P., 1983b. 'Le francoprovençal, son histoire, ses origines'. In: *Etudes de géographie linguistique*. Paris: Klincksieck.

Gardette, P., 1983c. 'La romanisation du domaine franco-provençal'. In: *Etudes de géographie linguistique*. Paris: Klincksieck.

Gardner, R., 1965. 'Some observations on syntax and morphology in the *Sottie des rapporteurs*, and the *Sottie des sots formés de malice*'. In: J. Mahoney and J. E. Keller (eds), *Medieval Studies in Honor of U. T. Holmes Jr*. Chapel Hill: North Carolina University Press.

Garmadi, J., 1981. *La Sociolinguistique*. Paris: PUF.

Gauchat, L., 1903. 'Gibt es Mundartgrenzen?' *Archiv für das Studium der Neuren Sprachen und Literaturen*, 111: 365–403.

Gazier, A., 1880. *Lettres à Grégoire sur les patois de la France (1790–1794)*. Paris: Durand.

Genicot, L. (ed.), 1973. *Histoire de la Wallonie*. Toulouse: Privat.

Giles, H., 1970. 'Evaluative reactions to accents', *Educational Review*, 22: 211–27.

Gilliéron, J. and Edmont, E., 1903–10. *Atlas linguistique de la France*. Paris: Champion.

Girault-Duvivier, C.-P., 1811. *Grammaire des grammaires*. Paris: Cotelle.

Glatigny, M., 1989. 'Norme et usage dans le français du XVIᵉ siècle'. In: P. Swiggers and W. van Hoeke (eds), *La Langue française au XVIᵉ siècle*. Louvain: Leuven University Press.

Gonon, M., 1973. 'Etat d'un parler franco-provençal dans un village forézien en 1974'. *Ethnologie Française*, 3: 271–86.

Gordon, D. C., 1978. *The French Language and National Identity*. The Hague: Mouton.

de Gorog, R. P., 1958. *The Scandinavian Element in French and Norman*. New York: Bookman.

Gossen, C.-T., 1957. 'Die Einheit der französischen Schriftsprache im 15. und 16. Jahrhundert'. *Zeitschrift für Romanische Philologie*, 73: 427–59.

Gossen, C.-T., 1962. 'Langues écrites du domaine d'oïl'. *Revue de Linguistique Romane*, 26: 271–308.

Gossen, C.-T., 1967. *Französische Skriptastudien*. Vienna: Österreichische Akademie der Wissenschaften.

Gossen, C.-T., 1969. Sprachgrenzen im Poitou. *Vox Romanica*, 29: 59–71.

Grafström, A., 1958. *Etude sur la graphie des plus anciennes chartes langue-dociennes avec un essai d'interprétation phonétique*. Uppsala: Almquist & Wiksells.

Green, J. N. and Hintze, M. A., 1988. 'A reconsideration of *liaison* and *enchaînement*.' In: C. Slater, J. Durand and M. Bate (eds), *French Sound Patterns: Changing Perspectives* (AFLS Occasional Papers 2). AFLS and Department of Language and Linguistics, University of Essex.

Grevisse, M., 1986. *Le Bon Usage*, 12th edn. Gembloux: Duculot.

Grillo, R., 1989. *Dominant Languages*. Cambridge: Cambridge University Press.

Guernes de Pont Sainte-Maxence, 1936. *La Vie de Saint Thomas Becket*, ed. E. Walberg. Paris: Classiques français du moyen âge, 77.

Gueunier, N., Genouvrier, E. and Khomsi, A., 1978. *Les Français devant la norme*. Paris: Champion.

Gueunier, N., Genouvrier, E. and Khomsi, A., 1983. 'Les Français devant la norme'. In: E. Bédard and J. Maurais (eds), *La Norme linguistique*. Quebec: Le Robert.

Guinet, L., 1982. *Les Emprunts gallo-romains au germanique (du 1er à la fin du Ve siècle)*. Paris: Klincksieck.

Guiraud, P., 1965. *Le Français populaire*. Paris: PUF (Que Sais-Je?).

Guiraud, P., 1966. *Le Moyen Français*. Paris: PUF (Que Sais-Je?).

Guiraud, P., 1968. *Le Jargon de Villon*. Paris: Gallimard.

Guiraud, P., 1976. *L'Argot*. Paris: PUF (Que Sais-Je?).

Gysseling, M., 1962. 'La genèse de la frontière linguistique dans le nord de la Gaule'. *Revue du Nord*, 44: 5–37.

Haarhoff, T. J., 1958. *Schools of Gaul*. Johannesburg: Witwatersrand University Press.

Hadjadj, D., 1983. *Parlers en contact aux confins de l'Auvergne et du Forez. Etude Sociolinguistique*. Clermont-Ferrand: Institut d'Etudes du Massif Central.

Hadjadj, D., 1989. 'La survie du parler dialectal'. In: D. Hadjadj (ed.), *Pays de Thiers. Le regard et la mémoire*. Clermont-Ferrand: Institut d'études du Massif Central.

Hagège, C., 1987. *Le Français et les siècles*. Paris: Odile Jacob.

Hall, R. A., 1949. 'The linguistic position of Franco-Provençal'. *Language*, 25: 1–14.

Hall, R. A., 1950. 'The reconstruction of Proto-Romance'. *Language*, 26: 6–27.

Hall, R. A., 1974. *External History of the Romance Languages*. New York: Elsevier.

Halliday, M. A. K., 1964. 'The users and uses of language'. Repr. in J. Fishman (ed.), *Readings in the Sociology of Language*, 1968, The Hague: Mouton.

Harris, M., 1978. *The Evolution of French Syntax*. London: Longman.

Harris, M. and Vincent, N. (eds), 1988. *The Romance Languages*. London: Croom Helm.

Hatt, J.-J., 1959. *Histoire de la Gaule romaine*. Paris: Payot.

Hatt, J.-J., 1972. *Celtes et Gallo-romains*. Paris: Nagel.

Haugen, E., 1962. 'Schizoglossia and the linguistic norm'. In: R.

REFERENCES

O'Brien (ed.), *Monograph Series on Languages and Linguistics*, vol. 15. Washington: Georgetown University.

Haugen, E., 1966. 'Dialect, language, nation'. Repr. in J. B. Pride and J. Holmes, *Sociolinguistics*, 1972, Harmondsworth: Penguin.

Haugen, E., 1972. *Ecology of Language*. Stanford: Stanford University Press.

Hausmann, F. J., 1979. 'Wie alt ist das gesprochene Französisch?' *Romanische Forschungen*, 91: 431–44.

Herman, J., 1967. *Le Latin vulgaire*. Paris: PUF (Que Sais-Je?).

Herman, J., 1978. 'Du latin épigraphique au latin provincial: essai de sociologie linguistique sur la langue des inscriptions'. In: *Etrennes de Septanaine: Travaux . . . offerts à Michel Lejeune*. Paris: Klincksieck.

Herman, J., 1985. 'La différentiation territoriale du latin et la formation des langues romanes'. *Linguistique comparée et typologie des langues romanes*. *Actes du XVIIᵉ Congrès internationale de linguistique et philologie romanes* (Aix-en-Provence, 29 août–3 septembre 1983), Aix-en-Provence, t. 2, pp. 13–62.

Hilty, G., 1968. 'La séquence de Sainte Eulalie et les origines de la langue littéraire française', *Vox Romanica*, 27: 4–18.

Hilty, G., 1973. 'Les origines de la langue littéraire française'. *Vox Romanica*, 32: 254–71.

Honey, J., 1989. *Does Accent Matter?* London: Faber and Faber.

Hope, T. E., 1971. *Lexical Borrowing in the Romance languages* (2 vols). Oxford: Blackwell.

Hubschmied, J. U., 1938. 'Sprachliche Zeugen für das späte Aussterben des Gallischen'. *Vox Romanica*, 3: 48–115.

Huchon, M., 1988. *Le Français de la Renaissance*. Paris: PUF (Que Sais-Je?).

Hudson, R. A., 1980. *Sociolinguistics*. Cambridge: Cambridge University Press.

Hugo, A., 1835. *La France pittoresque*. Paris: Delloye.

Hugues Faidit, 1969. *Donat proensal*, ed. J. H. Marshall. London: Oxford University Press.

von Humboldt, W , 1836. *Über die Kawi Sprache auf der Insel Java, nebst einer Einleitung über die Verschiedenheit des menschlichen Sprachbaues und ihren Einfluss auf die geistige Entwicklung des Menschengeschlechts*. Berlin: Akademie der Wissenschaften.

Hunnius, K., 1975. 'Archaische Züge des langage populaire'. *Zeitschrift für Französische Sprache und Literatur*, 85: 145–61.

Hymes, D., 1967. 'Models of the interaction of language and social settings'. *Journal of Social Issues*, 23: 8–28.

Hymes, D., 1971. 'On communicative competence'. Repr. in J. B. Pride and J. Holmes (eds), *Sociolinguistics: Selected Readings*, 1972, Harmondsworth: Penguin.

Jacob, P. L. (ed.), 1900. *Cyrano de Bergerac: Oeuvres comiques*. Paris: Garnier.

James, E., 1982. *The Origins of France, 500–1000*. London: Macmillan.

James, E., 1988. *The Franks*. Oxford: Blackwell.

Janson, T., 1979. *Mechanisms of Language Change in Latin*. Stockholm:

Almquist & Wiksells.

Jochnowitz, G., 1973. *Dialect Boundaries and the Question of Franco-Provençal*. The Hague/Paris: Mouton.

Jofre de Foixa, 1880. *Regles de trobar*, ed. P. Meyer. *Romania* 9: 51–86.

Johnson, J., 1946. *Etude sur les noms de lieu dans lesquels entrent les éléments 'court', 'ville' et 'villiers'*. Paris: Droz.

Joos, M., 1962. *The Five Clocks*. New York: Harcourt.

Joris, A., 1966. 'On the edge of two worlds in the heart of the new empire: the Romance regions of northern Gaul during the Merovingian period'. *Studies in Medieval and Renaissance History*, 3: 3–52.

Jouin, N., 1730. *Harangues des habitants de la paroisse de Sarcelles*. Aix: Girand.

Keller, H.-E., 1964a. 'Survivances de l'ancien saxon en Normandie'. In: *Mélanges de linguistique romane efforts à M. Delbouille, t. 1*. Gembloux: Duculot.

Keller, K. H., 1964b. 'The language of the Franks'. *Bulletin of the John Rylands Library*. 47: 101–22.

Krepinsky, M., 1958. 'La naissance des langues romanes et l'existence d'une période de leur évolution commune'. *Rozpravy CSAV*, Série SV, 13: 1–55.

La Ramée, P. de, 1562. *Gramère*. Paris: Wéchel.

Labov, W., 1970. 'The study of language in its social context'. Repr. in J. B. Pride and J. Holmes (eds), *Sociolinguistics*, 1972, Harmondsworth: Penguin.

Labov, W., 1973. *Sociolinguistic Patterns*. Pennsylvania: Pennsylvania University Press.

Lambley, K. R., 1920. *The Teaching and Cultivation of the French Language in England during Tudor and Stuart Times*. Manchester: Manchester University Press.

Lapierre, J.-W., 1988. *Le Pouvoir politique et les langues*. Paris: PUF.

La Rue, A. and Casciani, C., 1986. *Dictionnaire d'argot*. Paris: Flammarion.

Lefebvre, A., 1988. 'Les langues du domaine d'oïl'. In: G. Vermes (ed.), *Vingt-cinq communautés linguistiques de la France*. Paris: Logiques Sociales. L'Harmattan.

Leith, D., 1983. *A Social History of English*. London: Routledge and Kegan Paul.

Lemaire des Belges, J., 1611. *Concorde des deux langaiges*. Paris: Marnef et Viant.

Léon, P. R., 1973. 'Modèle standard et système vocalique du français populaire des jeunes Parisiens'. In: G. Rondeau (ed.), *Current Trends in Applied Linguistics*. Montreal: GEC.

Le Page, R. B. and Tabouret-Keller, A., 1985. *Acts of Identity*. Cambridge: Cambridge University Press.

Lévy, P., 1929. *Histoire linguistique d'Alsace et de Lorraine, t. 1: Des origines à la Révolution française; t. 2: De la Révolution à 1918*. Paris: Les Belles Lettres.

Lewicka, H., 1971. 'Langue d'oïl et langue d'oc dans le théâtre du midi de la France'. In: I. Cluzel and F. Pirot (eds), *Mélanges de philologie romane dédiés à la mémoire de Jean Boutière (1899–1967), t. 1*. Liège: Soledi.

Lewicka, H., 1974. *Etudes sur l'ancienne farce française*. Paris: Klincksieck.

Leys d'Amor, 1919, ed. J. Anglade. Toulouse: Bibliothèque méridionale.

Lhomond, Ch.-F., 1780. *Elémens de la grammaire françoise*. Paris: Colas.

Livet, Ch.-L., 1858. *Histoire de l'Académie française* (2 vols). Paris: Didier.

Lloyd, P., 1979. 'On the definition of Vulgar Latin'. *Neuphilologische Mitteilungen*, 80: 110–22.

Lloyd, P., 1991. 'On the names of languages (and other things)'. In: R. Wright (ed.), 1991, *Latin and the Romance Languages in the Early Middle Ages*. London: Routledge.

Lodge, R. A., 1979. *Etienne de Fougères: Le Livre des Manières*. Geneva: Droz.

Lodge, R. A., 1985. *Le Plus Ancien Registre de comptes des consuls de Montferrand en provençal auvergnat 1259–72, t. 49*. Clermont-Ferrand: Mémoires de l'Académie.

Lodge, R. A., 1989. 'Speakers' perceptions of non-standard vocabulary in French'. *Zeitschrift für Romanische Philologie*, 105: 427–44.

Lodge, R. A., 1991. 'Molière's peasants and the norms of spoken French'. *Neuphilologische Mitteilungen*, 92: 485–99.

Lodge, R. A. and Varty, K., 1989. *The Earliest Branches of the Roman de Renart*. Perthshire: Lochee Publications.

Löfstedt, E., 1959. *Late Latin*. Oslo: Aschebourg.

Lorian, A., 1967. 'Les latinismes de syntaxe en français'. *Zeitschrift für Romanische Philologie*, 77: 155–69.

Loriot, R., 1967. *La Frontière dialectale moderne en Haute-Normandie*. Amiens: Musée de la Picardie.

Lot, F., 1929. 'L'état des paroisses et des feux en 1328'. *Bibliothèque de l'Ecole des Chartes*, 90: 51–107, 256–315.

Lot, F., 1931. 'A quelle époque a-t-on cessé de parler latin?' *Archivum Latinitatis Medii Aevi (Bulletin du Cange)*, 6: 97–159.

Loyseau, C., 1614. *Traité des ordres et simples dignitez*. Paris: L'Angelier.

Lüdtke, H., 1962. 'Die Verkehrswege des Römanischen Reiches und die Herausbildung der romanischen Dialekte'. In: *Actes du Xe Congrès international de linguistique et philologie romanes Strasbourg 1962, t. II*. Paris.

Lugge, M., 1960. *'Gallia' und 'Francia' im Mittelalter*. Bonn: Röhrscheid.

Lusignan, S., 1987. *Parler vulgairement. Les Intellectuels et la langue française aux XIIIe et XIVe siècles*. Paris/Montreal: Vrin.

Malherbe, F. de, 1630. *Les Oeuvres de M. de Malherbe*. Paris: Chappellain.

Marchello-Nizia, C., 1979. *Histoire de la langue française aux XIVe et XVe siècles*. Paris: Bordas.

Marot, C., 1533. *Les Oeuvres de François Villon de Paris*. Paris: du Pré.

Martinet, A., 1945. *La Prononciation du français contemporain*. Geneva: Droz.

Martinet, A., 1969. *Le Français sans fard*. Paris: PUF.

Marzys, Z., 1974. 'La formation de la norme du français cultivé'.

Kwartalnik Neofilologiczny, 21: 315–32.

Matoré, G., 1968. *Histoire des dictionnaires français*. Paris: Larousse.

Mauger, C, 1706. *Nouvelle Grammaire françoise*. Rouen: Besogne.

Maurand, G., 1981. 'Situation linguistique d'une communauté rurale en domaine occitan'. *International Journal of the Sociology of Language*, 29: 99–119.

Meigret, L., 1550. *Le Trętté de la grammęre françoęze*. Paris: Wéchel.

Meillet, A., 1928. *Esquisse d'une histoire de la langue latine*. Paris: Hachette.

Merle, P., 1986. *Dictionnaire du français branché*. Paris: Seuil.

Meyer, P., 1875. Review of G. T. Ascoli, *Schizzi franco-provenzali*. *Romania*, 4: 294–6.

Meyer, P., 1889. 'La langue romane du midi de la France et ses différents noms'. *Annales du Midi*, 1: 11.

Millardet, G., 1922. 'Linguistique et dialectologie romanes'. *Revue des langues romanes*, 61: 1–160, 193–386; 62: 1–157.

Milroy, J. and Milroy, L., 1985a. *Authority in Language*. London: Routledge & Kegan Paul.

Milroy, J. and Milroy, L., 1985b. 'Linguistic change, social network and speaker innovation'. *Journal of Linguistics*, 21: 339–84.

Milroy, L., 1987. *Language and Social Networks* (2nd edn). Oxford: Blackwell.

Molière, J. P. de, 1971. *Les Précieuses ridicules*, ed. G. Couton. In *Oeuvres complètes*, Paris: Gallimard.

Monfrin, J., 1963. 'Humanisme et traductions au moyen âge'. *Journal des Savants*, 161–90.

Monfrin, J., 1964. 'Les traducteurs et leur public en France au moyen âge'. *Journal des Savants*, 5–20.

Monfrin, J., 1968. 'Le mode de tradition des actes écrits et les études en dialectologie'. *Revue de Linguistique Romane* 32: 17–47.

Monfrin, J., 1972. 'Les parlers en France'. In: A. François (ed.), *La France et les Français*. Paris: Pléiade.

de Montaigne, M., 1967. *Essais*, ed. R. Barral. Paris: Seuil.

Moore, A. P., 1935. *The 'Genre poissard' and the French Stage of the Eighteenth Century*. New York: Columbia University Press.

Mounin, G., 1975. 'La répression linguistique dans les groupes humains'. *Archivum Linguisticum*, 6: 65–70.

Müller, B., 1971. 'La bi-partition linguistique de la France'. *Revue de Linguistique Romane*, 35: 17–30.

Müller, B., 1974. 'La structure linguistique de la France et la romanisation'. *Travaux de Langue et de Littérature de Strasbourg*, 12: 7–29.

Müller, B., 1985. *Le Français d'aujourd'hui*. Paris: Klincksieck.

Muller, H. F., 1921. 'When did Latin cease to be a spoken language in France?' *Romanic Review*, 12: 318.

Muller, H. F., 1929. *A chronology of Vulgar Latin*. (Zeitschrift für Romanische Philologie, Beiheft 78). Tübingen: Niemeyer.

Musset, L., 1975. *The Germanic Invasions*, trans. E. and C. James. London: Paul Elek.

Nezirovic, M., 1980. *Le Vocabulaire dans deux versions du Roman de Thèbes*.

Clermont-Ferrand: Association des Publications de la Faculté des Lettres de Clermont-Ferrand.

Nicot, J., 1606. *Trésor de la langue françoise*. Paris: Douceur.

Nisard, C., 1872. *Etude sur le langage populaire ou patois de Paris et de sa banlieue*. Paris: Franck.

Norberg, D., 1966. 'A quelle époque a-t-on cessé de parler latin en Gaule?' *Annales ESC*, 2: 346–56.

Nouguier, E., 1987. *Dictionnaire d'argot*. Paris: Even.

Offord, M., 1990. *Varieties of Contemporary French*. London: Macmillan.

Padley, G. A., 1976. *Grammatical Theory in Western Europe 1500–1700: the Latin Tradition*. Cambridge: Cambridge University Press.

Padley, G. A., 1983. 'La norme dans la tradition des grammairiens'. In: E. Bédard and J. Maurais (eds), *La Norme linguistique*. Quebec: Le Robert.

Palsgrave, J., 1530. *Lesclarcissement de la Langue Francoyse*. London: Hawkins.

Paris, G., 1888. *Les Parlers de France*. Discours prononcé à la réunion des sociétés savantes, le samedi 26 mai, Paris.

Pasturel, J., 1733. *Poésies auvergnates*. Riom: Thomas.

Pei, M. A., 1932. *The Language of 8th-Century Texts in Northern France*. New York: Columbia University Press.

Peletier du Mans, J., 1550. *Dialogue de l'ortografe é prononciacion françoese*. Poitiers: J. et E. de Marnef.

Pernoud, R., 1966. *La Formation de la France*. Paris: PUF (Que Sais-Je?).

Perrenot, T., 1942. *La Toponymie burgonde*. Paris: Payot.

Perrin, O., 1968. *Les Burgondes*. Neuchatel: Baconnière.

Petit-Dutaillis, C., 1950. *La Monarchie féodale en France et en Angleterre*. Paris: Albin Michel.

Petri, F., 1937. *Germanische Volkserbe in Wallonien und Nordfrankreich. Die fränkische Landnahme in Frankreich und den Niederlanden und die Bildung der westlichen Sprachgrenze* (2 vols). Bonn: Röhrscheid.

Petri, F., 1973. *Siedlung, Sprache und Bevolkerungstruktur*. Darmstadt: Wissenschaftliche Buchgesellschaft.

Peyre, H., 1933. *La Royauté et les langues provinçales*. Paris: Presses modernes.

Pfister, M., 1973a. 'La répartition géographique des éléments franciques en gallo-roman'. *Revue de Linguistique Romane*, 37: 126–49.

Pfister, M., 1973b. 'Die sprachliche Bedeutung von Paris und der Ile-de-France vor dem 13. Jahrhundert'. *Vox Romanica*, 32: 217–53.

Picoche, J. and Marchello-Nizia, C., 1989. *Histoire de la langue française*. Paris: Nathan.

Pignon, J., 1960. *Evolution phonétique des parlers du Poitou*. Paris: Artrey.

Pillot, J., 1550. *Gallicae Linguae institutio*. Paris: Grouleau.

Poerck, G. de, 1963. 'Les plus anciens textes de la langue française comme témoins d'époque'. *Revue de Linguistique Romane*, 27: 1–34.

Polomé, E. C., 1980. 'Creolization and diachronic linguistics'. In: A. Valdman and A. Highfield (eds), *Theoretical Orientations in Creole Studies*. New York: Academic Press.

Polomé, E. C., 1983. 'The linguistic situation in the western provinces of the Roman Empire'. In: H. Temporini and W. Haase (eds), *Aufstieg und Niedergang der Römischen Welt*, t. 29. Berlin/New York: de Gruyter.

Pope, M. K., 1952. *From Latin to Modern French*. Manchester: Manchester University Press.

Pottier, B., 1968. 'La situation linguistique en France'. In: A. Martinet (ed.), *Le Langage*. Paris: Pléiade.

Price, G., 1984. *The Languages of Britain*. London: Arnold.

Pride, J. B. and Holmes, J. (eds), 1972. *Sociolinguistics: Selected Readings*. Harmondsworth: Penguin.

Pulgram, A., 1950. 'Spoken and written Latin'. *Language*, 26: 458–66.

Quemada, B., 1968. *Les Dictionnaires du français moderne, 1539–1863*. Paris: Didier.

Quemada, B., 1972. *Matériaux pour l'histoire du vocabulaire français*. Paris: Didier.

Quéré, L., 1987. 'Le statut duel de la langue dans l'état-nation'. In: G. Vermes et J. Boulet (eds), *France, pays multilingue*. Paris: Logiques Sociales. L'Harmattan.

Rabelais, F., 1533. *Pantagruel*, ed. P. Jourda, 1962. Paris: Garnier.

Raimon Vidal de Besalu, 1878, *Razos de trobar*, ed. E. Stengel. Marburg: Marburg University Press.

Rauhut, F., 1963. 'Warum wurde Paris die Hauptstadt Frankreichs?' In: H. Bihler and A. Noyer-Weidner (eds), *Medium Aevum Romanicum Festschrift für H. Reinfelder*. Munich: Hüber.

Reichenkron, G., 1965. *Historische latein–altromanische Grammatik*. Wiesbaden: Harrassowitz.

Reichstein, R., 1960. 'Etude des variations sociales et géographiques des faits linguistiques.' *Word*, 16: 55–99.

Reid, T. B. W., 1958. *Twelve fabliaux*. Manchester: Manchester University Press.

Remacle, L., 1948. *Le Problème de l'ancien wallon*. Liège: Bibliothèque de la Faculté de Philosophie et Lettres.

Restaut, P., 1730. *Principes généraux et raisonnés de la langue françoise*. Paris: Le Gras.

Richelet, P., 1680. *Dictionnaire françois*. Geneva: J.-H. Widerhold.

Richter, M., 1975. 'A socio-linguistic approach to the Latin Middle Ages'. In: D. Baker (ed.), *Materials, Sources and Methods of Ecclesiastical History*. Oxford: Blackwell.

Richter, M., 1983. 'A quelle époque a-t-on cessé de parler latin en Gaule? A propos d'une question mal posée'. *Annales ESC*, 3: 439–48.

Rickard, P., 1968. *La Langue française au 16ᵉ siècle*. Cambridge: Cambridge University Press.

Rickard, P., 1976. *Chrestomathie de la langue française au XVᵉ siècle*. Cambridge: Cambridge University Press.

Rickard, P., 1981. *The Embarrassments of Irregularity: the French Language in the 18th Century*. Cambridge: Cambridge University Press.

Rickard, P., 1989. *A History of the French Language* (2nd edn). London: Hutchinson.

de Rivarol, A., 1784. *De l'Universalité de la langue française; discours qui a*

remporté le prix à l'Académie de Berlin, ed. H. Juin. Paris: Belfond.
Robertson, D. M., 1910. *The French Academy*. London: Fisher Unwin.
Robson, C. A., 1963. 'L'*Appendix Probi* et la philologie latine'. *Le Moyen Age*, 69: 39–54.
Rohlfs, G., 1970. *Le Gascon, études de philologie pyrénéenne*. (Zeitschrift für Romanische Philologie, Beiheft 85). Tübingen: Niemeyer.
Romaine, S. and Reid, E., 1976. 'Glottal sloppiness? – a sociolinguistic view of urban speech in Scotland'. *Teaching English*, 9: 3.
de Ronsard, P., 1565. 'Art poétique'. In: P. Laumonier (ed.), *Oeuvres complètes, t. XIV*. Paris, 1914: Hachette.
de Ronsard, P., 1578. 'Préface sur la Franciade'. In: P. Laumonier (ed.), *Oeuvres complètes, t. XVI*. Paris, 1914: Hachette.
Rosset, T., 1911. *Les Origines de la prononciation moderne étudiées au XVIIe siècle, d'après les remarques des grammairiens et les textes en patois de la banlieue parisienne*. Paris: Colin.
Rouche, M., 1979. *L'Aquitaine des Wisigoths aux Arabes, 418–781*. Paris: Touzot.
Ryan, E. B., 1979. 'Why do low-prestige language varieties persist?' In: H. Giles and R. Sinclair (eds), *Language and Social Psychology*. Oxford: Blackwell.
Ryan, E. B. and Giles, H., 1982. *Attitudes towards Language Variation*. London: Edward Arnold.
Sainéan, L., 1907. *L'Argot ancien*. Paris: Champion.
Sainéan, L., 1920. *Le Langage parisien au XIXe siècle*. Paris: Boccard.
Sandry, G. and Carrière, M., 1980. *Dictionnaire de l'argot moderne*. Paris: Dauphin.
de Saussure, F., 1915. *Cours de linguistique générale*. Paris: Payot.
Sauvageot, A., 1964. *Portrait du vocabulaire français*. Paris: Larousse.
Sauzet, P., 1988. 'L'occitan. Langue immolée'. In: G. Vermes (ed.), *Vingt-cinq communautés linguistiques de la France, t. 1*. Paris: L'Harmattan.
Schlieben-Lange, B., 1976. 'L'origine des langues romanes – un cas de créolisation'. In: J. M. Meisel (ed.), *Langues en contact – Pidgins-créoles*. Tübingen: Gunter Narr.
Schlieben-Lange, B., 1977. 'The language situation in southern France'. *International Journal of the Sociology of Language*, 12: 101–9.
Schmidt, C., 1974. *Die Sprachlandschaften der Galloromania*. Frankfurt: Lang.
Seguin, J. P., 1972. *La Langue française au XVIIIe siècle*. Paris: Bordas.
Séguy, J., 1950. *Le Français parlé à Toulouse*. Toulouse/Paris: Privat.
Simoni-Aurembou, M.-R., 1989. 'La couverture géolinguistique de l'Empire Français: l'enquête de la Parabole de l'Enfant Prodigue'. In: *Espaces romans. Etudes de dialectologie et de géolinguistique offertes à Gaston Tuaillon, t. II*. Grenoble: Ellug.
Steinmeyer, G., 1979. *Historische Aspekte des français avancé*. Geneva: Droz.
Stimm, H., 1980. *Zur Geschichte des gesprochenen Französisch und zur Sprachlenkung im Gegenwartsfranzösischen*. Wiesbaden: Steiner.
Straka, G., 1956. 'La dislocation linguistique de la Romania et la forma-

tion des langues romanes à la lumière de la chronologie relative des changements phonétiques'. *Revue de Linguistique Romane*, 20: 249–67.

Swiggers, P., 1987. 'A l'ombre de la clarté française'. *Langue Française*, 75: 5–21.

Swiggers, P. and van Hoecke, W., 1989. *La Langue française au XVI* siècle: usage, enseignement et approches descriptives*. Louvain: Leuven University Press.

Tabouret-Keller, A., 1981. 'Introduction: regional languages in France. Current research in rural situations'. *International Journal of the Sociology of Language*, 29: 5–14.

Thévenot, E., 1948. *Les Gallo-Romains*. Paris: PUF.

Thurot, C., 1881. *De la Prononciation française depuis le commencement du XVI* siècle, d'après les témoignages des grammairiens*, 3 vols. Paris: Imprimerie Nationale Hachette.

Tory, G., 1529. *Champfleury*, facsimile edition, 1931. Paris: Bosse.

Trudeau, D., 1983. 'L'Ordonnance de Villers-Cotterêts, histoire ou interprétation'. In: *Bibliothèque d'Humanisme et Renaissance*, 45: 461–72.

Trudgill, P., 1983. *Sociolinguistics*. Harmondsworth: Pelican.

Trudgill, P., 1986. *Dialects in Contact*. Oxford: Blackwell.

van Uytfanghe, M., 1976. 'Le latin des hagiographes mérovingiens et la protohistoire du français'. *Romanica Gandensia*, 16: 5–89.

Väänänen, V., 1959. *Le Latin vulgaire des inscriptions pompéiennes*, 2nd edn. Berlin: Abhandlungen der Deutschen Akademie der Wissenschaften zu Berlin.

Väänänen, V., 1983. 'Le problème de la diversification du latin'. In: W. Haase (ed.), *Aufstieg und Niedergang der römischen Welt, t. 11*. Berlin/ New York: de Gruyter.

Vadé, J.-J., 1759–60. *Oeuvres*. The Hague: Gosse.

Valdman, A., 1976. *Introduction to French Phonology and Morphology*. Rowley, Mass.: Newbury House.

Valdman, A. (ed.), 1979. *Le Français hors de France*. Paris: Champion.

Valdman, A., 1988. 'Introduction'. In: G. Vermes (ed.), *Vingt-cinq Communautés linguistiques de la France, t. 1*, pp. 7–28. Paris: Logiques Sociales. L'Harmatton.

Van de Vyver, A., 1939. 'Les traductions du "De Consolatione philosophie"', *Humanisme et Renaissance*, 6: 247–73.

de Vaugelas, C. V., 1647. *Remarques sur la langue française*, ed. J. Streicher. Geneva: Slatkine Reprints, 1970.

Verlinden, C., 1956. *Les Origines de la frontière linguistique en Belgique et la colonisation franque*. Brussels: Renaissance du Livre.

Vermes, G. (ed.), 1988. *Vingt-cinq Communautés linguistiques de la France, t. 1*. Paris: Logique Sociales. L'Harmattan.

Vermes, G. and Boulet, J. (eds), 1987. *France, pays multilingue, t. 1: Les Langues en France, un enjeu historique et social; t. 2: Pratiques des langues en France*. Paris: Logiques Sociales. L'Harmattan.

Vial, E., 1983. *Les Noms de villes et de villages*. Paris: Belin.

Vielliard, J., 1927. *Le Latin des diplômes royaux et chartes privées de l'époque mérovingienne*. Paris: Champion.

Vigier, P., 1979. 'Diffusion d'une langue nationale et résistance des patois en France au XIXe siècle'. *Romantisme*, 25–6: 191–208.

Wacker, G., 1916. *Über das Verhältnis von Dialekt und Schriftsprache*. Halle: Niemeyer.

Walter, H., 1982. *Enquête phonologique et variétés régionales du français*. Paris: PUF.

Walter, H., 1984a. 'Patois ou français régional?' *Français Moderne*, 52: 183–90.

Walter, H., 1984b. 'L'innovation lexicale chez les jeunes Parisiens'. *La Linguistique*, 20: 69–84.

Walter, H., 1987. 'Toponymie, histoire et linguistique: l'invasion franque en Gaule'. In: *Actes du XIIIe Colloque international de linguistique fonctionnelle (Corfou 1986)*. Paris: SILF.

Walter, H., 1988. *Le Français dans tous les sens*. Paris: Laffont.

Wardhaugh, R., 1986. *An Introduction to Sociolinguistics*. Oxford: Blackwell.

Wardhaugh, R., 1987. *Languages in Competition*. Oxford: Blackwell.

Warnant, L., 1973. 'Dialectes ou français régionaux'. *Langue Française*, 18: 100–25.

von Wartburg, W., 1939. *Die Entstehung der romanischen Völker*. Halle-Saale: Niemeyer.

von Wartburg, W., 1951. *Ausgliederung der romanischen Sprachraüme*. Berne: Francke.

von Wartburg, W., 1962. *Evolution et structure de la langue française*, 6th edn. Berne: Franke.

von Wartburg, W., 1967. *La Fragmentation linguistique de la Romania*. Paris: Klincksieck.

Weber, E., 1977. *Peasants into Frenchmen. The Modernization of Rural France, 1870–1914*. London: Chatto and Windus.

Weinreich, U., 1968. *Languages in Contact*. Paris: Mouton.

Weinreich, U., Labov, W. and Herzog, M., 1968. 'Empirical foundations for a theory of language change'. In: U. Lehmann and Y. Malkiel (eds), *Directions for Historical Linguistics*. Austin: Texas University Press.

Whatmough, J., 1970. *The Dialects of Ancient Gaul*. Harvard: Harvard University Press.

Williamson, R. C. and van Eerde, J. A. (eds), 1980. 'Language maintenance and language shift'. *International Journal of the Sociology of Language*, 25.

Woledge, B., 1970. 'Un scribe champenois devant un texte normand: Guiot copiste de Wace'. In: *Mélanges offerts à Jean Frappier, t. 2*. Geneva: Droz.

Wolf, L., 1983. 'La normalisation du langage en France. De Malherbe à Grevisse'. In: E. Bédard and J. Maurais (eds), *La Norme linguistique*. Quebec: Le Robert.

Wolff, P., 1971. *Western Languages AD 100–1500*, trans. F. Partridge. London: Weidenfeld and Nicolson.

Wright, R., 1982. *Late Latin and Early Romance*. London: Francis Cairns.

Wright, R. (ed.), 1991. *Latin and the Romance Languages in the Early Middle Ages*. London: Routledge.

Wüest, J., 1969. 'Sprachgrenzen im Poitou'. *Vox Romanica*, 29: 14–58.
Wüest, J., 1979. *La Dialectalisation de la Gallo-Romania*. Berne: Francke.
Wüest, J., 1985. 'Le patois de Paris et l'histoire du français'. *Vox Romanica*, 44: 234–58.
Wyld, H. C., 1920. *A History of Modern Colloquial English*. Oxford: Oxford University Press.
Yaguello, M., 1978. *Les Mots et les femmes*. Paris: Payot.
Yaguello, M., 1988. *Catalogue des idées reçues sur la langue*. Paris: Seuil.
Yates, F. A., 1947. *The French Academies of the Sixteenth Century*. London: Warburg Institute.
Zinc, M., 1976. *La Prédication en langue romane avant 1300*. Paris: Champion.

INDEX

Académie Française 3, 134, 159–61, 174, 210, 236; and provincial academies 196
Accademia della Crusca 134, 160
acceptance, of the standard language 25, 188–229
accommodation, between dialects 13, 90
adstratum influences 20
Agde 39, 47
age, a factor in language variation 240–1
Aix-en-Provence 125
Alamans 47, 50, 59, 61, 69
Albigensian heresy 122, 132
Alcuin 91
Alps 30, 39, 41, 45, 47, 69, 77, 78, 81
Alsace 54, 59, 61, 199, 211, 244; Alsatian language 5, 61, 202, 206
analogical changes 19
Anglo-Norman 6, 28, 65, 100, 113
Anglo-Saxon 91, 118
Antibes 39, 47
Appendix Probi 88
Aquitania, Aquitaine 39, 45, 47–9, 65–8, 69, 83; Aquitani 42, 52; Aquitanian language 48, 53, 68
Arab-speaking countries 13; Arabs 56, 67, 109
argot 4, 86, 146, 198, 229, 235, 250, 251, 252

Arian heresy 66
Arles 68, 93, 102
Armorica *see* Brittany
Arras 98, 143, 144
Asia Minor 30, 50
Austrasia 59–60, 63, 67, 69, 70
Autun 45, 102
Auvergne 48, 120, 191, 196–7, 204; Auvergnat dialect 68, 74, 77, 196–7, 244

Babel, Tower of 162, 214
Basque: language 5, 17, 23, 39, 48, 68, 202, 214, 215, 219; people 67, 206
Béarn 211
Belgae 40, 42; Belgica 45, 49–51, 52, 83
Belgium 20, 23, 24, 28, 39, 54, 60, 86, 215
Beurs 250
Bible 36, 130
bilingualism 14–15, 61, 192, 202, 205
bon usage 99, 171, 175–7, 180, 190, 196, 198, 217
Bordeaux 45, 47, 67, 102, 143, 245; *parlement* 125
bourgeois, emergence of the term 109
Britain 5, 16, 33, 39, 54, 57, 222–3, 234; Britons 56, 57
Brittany 49, 54, 57, 65, 122, 198, 199; Breton language 5, 57, 86,

279

202, 206, 215, 219; decline of 227

Burgundia, Burgundy 69–71, 83, 122; Burgundians 56, 59, 69–71, 77, 79; development of the name 70; Romance dialect of Burgundy 77, 96, 97, 100, 195

Caesar, Julius 31, 40, 42, 47

Canada 6, 23, 24, 28, 86

Carolingians 59, 63, 70; educational reforms 91, 108, 129

Carthaginians 30

Castilian (cf. Spanish) 18

Catalonia 66; Catalan language 5, 18, 29, 55, 127, 202, 206, 215, 219; Catalan troubadours 111

Celts 39, 42; Celtic language 30, 33, 40, 50, 52 see also Gaulish

Cévennes 39, 211

Chalon-sur-Saône 93

Champagne 122; dialect 74, 113; markets of 103

Charlemagne 11, 91

Chartres 110, 168

chtimi 245

Church 36, 56, 68, 109; exclusive attitude to Latin 91–2, 108, 127; and the ideological cohesion of the Ancien Régime 210–1

Cicero 31, 35, 129

civitates 40, 45

class-based variation 245–50

'Classical Latin' 31, 89; 'Classical French' 135–7

Claudius Terentianus 35

Clermont-Ferrand 67, 106, 124–5, 196–7, 204, 247

Clovis 59, 102

code-switching 13, 142, 202

codification 26, 153–87, 233, 257

Collège de France 127, 129

Cologne 49, 59, 143

communicative competence 251

conscription 202, 217, 229

consonants, medial, evolution of Latin 73

contact of languages (interference phenomena) 20, 53, 55

continua 16; social 17; spatial 16, 72, 75–7; stylistic 17, 89–90, 256, 259; temporal 88

convergence of dialects 190–2

Coquebert-Montbret, E. 17–18, 200

Corsica 30, 33, 211; Corsican dialect 5, 202, 206, 219

Cour 143, 169–71, 176, 179

courtliness 109, 144

creolisation 51

'Croissant' (Crescent), dialect area 68, 77

Crusades 110, 112

cultural boundaries within France 81–2

Danish 18

Dante 96, 131

defence of the French language 236–7

developed v. undeveloped languages 22–3, 40, 118

dialect 5, 12, 14, 15–19; dialect boundaries 71–3, 78; difference between 'dialect' and 'language' 17–19; myth of 'pure dialect' 114

dictionaries, French 161–2, 257

diffusion of linguistic innovations 20–1, 42, 80–4; functional 42–4, 120–30; general conditions 190–2; of non-standard forms 33–4, 150, 189–90, 217, 229, 240; social 44; spatial 45; of the standard 188–229

diglossia 13–14, 33, 44, 89, 94–5, 116–17, 118–20, 148–52, 205, 233, 257–60

Druids 40, 44

Dutch 18

economy of effort, principle of in language change 19

Egypt 31

elaboration of function 26, 118–52, 252–3

elites 86, 130, 133, 169, 175, 196, 209–10

England, medieval 6, 20, 65, 91; English 6, 12, 17, 22, 23; American English 105, 240; Middle English 6, 86, 158
Etruscan 33

Fauchet, Claude 8, 136
Ferguson, C. A. 13–14, 150–1
Ferry, Jules 217, 219, 224
field 13, 252
Flanders 50, 62, 109, 198, 199, 211; Flemish language 5, 20, 60, 206
focused communities 24, 85–6, 178, 233
foederati 59, 65, 69
français familier 4, 17, 231–2, 246
français populaire 5, 17, 148, 231–2, 235; difficulties with the term 246–7
français régional 5, 231–2, 242–5
France, meanings of the term 97, 122
Franche-Comté 211
Francian 7, 97
François I 126, 134
Francophone Africa 28
Franco-Provençal 55, 71, 77–8, 83, 96, 194
Franks 47, 50, 56, 57–65, 66, 67, 68, 79; development of the name 63
French: names for the language 97, 101, 126–7; Old French 19; only codified form of language entitled to call itself 'French' 179, 184, 234; teaching of 149, 211–13, 217–18, 235–6, 254
French Revolution 6, 11, 24, 187, 198, 213
functions of language 22; functional diffusion 42–4, 120–30, 190

Galatia 50
Galician dialect 18
Galli (Gauls) 40; Gallo-Romans 66
Gallo dialect 242
Garonne, river 39, 48, 49, 66, 67
Gascony 67, 122, 175; French

speech influenced by Gascon (*gasconisme*) 171, 181, 193; Gascon dialect 18, 68, 74, 96, 127
Gaul 21, 29, 33, 39; Cisalpine Gaul 30, 39; Gaulish 29, 39, 40, 42, 44, 49, 57; Transalpine Gaul 31, 39
Geneva 39, 69, 77, 221, 224
Germany 31, 39, 91, 93, 101, 222–3, 234; German 18, 33, 214, 215; Germania 50; Germanic 21, 40
grammarians 146–8; their motivations 172–3; 'tyranny' of 157, 238
grammars of French 162–3
graphisation 23, 26, 104–16
Greece 30; Greek 8, 33, 36, 47, 134, 162; Greek alphabet 39; Greeks 39, 47; influence of Greek on literary Latin 31
Grégoire (Abbé) 198–200, 215
Gregory of Tours 88
Grenoble 125
Guarani 14, 258

Halliday, M. A. K. 13, 232, 255
Hebrew 36, 162
Henry IV 171–2
Hindi 6
honnête homme 177, 252
Humboldt, W. von 9
Hundred Years War 122, 125
hypercorrectness 248

Iberians 39
idealisation 9
idiolect 16
Ile-de-France 59, 62, 97, 114, 199
Illyria *see* Yugoslavia
India 6
Indo-European 39
Ireland 39; Irish 118
isogloss 71, 75–7, 88
Italy 30, 33, 36, 39, 41, 49, 56, 91, 109; Italian 8, 18, 29, 55, 87, 96, 100, 111, 131, 214, 215; prestige in early modern period 134–5,

159, 162

Jacobins 214, 237
jargon 145

King's French 95, 98, 120, 124, 125, 131, 133, 144, 149, 211
koine 111, 114

laeti 50, 59
Lake Constance 39
language change 19–22
language death 15, 190–1, 227
language loyalty 24, 86, 133, 135
language planning 23, 210, 215, 216
language shift 15, 42, 51, 63–4, 190–2, 205
language system *v.* language use 186
languages, delimitation of 17–19, 87–95
Languedoc, region of southern France 66, 218, 244; Languedocian dialect 68, 73, 74
langue d'oc 54, 71; development of writing systems 110–13; differences between *langue d'oc* and *langue d'oil* 73–7; their elimination by Parisian French 120, 123–7; their variability 113–16 *see also* Occitan, Provençal
langue d'oil 54, 71; development of writing systems 113
Latin 1, 8, 10, 19, 22; Classical 31, 34, 89; clung to by Church and legal profession 126–30; latinisation of Gaul 29–53; Low 36, 89; medieval attitudes to 108, 116; myth 31, 35, 158; provides model for French grammarians 163; translation from to French 127–8; Vulgar 34–9
Latino-Celtic inscriptions 51
Latium 30
lexical changes, in Latin 38–9
Ligurians 39, 47

Lille 143, 245
Limousin region 111, 112; dialect 68, 74, 112, 194; *lemosi* 96, 119
lingua franca 25, 112, 127, 131
listener-oriented discourse *v.* message-oriented discourse 13, 255
literacy 104, 119, 130, 149–50, 181, 224, 253
literary authors, felt to be creators of standard language 3, 236
loan-words 3; English 135, 237; Frankish 64–5; Italian 134; Latin 137–8
Loi Deixonne 219
Loire, river 49, 52, 53, 59, 62, 65, 66; Loire valley seen as home of 'best French' (cf. Tours) 167; seen to represent boundary between *langue d'oil* and *langue d'oc* 175
London 143; London English 166–7, 195, 229
Lorraine 50, 54, 61, 62, 122, 124, 127, 211; dialect 200
Louis IX 11
Louis XII 125
Louis XIII 148
Louis XIV 11, 135, 136, 173, 178, 179, 180, 181, 211
Lugdunensis 45, 49, 52
Lyon 45, 49, 69, 70, 78, 91, 99, 102, 134, 143, 222, 245; Lyonnais 71, 77, 122

male/female speech 45, 177, 197, 204, 238–40
Malherbe, F. de 173–4
Marne, river 40
Marseille 39, 47, 143, 194, 222, 245
Martel, Charles 67, 69, 91
Massif Central 77, 81, 112
'maternal language' 94, 101, 126
Mazarin, Cardinal 172
Mediterranean 31, 33, 39, 53, 66, 68, 81, 83
Merovingians 59, 63, 66, 83, 102
message-oriented (*v.* listener-

oriented) discourse 13, 255
Mistral, F. 218
mode 13, 252–4
Montpellier 143
morpho-syntactic change: in
    French 139–40; in Latin 37–8
Moselle, river 45, 49, 83

Napoleon 11, 153, 215, 217
Narbonensis 41, 45, 46–7
Narbonne 41, 45, 143
nation 3, 18, 24, 61; eighteenth-
    century re-thinking of term
    209; medieval meanings of
    term 130–1; national identity 6,
    9, 19, 25, 130–1, 134, 213–15,
    217, 237
Neogrammarians 114
network ties 21, 53, 64, 68; loose
    networks and diffusion of
    standard 225; relationship with
    language change 21, 83–4
Neustria 59, 63, 70
New Mexico 23
Nice 39, 47
Normandy 65, 120, 132, 175;
    dialect 16, 65, 74, 97, 100, 113,
    200, 202
norms 6, 21, 53, 84, 86;
    artificiality 186; association
    with group identity and status
    169, 173, 232–3, 241–2, 249–50;
    local, supralocal, regional,
    supraregional 86, 95, 233;
    norme v. surnorme 154–5;
    selection of 85–117; social v.
    community 27, 233–4, 239–40;
    spoken v. written 24, 86–7, 95,
    155–6, 166, 181–2, 253–4
Norse language 65 see also Viking
North Africa 30, 54, 245, 250
Norwegian 18
Novempopulania 48, 67

Occitan 5, 18, 20, 29, 55, 73–8;
    codification 133; general use in
    south in seventeenth-century
    194–5; medieval names for 96;
    modern attempts at

standardisation and promotion
    of language 218–19; prestige
    dialect 103; shift to French 205,
    227; strong persistence in
    eighteenth century 199–200;
    sixteenth-century writers
    prefer French to Occitan 133;
    use as an administrative
    language 112–13
Orléans 91, 102, 103, 110, 122,
    143, 168, 171, 244
Ovid 31

pagi 40, 45
Palais (de Justice) 143, 169–71, 175
palatalisation 73
Paraguay 14, 258
Paris 6, 7, 102–4, 110, 114, 235;
    crucial importance of
    merchant/business class 169,
    172, 180; expansion of power
    120–3, 206, 215, 228; growth in
    later Middle Ages 142–4;
    lower-class vernacular 195, 198,
    228–9, 246, 250–1; origins of
    upper-class speech norms
    167–9; Parisian French 5, 11,
    95–104; reflects social
    stratification 144–8, 166–7,
    189–90; site of social conflict
    172, 229; university 103, 127
patois 4, 5, 18 and passim;
    persecution of patois speech
    217–18
peasant economy 220–1
perfectibility of French language
    v. linguistic relativism 136, 178
Petronius 34
Peuple (de Paris) 143, 169, 175, 229
Philippe-Auguste 11
phonological change 36–7
Picardy 62, 122, 244; dialect 16,
    74, 97–8, 100, 132, 195, 200,
    202; towns 113, 124
pidgins 20, 22; pidginisation 51,
    63
Pilgrimage to the Holy Places, A 36,
    88
Pivot, Bernard 253

planned *v.* unplanned discourse 13, 181–2, 254
Plautus 34
Pléiade poets 136, 174
Poissard dialect 195
Poitiers, counts of 111
Poitou 49, 77, 120, 122, 175
Portuguese 18, 29, 55
preciosity 177, 249
prescriptivism 3, 7, 200, 234; in histories of French 10–11, 140
prestige, overt *v.* covert 27, 233, 239; growth in prestige of French 130–5
Protestants: espousal of French 128; hostility to Italianate Court 171; persecution of 211
Proto-Romance 87–91
Provence 41, 68, 122, 127; dialect 18, 74, 77, 218; old name for Occitan 71
purism 3; purists 259
Pyrenees 30, 39, 41, 47, 48, 65, 66, 67, 68, 81

Quintilian 34

Reichenau Glossary 88, 89
Reims 49, 93, 110, 143
Renaissance 10, 129, 133, 135
repertory, repertoire, verbal 13, 14, 251–2, 256, 258, 259
Rheto-Romance 23, 29, 33, 55
Rhine, river 39, 45, 47, 49, 50, 52, 57, 59, 60, 61, 69, 83
Rhône, river 45, 47, 49, 52, 66, 68, 69, 77, 81, 83
Richelieu, Cardinal 160, 172
Rodez 67, 112
Romance: continuum 18; languages 1, 29, 54, 55, 257; linguists 33; speech 61
Romansh *see* Rheto-Romance
Rome 30, 33; Roman Empire 29–53
Rouen 65, 98, 143, 144
Roussillon 211
rules, descriptive *v.* prescriptive 154
Rumanian 29, 55

Saint Augustine 36
Saint-Denis, Abbey of 102
Saint Jerome 36, 50
Salian Franks 59; Salic law 63
Sanskrit 257
Saône, river 49, 77, 83
Sardinia 30, 33; Sardinian language 29, 55
Savoy 69, 127, 177, 244
Saxons 57; West Saxon, dialect of Middle English 86
Schwyzertutsch 33
scripta theory 114–16
Seine, river 40, 49, 59, 62, 65, 167
selection, of norms 25, 85–117, 188
Septimania 66
Sicily 30, 33, 65
sociolect 16
Somme, river 62
Spain 30, 33, 39, 41, 45, 56, 66, 91; Spanish 14, 18, 23, 29, 55, 87
speaker variables *see* variation: user
speech community 95, 151
spelling: influence upon pronunciation 164; latinisation 141; value set on correctness 106, 164, 225, 235–6
standardisation 2, 11, 22–7; ideology 25, 156–7, 165, 178–87, 216, 251–2; languages 3, 4, 5–6, 8, 15–16, 189; social aims of 85, 214
stereotypes, sociolinguistic 5, 187; social 246–7
Strasbourg Oaths 10, 88, 106, 108
style 13, 255–7; labels 255; shifting 13, 248–9, 256; stylistic variation 231, 233
subjective attitudes to language 3, 12, 95, 102, 165, 186–7, 241–2, 253
substratum influences 20, 29, 55, 68, 79, 243
superstratum influences 20, 29, 55, 68, 79–80
Swedish 18
Switzerland 23, 28, 33, 39, 50, 61,

69, 91, 215; example of a diglossic community 13
Syagrius 59, 70

Terence 34
'third-century crisis' 47, 50, 53, 59
Toulouse 47, 66, 67, 98, 112, 133, 143; counts of 96, 103, 111, 120; *parlement* 125
Tours 91, 110, 247; Council of 89, 93–4; home of 'the best French' 167–9, 171, 175
transport revolution 225
Trier (Trèves) 49, 50, 61, 102
troubadours 111

urbanisation 221–3

variation: according to use 13–15, 251–7; according to user (speaker variables) 15–16, 238–51
variety 13, 16
Varro 34–5
Vascones *see* Basques; Vasconia *see* Gascony
Vaugelas, C. V. de 174–8, 179, 182, 196
verlan 250

vernacular 22, 33, 40, 44, 94, 209, 240
Via Aurelia 41
Via Domitia 41
vici 45
Vienne 49, 70
Vieux Rouen 245, 249–50
Vikings 56, 65, 102, 109
Ville (de Paris) 143, 170, 175
Villers-Cotterêts, Ordinance of 126–7, 160, 165, 210
Virgil 31, 195
Visigoths 56, 59, 65–8, 153
Vosges 61
vowels, stressed, evolution of Latin 73, 80

Wallonia 62, 124, 127; Walloon language 60, 114
wave theory 81
Welsh 17
Winegrowers' Revolt 218
writing systems 23, 26, 90, 104–16

Yugoslavia 30